D0290340

Soundscape in Early French Literature

by Brigitte Cazelles

ACMRS
(Arizona Center for Medieval and Renaissance Studies)
Tempe, Arizona
in collaboration with
BREPOLS
2005

ASMAR Volume 17: ISBN 2-503-52361-7

Library of Congress Cataloging-in-Publication Data

Cazelles, Brigitte.
Soundscape in early French literature / by Brigitte Cazelles.
p. cm. -- (Medieval and Renaissance texts and studies ; v. 295)
Includes bibliographical references and index.
ISBN-13: 978-0-86698-339-6 (alk. paper)
ISBN-10: 0-86698-339-2 (alk. paper)
1. French literature--To 1500--History and criticism. 2. Sounds in literature.
I. Title. II. Series: Medieval & Renaissance Texts & Studies (Series) ; v. 295.

PQ155.S76C39 2005
840.9'36--dc22

2005031639

∞
This book is made to last.
It is set in Adobe Caslon Pro,
smyth-sewn and printed on acid-free paper
to library specifications.
Printed in the United States of America

Contents

About the Cover

Submission of the City of Bruges to Philippe VI, King of France

Koninklijke Bibliotheek (National Library of The Netherlands)

INTRODUCTION

NOISE AS GLOSS

The realm of sensory perception has long attracted the attention of philosophers and scientists, leading to a plethora of theories from various perspectives, including cognition, psychology, psychoanalysis, sociohistory, and anthropology. By contrast, the field of literature does not seem to provide any greatly useful information on the subject, in part because its medium, the written word, appears by definition to deny such experiences as taste, touch, smell, and hearing. That we absorb a literary work via the eyes has also contributed to the prevalence of vision as a mental rather than sensorial type of perception and, hence, of visual imagery as the metaphor of knowledge and understanding. Yet many premodern or non-Western cultures register and express the world on the basis of a different sensory order, signaling the presence of a less or even non-visual-centered mode of perception. The full appreciation of these cultures thus entails an approach correspondingly attentive to the import of non-visual senses, and such is the goal of *The Soundscape of Early French Literature.* My main source of documentation, French literature in its formative period,[1] consists of works that were transmitted orally to a community of listeners, whence the prevalence of verse over prose as a form facilitating the process of aural communication and retention. Accordingly, many of the texts analyzed in this book will be borrowed from the verse vernacular repertoire. Yet, to the extent that the metrical pattern of these texts has a primarily mnemonic function, their verse form is not an index of sophistication or artistic excellence and is not, therefore, in itself significant. What distinguishes the documents considered in this book is their specificity in constructing, intentionally or not, a cosmology in the main governed by inconstancy and fluctuation. Regardless of form (verse or prose), genre (e. g., epics or romance), language (Latin or vernacular), date (medieval or not), or even origin (European or non-Western), most of my primary sources belong to mythical and imaginative literature in that their depiction of the world tends to run counter to the stable view developed by medieval theologians and moralists.

[1]For the sake of those readers who may not be familiar with some of the texts considered in this book, I will provide plot summaries and translate my quotations of the original language. And for the sake of brevity, I will cite only passages that best illustrate the meaning of the sounds and soundscapes of my textual examples.

My aim in exploring these mythical and imaginative artifacts is to assess the meaning and value they impart to the sense of hearing in conditioning experience of the world and interaction with others. While I hope thus to bring new insight into French literature in its formative period, I also recognize the challenging aspect of my endeavor. Indeed, the visual character of both this book and the literary documents which it considers is bound to textualize and thus adulterate what is in essence a sonorous mode of perception. Acknowledging the silencing effect of the written word, I can only reiterate David Howes' hope that "the medium will *not* be the message"[2] and that such incursion into the realm of the auditory will succeed in echoing the resonance and vibrancy of the Old French tradition. Therein lie the necessary limits of my book: it analyzes a variety of textually-transcribed sounds in an attempt to disclose their significance in enriching our understanding of literature and, in parallel fashion, in an attempt to assess the value of literature in enriching our understanding of aural and oral phenomena.

The history of perception developed by Western thought displays a constant distrust of those senses whose function seems useless or even detrimental to cognition. The result is a hierarchical view of the sensorium within which touch and the two chemical senses of smell and taste came to represent a lower, because more animalistic, mode of perception inasmuch as these senses evoke proximity and even promiscuity.[3] Gradually, seeing and hearing became the leading senses both in terms of perceptual functionality (the absorbing and processing of information) and in terms of aesthetic production and theory.[4]

---

[2] David Howes, ed., *The Varieties of Sensory Experience* (Toronto, Buffalo, and London: University of Toronto Press, 1991), 285.

[3] These three senses began to play a lesser role with the emergence of "homo erectus," when man's upright position favored the functions of fabrication and tool-making, thus fostering the development of the two distance senses of seeing and hearing. (For Edward T. Hall, however, [*The Hidden Dimension* (Garden City, NY: Anchor Books, 1982), 39] vision played a part even before hominids stood on their hind legs, considering the importance of this mode of sensory perception during arboreal life.) Henceforth, prehension (the hand), apprehension (seeing and hearing), and comprehension formed the three stages of man's cognitive process: André Leroi-Gourhan, *Le geste et la parole* (Paris: Albin Michel, 1964).

[4] See Hans J. Rindisbacher, *The Smell of Books: A Cultural-Historical Study of Olfactory Perception in Literature* (Ann Arbor: University of Michigan Press, 1992), vi. A number of philosophers, e. g., Kant and Hegel, thus exclude olfactory perception from both the aesthetic realm and cognitive science. Significantly, however, the distrust of olfactory perception and the attendant preference for the visual no longer characterize German philosophy, whose current hermeneutics is marked, as Martin Jay notes, by a "general privileging of the ear over the eye": *Downcast Eyes: The Denigration of Vision in Twentieth-Century French Thought* (Berkeley, Los Angeles, and London: University of California Press, 1993), 14 n. 41. The trend in contemporary philosophy to denigrate the ocularcentric tradition of Western thought is discussed in the concluding chapter of this book.

But this equation of vision and audition in their capacity to make sense of the world does not entirely cohere with the traditional preeminence of the visual in the Western episteme.[5] Evidence of this preeminence is provided in many modern languages, for example English.[6] Although its vocabulary may express a tactile approach to understanding (such that we apprehend, cogitate, conceive, comprehend, grasp, perceive, ponder, meditate, and understand), thought processes are expressed through metaphors that are primarily visual (such that we consider, contemplate, muse, reflect, and speculate). The reason for the priority of vision lies in the fact that, unlike other modes of cognition, like touch, this sensory perception presupposes detachment and objectivity, that is, a minimal involvement and contact with the object of observation.[7] Vision thus contributes to the development of the "observer" into a sentient and autonomous individual, leading Augustine's association of the eye with the concept of freedom, as opposed to the ear in indicating "the limits or even suspension of freedom."[8] Considering that the ear is by nature open, this organ does indeed render us vulnerable

[5] Augustine provides an illustration of the pervasive use of the verb "to see" in its cognitive implications. Whereas one never says "listen how this sparkles," or "smell how this shines," or "taste how this explodes," one is accustomed to exclaim, "see this sound, see this smell, see this taste, or see this consistency" (*Confessions*, 10.35.54, ed. and trans. de Labriolle [281]). On the oft-noted centrality of the eyes in Western thought, see, among many others, *Visuality Before and Beyond the Renaissance* (Cambridge: Cambridge University Press, 2000), ed. Robert S. Nelson; Chris Jenks, "The Centrality of the Eye in Western Culture: An Introduction," in *Visual Culture*, ed. idem (London: Routledge, 1995), 1–25; Marcel Denasi, "Thinking is Seeing: Visual Metaphors and the Nature of Abstract Thought," *Semiotica* 80 (1990): 221–37; Martin Jay, "Scopic Regimes of Modernity," in *Vision and Visuality*, ed. Hal Foster (Seattle: Bay, 1988), 3–28; Stephen Tyler, "The Vision Quest in the West, or What the Mind's Eye Sees," *Journal of Anthropological Research* 40 (1984): 23–40; Richard Rorty, *Philosophy and the Mirror of Nature* (Princeton: Princeton University Press, 1979); Walter Ong, *Interfaces of the World: Studies in the Evolution of Consciousness and Culture* (Ithaca: Cornell University Press, 1977); and Suzannah Biernoff, *Sight and Embodiment in the Middle Ages* (Houndmills: Palgrave Macmillan, 2002).

[6] See Constance Classen, *World of Sense: Exploring the Senses in History and Across Cultures* (London and New York: Routledge, 1993), 50–76.

[7] The preeminence of visual imagery as a cognitive modality developed with particular intensity during the Italian Renaissance, when linear perspective became the model of a type of inquiry which calls upon the agency of a dispassionate and detached eye (Jay, "Scopic Regimes of Modernity"). Linear perspective fostered a scientific approach to reality, wherein conceptions of knowledge tended to reduce the world to "objects of quasi-observation" (Rorty, *Philosophy and the Mirror of Nature*, 50). Replacing the language of civilization (letters), the language of science (numbers) resulted, not in the creation of a new knowledge, but in the triumph of print culture "as a consumer's paradise of applied knowledge": Marshall McLuhan, *The Gutenberg Galaxy* (Toronto: University of Toronto Press, 1962), 151.

[8] Hans Blumenberg, "Light as a Metaphor for Truth," in *Modernity and the Hegemony of Vision*, ed. David Michael Levin (Berkeley, Los Angeles, and London: University of California Press, 1993), 30–62, here 47–48.

to any sonic production that is either unsolicited or harmful.[9] This physiological fact may in turn explain the semantic equation between to "hear" and to "obey" by virtue of their common etymological root (the Latin verb "audire"). Yet, while *hearing* may imply passivity and obedience, this is not necessarily the case with *listening*. Aristotle, for example, invests audition with cognitive value inasmuch as, like any one of our sensory organs, the ears enable us to perceive and appreciate reality as it is inscribed in the physical world.[10] The Aristotelian foundation of knowledge is in that respect diametrically opposite to Platonic thought, wherein reality lies in the essence of things rather than in their appearance.[11] In Socrates' definition, sentience entails the ability to transcend the tangible world in order to perceive its abstract, immutable, and invariable nature.[12]

---

[9] In contrast to *listening*, which presumes a willingness to register on the part of the auditor, *hearing* can be said to describe an involuntary type of acoustic reception. The distrust of hearing invokes the capacity of this particular sense to signal, not only exposure and vulnerability, but also refusal and rejection. As Blumenberg remarks, "the attitude of not wanting to hear is marked, even if only metaphorically, as more serious than the attitude of not wanting to see, since the ear is, by nature, always open and cannot be shut. Thus, not hearing presupposes a greater degree of contrariness and of intervention in nature than does not seeing" ("Light as a Metaphor for Truth," 48).

Audition is also placed lower than vision by virtue of the archaic and primitive character of the modality of hearing. This is what transpires from the myth of Narcissus and Echo in evoking two successive phases in the constitution of the self. In Didier Anzieu's psychoanalytical interpretation (*Le Moi-peau* [Paris: Dunod, 1995]), Echo thus illustrates the both anterior and feminine character of the "sound mirror" by means of which the infant first learns how to perceive and communicate, while Narcissus represents a more advanced mode of apprehension (the "visual mirror").

[10] Aristotle, who organizes the five senses on the basis of their position in the body, acknowledges their usefulness in providing "the most authoritative knowledge of particulars," while enjoying the *pleasure* they may produce (*Metaphysics*, 1, 981 g 10–23 in *Complete Works*, ed. Barnes, 1552; emphasis added).

[11] The distrust of the senses in Platonic and neo-Platonic thought addresses the potentially alienating effect of sensory perception as well as its pleasure-giving function. Concerning hearing, for example, what Augustine fears is the alienating effect of beautiful sounds (including the melodies of the liturgy) in that they often cause him to be moved by the song rather than by its words. In a progressive enumeration—from tasting, to smelling, to hearing, to seeing—he cites vision as his worst tempter ("my eyes enjoy beautiful and varied forms, bright and fresh colors": *Confessions*, 10.34.51, ed. and trans. de Labriolle, 278). It is probably Augustine's predilection for sight that accounts for his glorification of God as light and for his desire to raise invisible eyes toward Him ("erigo ad te inuisibiles oculos" [279]). On Augustine's view on music and sound, see N. van Deusen, "Music, Rhythm," in *Augustine Through the Ages*, ed. A. D. Fitzgerald et al. (Grand Rapids: Eerdmans, 1999), 572–74, and "Musica, De," 574–76.

[12] With regard to the effects of sounds, for example, Socrates distinguishes the inferior individual, to whom sounds bring only pleasure, from the rational individual, in whom they elicit spiritual joy inasmuch as he thus perceives the "divine harmony" (*Timaeus*, 80b).

A similarly transcendental perspective characterizes Christian thought, although the emphasis there is less on human reason, because of its imperfect nature, than on faith. Sharing nonetheless the Platonic distrust of the senses, the Christian tradition equates knowledge with illumination,[13] which the believer attains to the extent that he avoids the seduction of the tangible world in order thus to perceive God as absolute reality. According to moralist writers from Augustine to Bonaventure and beyond, enlightenment, which is achieved through the eyes of the soul,[14] calls upon the believer's capacity to contemplate God in silence and solitude, away from the noise of the world.[15] Not only does this world

---

[13] From the early period of Christianity, theologians tend to give priority to sight as the noblest of all senses. According to Cyril of Jerusalem, "sight is more trustworthy than hearing"; for Nemesius of Emesa, sight comes first, followed by touch, and only then by taste, hearing, and smell. See Georgia Frank, *The Memory of the Eyes* (Berkeley, Los Angeles, and London: University of California Press, 2000), 111, 132; and eadem, "The Pilgrim's Gaze in the Age Before Icons," in *Visuality Before and Beyond the Renaissance*, ed. Nelson, 98–115. For a more detailed examination of the history of the senses from Greco-Roman science and ethics to medieval symbolism, see Louise Vinge, *The Five Senses* (Lund: Royal Society of Letters, 1975), 15–70.

[14] Echoing Paul in 1 Cor 13:12 ("through a glass, darkly"), Augustine describes human existence in terms of an obscure mirror ("per speculum in aenigmate": *Confessions*, 10.4.7, ed. and trans. de Labriolle, 244). To reach God, "the permanent light," requires that one may overcome temptations as they arise through "the delectation of the senses." Bonaventure expresses his conception of spiritual enlightenment in similar terms: "Observe, not with the bodily eye, but with the eye of the mind [...] and you will be able to see God through yourself as through an image; and this indeed is to see through a mirror in an obscure manner" ("per speculum in aenigmate"): *Itinerarium Mentis in Deum*, ed. and trans. Boehner, 62–63.

[15] For Augustine, illumination of the soul will result from the introspective analysis of his imperfect self and, diachronically, from the retrospective examination of his sinful existence. The speculative value of his *Confessions* is thus linked to Augustine's capacity to retire and meditate away from the noise of the world. Similarly, Bonaventure's journey toward God's light requires, to be successful, that the traveler recover "the quiet of contemplation" which he enjoyed before the Fall (*Itinerarium*, ed. and trans. Boehner, 43).

However, although Christian thought placed vision first in the hierarchy of the senses, it also viewed this particular sensory modality as a potential source of error and distortion. The source of this ambivalent view was a distinction between sensory experience (wherein each sense has a unique and specific function) and religious experience (wherein divine truth is expressed by means of a "symbolic synesthesia"; see David Chidester, *Word and Light* [Urbana and Chicago: University of Illinois Press, 1992], 57). Thus Augustine defines God's truth as "a light that is heard." Such interpenetration is, by contrast, unthinkable with respect to the human sensorium because it "would violate the ordered structure of perception and the basic perceptual logic of ordinary language" (Chidester, *Word and Light*, 56).

Noting the paradoxical status of vision during the Middle Ages, Suzannah Biernoff analyzes the way the eyes of the flesh could lead to redemption (what she terms "ocular communion" and "carnal mediation"), but could also be used as "a means of grasping, devouring, adhering to the object of one's sensual appetite": *Sight and Embodiment*, 59, 140–51.

view posit a rivalry between the eye and the ear,[16] it also interprets each of those two modes of perception in cultural terms. To a sensory order that gives vision pride of place over audition thus corresponds a social order that gives intellect priority over ignorance. The result is a distinction between, on the one hand, the mentally able members of society (a select community of thinkers each endowed with the power to read and reflect in silence) and, on the other hand, the unrefined masses. Deprived of the expertise required to enter the realm of thoughts and letters, the latter are assigned the formless and noisy[17] appearance of a crowd that evolves of necessity in the realm of the auditory. The world view developed by medieval thought thus places vision in a privileged position as the ultimate sensory modality with respect to the acquisition of knowledge,[18] in contrast to audition in its capacity to disturb or distract the individual.[19]

At the basis of this distinction between the eyes and the ears lies, in reality, a distinction between the individual and the collectivity. Access to knowledge is an individual experience only in the case of those select few who are endowed with the capacity to read and meditate on their own, like the thinkers of the Middle Ages whose writings have come down to us. Access to knowledge is, by

[16] Cf. W. J. T. Mitchell, "Eye and Ear: Edmund Burke and the Politics of Sensibility," in *Iconology: Image, Text, Ideology*, ed. idem (Chicago: University of Chicago Press, 1986), 116–49.

[17] In this context, *noise* refers to any sonic manifestation which alters or puts an end to silence. However, although noise is almost always a sound, not every sound is a noise—as I further clarify in a subsequent section of this introduction. With regard to the opposition between silence and noise, a key concept is *askesis* (self-discipline) understood either in religious or in secular terms. For example, much like the contemplative thinkers of the medieval period, learned men in early modern France cultivate silence "as an exercise that allows the practitioner to acquire self-control." Then and now, in reality, silence "constitutes a process of distinction" that serves to separate the elite and the mass. See Jean-Pierre Gutton, *Bruits et sons dans notre histoire: essai sur la reconstitution du paysage sonore* (Paris: Presses Universitaires de France, 2000), 48, 69, 120.

[18] However, this is not the case in medieval theories of aesthetics (see Edgar de Bruyne's monumental work on the subject, *Etudes d'esthétique médiévale*, 3 vols. [Bruges: De Tempel, 1946]), where the organization of the sensorium varies according to personal preference; hence, for example, the priority of hearing with Bernard of Clairvaux, of seeing with Hugh of Saint-Victor, of touching with John Scotus or, with Thomas Aquinas, of seeing and hearing as two intellectual senses conducive to the perception of that which is beautiful (in contradistinction to the other senses, associated with the perception of that which is good). Individual temperament may similarly determine the organization of the sensorium within each literary work and foster the preeminence of a particular modality in accordance with the author's way of sensing the world. Just as the priority of one natural element over the others, in Gaston Bachelard's perspective, constitutes a telling element for the interpretation of texts, so may the priority of one sensorial perception open new vistas on the significance of literary artifacts.

[19] Seeing is viewed as superior to hearing in that the eyes function as a medium that ensures "unmediated knowledge": Frank, "The Pilgrim's Gaze in the Age Before Icons," 125.

contrast, a collective experience for all those people who learn and communicate via audition, like the listeners edified or entertained by Old French literature, or by the experience of the liturgy. The aural character of cultural transmission, combined with a corporate rather than individualistic experience of selfhood, are two characteristics shared by the "illiterate" audiences of premodern Europe as well as by many non-Western societies.[20] That these societies belong to a pre-literate or non-literate culture does not, however, signify that they are by the same token ear-minded rather than eye-minded, as is confirmed by the visualism that governs the cosmological world of the Desana Indians of the Colombian Amazon.[21] Thus, approaching culture from the angle of what David Howes calls the "orality/literacy divide" (*The Varieties of Sensory Experience*, 12) errs to the extent that it develops an arbitrary contrast between illiteracy as necessarily the realm of the oral, and literacy as necessarily the realm of the visual. Too reductive and at the same time too universal, such division posits a historical evolution from the ear to the eye which is fundamentally Eurocentric and, consequently, of limited use with regard to the analysis of many non-Western societies. At the same time, because the documents explored in this book are in the main borrowed from the literary tradition of premodern Europe, it may be that the distinction between orality and literacy adequately reflects the gradual process whereby, to paraphrase McLuhan (*The Gutenberg Galaxy*, 19), the "neutral visual world" of contemporary society came to supplant and replace the "magical world of the ear" in which Western man used to live. Still, this does not mean that literacy ignores the realm of sounds, nor that orality equates with illiteracy. In the case of premodern Europe, we are dealing with what Brian Stock has aptly described

[20] The medieval notion of "illiteratus" does not imply ignorance but designates the various levels of cognition (and/or language competence) that exist within a given collectivity, or even, the various attitudes and behavior that may coexist in an individual (Paul Zumthor, *La lettre et la voix* [Paris: Seuil, 1987], 137; cf. William V. Harris, *Ancient Literacy* [Cambridge, MA: Harvard University Press, 1989], 140–46). While the "illiteratus" has lesser control over words than the "literatus," he is also closer to them and experiences their power more deeply. The very title of Zumthor's book implicates a "conversion" regarding his approach to the medieval vernacular production, from the structuralist bent of his 1968 *Essai de poétique médiévale* (everything is text) to the culturalist bent of *La lettre et la voix* (every text is a voice). I would amend this latter view by suggesting the presence of a transformation, from voice to text, which articulates the evolution from a textuality transmitted orally (primarily, the verse production of Old French literature) to a textuality of private reading (from the mid-thirteenth century; as suggested by Suzanne Lewis, *Reading Images: Narrative Discourse and Reception in the Thirteenth-Century Illuminated Apocalypse* [Cambridge: Cambridge University Press, 1995]).

[21] Cf. Constance Classen, "Creation by Sound/Creation by Light: A Sensory Analysis of two South American Cosmologies," in *The Varieties of Sensory Experience*, ed. David Howes (Toronto: University of Toronto Press, 1991), 239–55, here 253.

as a culture of "literate orality,"[22] considering the function of the written text in guaranteeing the authority of the narrator and in contributing to the cohesiveness of the listeners in terms of "textual communities." Whether literate or not, members of medieval society shared a concept of authenticity and veracity grounded in the written tradition,[23] a tradition inherited from both Greco-Roman antiquity and early Christian thought and associated with Latin as the language and repository of knowledge.

This tradition accounts for a hierarchical assessment of languages wherein Latin was assigned a preeminent position by virtue of its scientific quality.[24] Just as hierarchical, in the moralistic perspective,[25] is the assessment of inferior forms of cultural transmission, like Old French literature. A vernacular artifact

[22] Brian Stock, *The Implications of Literacy* (Princeton: Princeton University Press, 1983). The hybrid character of this culture complicates the task of determining its authors' degree of literacy. In an article significantly entitled "Was There a Song of Roland?," *Speculum* 76 (2001): 28–65, Andrew Taylor contends that French epics were essentially the creation of learned clerics rather than illiterate minstrels. In Evelyn Birge Vitz's notably different perspective (*Orality and Performance in Early French Romance* [Cambridge: Boydell and Brewer, 1999]), epic songs were composed and transmitted orally, and so were, she argues, many Old French verse romances (building on the "Parry-Lord Hypothesis"). Adhering to Vitz's contention that artistic talent is not a matter of literacy or clerical training, I also suggest that imaginative literature in its orally-transmitted form often displays a high degree of sophistication. An example, which I explore in Chapter Four, is the way vernacular storytellers cultivate and revel in the ambiguity of language through double-entendres that playfully disclose the slippery character of human interaction. Compare also Katherine O'Brien O'Keeffe, *Visible Song: Transitional Literacy in Old English Verse* (Cambridge: Cambridge University Press, 1990).

[23] Evidence of the centrality of the written text is the way medieval culture "commonly represented the human subject in terms of the manuscript book": Eric Jager, *The Book of the Heart* (Chicago and London: University of Chicago Press, 2000), xviii.

[24] As Jeffrey Burton Russell shows (*Chaucer and the Trivium* [Gainsville: University Press of Florida, 1998], 11–19), medieval grammar texts teach that Latin is pure, precise, stable, and clear, whereas vernacular languages are chaotic and clumsy, always entailing a compromise of quality for the sake of communication. The result is a hierarchy of languages with English, for example, at or near the bottom. See also Vivien Law, *Grammar and Grammarians in the Early Middle Ages* (London: Longman, 1997) and *The Insular Latin Grammarians* (Woodbridge: Boydell Press, 1982).

[25] By "moralistic perspective," I refer to the definition—articulated by theologians, preachers, and grammarians—of what constitutes a worthy form of aural transmission. Among the numerous scholarly books on the subject, Christopher Page, *The Owl and the Nightingale* (Berkeley and Los Angeles: University of California Press, 1989) is for me particularly relevant in that its focus is the ecclesiastical view on minstrels as expressed in France between 1100 and 1300. Page's analysis calls into question the traditional claim (by Edmond Faral and Edmund Bowles, among other scholars) that the Church's attitude towards secular performers was one of open hostility and "never varied throughout the Middle Ages" (cited by Page, *The*

is deemed evil when its goal is to induce improper desires (*voluptas*), but worthy when it relaxes its audience or instructs it pleasantly and profitably (Page, *The Owl and the Nightingale*, 28). Indeed, each of the preachers and theologians reviewed by Page emphasizes usefulness as the ultimate criterion to distinguish between good and bad secular entertainers. At the top of their scale is the musician inasmuch as music may inspire devotion (Peter the Chanter, late twelfth century), bring comfort against anger and sadness (Thomas Docking, ca. 1265), and restrain the specific vices associated with each social class (John of Freiburg, late thirteenth century). Aware of a contemporary musical climate wherein "the strings were regarded as the most subtle and artistic of all instrumental resources" (as Page observes: *The Owl and the Nightingale*, 26), preachers (like Thomas of Chobham, ca. 1216) show a marked predilection for the *joculatores*, or string-players, who sing of religious heroes (saints) and secular ones (princes).[26] Along with usefulness, another important criterion is historical authenticity, on the basis of which moralists differentiate between good singer-narrators and bad ones. Echoing Thomas of Chobham's criticism of the minstrels who go to taverns and sing "wanton songs" (cited by Page, *The Owl and the Nightingale*, 70), Thomas Docking condemns those musicians (*histriones*) who "exercise their trade so that they may provoke people to sloth or wantonness" (24). Because they accompany their recitation of obscene and false stories with gestures that incite people to shameful behavior, storytellers (*histriones*) are as harmful as the acrobats and contortionists who "follow the courts of magnates" (Thomas of Chobham: Page, *The Owl and the Nightingale*, 23). At the bottom of the moralists' scale, therefore, is any secular entertainer who acts against modesty and decency through bodily movements that deform the image of God (Peter the Chanter) and incite people to foul things (Thomas of Chobham: Page, *The Owl and the Nightingale*, 21).[27]

Owl and the Nightingale, 8). In reality, clerical opinions kept evolving (cf. James McKinnon, ed., *Music in Early Christian Literature* [Cambridge: Cambridge University Press, 1987]) and were especially influenced by the intellectual and spiritual renaissance of the twelfth century, whose effect was to soften the rigor of patristic thinking (Page, *The Owl and the Nightingale*, 6, 14). This new spirit of tolerance accounts for a view of vernacular literature which distinguishes between a good and a bad form of secular entertainment. It is that view which I propose to summarize in this section of my introduction.

[26] The reason for this connection between saints and princes is that both the hagiographic and the epic traditions are viewed as being the most truthful narrative material. For, as Page notes (*The Owl and the Nightingale*, 215, n. 68), the "sacred" and the "secular" are not so easily distinguished in an age which tends to sanctify its heroes—like Roland, designated in Old Passionals as "Sanctus Rolandus." Contemporary evidence associates narrative song with a stringed instrument, usually the fiddle or *vielle*, which often accompanies the reciting of epics (Page, *The Owl and the Nightingale*, 25).

[27] Public dancing is an example of shameful behavior, when the intention is to inspire lust (John of Freiburg; cited by Page, *The Owl and the Nightingale*, 132).

Even more noteworthy in the context of my acoustemological[28] journey is the moralists' association between shameful minstrelsy and speech acts, evidence of which is the way sermons and theological treatises designate minstrels as talkers ("joculatores loquentes") more often than as musicians (Page, *The Owl and the Nightingale*, 45).[29] Among the forms of secular entertainment which use language indecently is the love-poetry sung by troubadours and trouvères, given the element of pervasive eroticism characteristic of this particular form of literary creation.[30] Just as blameworthy are the backbiters and flatterers who spread "malicious gossip" (Thomas of Chobham, cited by Page, *The Owl and the Nightingale*, 21) and seduce people away from the right path.[31] Instead of having a relaxing or instructive effect, the language of love-singers and sycophants acts as parasitic interference inasmuch as it generates or increases "the loud *noise* and restlessness of court activities."[32] Far from serving the cause of truth and history, as is the case with the string-players who sing of saints and heroes, court parasites manipulate orality in ways that foster disorder and discord. The result of this hierarchical perspective is, simply put, a distinction between narrative chants and

[28] The word "acoustemology" was coined by the anthropologist Steven Feld to express the role of acoustic experience and epistemology in establishing personal and cultural identity: "Waterfalls of Song: Acoustemology of Place Resounding in Bosavi, Papua New Guinea," in *Senses of Place*, ed. idem and K. H. Basso (Santa Fe: School of American Research Press, 1996), 91–135.

[29] It is the vocal power of secular minstrelsy that churchmen have in mind when they evoke repeatedly the sacred faculty of "speech" (*vox*, *auris*, *lingua*, *sonus*, *verbum*, and *loquor*: Page, *The Owl and the Nightingale*, 68) as their means to silence impious manipulation of orality. Early Christian monasticism displays a similar acknowledgment of the power of words (which desert monks described as the "sounds of the world"), leading to a distinction between good (edifying) words and useless (slanderous) ones: see Douglas Burton-Christie, *The Word in the Desert* (New York and Oxford: Oxford University Press, 1993), 143, 137.

[30] One of the disruptive effects of secular love-songs is that they incite knights to grow lazy and dissolute, thus preventing them from fulfilling their martial function. See Stephen Jaeger, *The Origins of Courtliness* (Philadelphia: University of Pennsylvania Press, 1985), 177.

[31] Likened to dogs and serpents and called enviers, intriguers, and manipulators (Jaeger, *The Origins of Courtliness*, 55), these courtiers are parasites governed by *ambitio* (greed and venality) and *adulatio* (hypocrisy, mendacity, and slander: see Joachim Bumke, *Courtly Culture* [Berkeley, Los Angeles, and Oxford: University of California Press, 1991], 416–17). According to John of Salisbury (mid-twelfth century), who uses hunting as the metaphor of all the excesses induced by "the immoderate impulse for pleasure," their presence at court contributes to such dissolute activities as "feast, drinking, eating, songs and games, overrefined luxury, excesses and every kind of dissipation" (Bumke, *Courtly Culture*, 416).

[32] Bumke, *Courtly Culture*, 421 (my emphasis). Music as "noise" is of course a subjective experience. From a monastic perspective, secular musicians are bound to sound indifferently loud and noisy; but not so, as Page notes, for preachers who live in the city and know how to appreciate good professional musicians (*The Owl and the Nightingale*, 79–80).

courtly songs as two opposite types of speech with regard to usefulness and authenticity.[33]

In this context, vernacular hagiography represents a good and useful form of orality[34] in that its listeners are provided with exemplary models of behavior. The resulting collection of verse narratives commemorates and praises the saints for having forsaken the pleasures of the temporal world to such an extent that they are now granted to contemplate God in heaven. Although vernacular hagiographers thus espouse or, more to the point, seek to espouse the predominant world view and its attendant visual paradigm, as we will see they are not altogether successful in their attempt to reproduce the visual cosmology of the Christian tradition. The reason for this relative failure lies in part in the hagiographers' mandatory reliance on a communication process that requires vocalization and therefore entails an aural translation of the visual metaphor. If the saint pursues revelation in the silence of his soul, the commemoration of this achievement will of necessity be 'noisy.' A second, more significant reason emerges from the hagiographers' patent hostility toward any form of cultural manifestation that seeks to entertain rather than edify its audience. Echoing the moralists' implicit or outright contempt for the unsophisticated masses, vernacular hagiographers defend the illuminating quality of their works through diatribes the noisy character of which interferes with, and to a degree contradicts, the moral lesson they intend to convey. Just as problematic is, thirdly, the hagiographers' antipathy toward secular literature, considering that they are prone to borrow their narrative techniques from the then most popular forms of imaginative literature, that is, epics, courtly lyrics, and romances. In this context, the orality/literacy divide does not presume a historical evolution from the ear to the eye but, rather, a coexistence of and, at times, rivalry between different modes of knowledge acquisition, for example, juxtapositions such as literate orality and written textuality, Latin culture and vernacular culture, and, within the latter, didactic and secular literature.

At the heart of the moralists' distrust of audition is, as we saw, their opinion that this is an unrefined and at times noisy mode of communication. One could of course argue that vision is not always conducive to revelation (witness the confusing effect of mirages and illusions), any more than audition is a necessarily inferior

[33] A similar distinction appears to characterize sermons composed in the vernacular, which denounce any literary creation that seeks to stir the listeners' evil impulses (like secular love songs; see Michel Zink, *La Prédication en langue romane avant 1300* [Paris: Champion, 1976], 374), but praise the reciting of epic poems inasmuch as these support the principles of the Christian faith (Zink, *Prédication*, 383).

[34] Among the means employed by verse hagiographers to facilitate the process of communication and retention are many of the mnemonic devices—analyzed by Walter Ong (*Orality and Literacy* [London and New York: Routledge, 1995], 31–77)—marking the style and syntax of aural transmission, such as rhythmic and balanced patterns, repetitions or antitheses, alliteration and assonance, and formulaic expressions and proverbs.

mode of transmission. In the context of the culture of literate orality which is the focus of this book, a central question concerns the value of hearing (Old French "oïr") in the process of cognitive acquisition. A poet like Marie de France at the end of the twelfth century uses the verb in a manner that underscores the significance of audition in promoting knowledge. Appearing five times in the general prologue to her collection of courtly novellas (*Lais*),[35] "oïr" serves in its first occurrence to amplify the value of public recitations in guaranteeing the survival of worthy texts, such as Marie's *Lais*, whose merit lies in both science and eloquence. Yet transmission via memory alone is insufficient and unreliable, hence Marie's determination to ensure the survival of those stories, first, by assembling them, and second, by composing and recounting them in rhyme. She now offers to the "noble king" (Henry II Plantagenet?) and his court oral utterances that will provide them with knowledge and understanding. In this orally-communicated mode of textuality, to hear means at the same time to remember, to understand, and to reflect, reflection being the ultimate stage of aural reception that will enable Marie's listeners to interpret the figurative meaning hidden in her novellas. Thus transformed into a textual body and endowed with intellectual value, her stories become part of the body social to which they are addressed, proof of the aristocracy's interest in, and disposition for, learning and knowing. Along with the many works sponsored by noble courts, Marie's *Lais* praise literate orality as a culture wherein aural signs lead to mastery in the art of interpretation, enabling any attentive listener to "see" the meaning of the world and its organizational principles.

---

[35] Marie's successive use of the verb "oïr" refers, first, to the value of transmitting worthy subject matter: "Quan uns granz biens est mult oïz / dunc a primes est il fluriz" ("When a good thing is heard often, it begins to blossom": ll. 5–6). Second, the verb evokes the aural circumstances which led Marie to hear the tales she is about to transmit ("qu'oïz aveie" and "oïz conter," ll. 33 and 39), from storytellers who had themselves learned those stories through oral recitations ("aventures qu'ils oïrent," l. 36). The fifth and last occurrence of the verb (l. 56) invites Marie's noble public to lend an attentive ear to her stories: "Ore oëz le comencement!" ("Listen now, the story begins"). As Mathilda Tomaryn Bruckner notes (*Shaping Romance* [Philadelphia: University of Pennsylvania Press, 1993], 206), Marie intertwines the process of traditional storytelling with "the textual traditions of romance and the written text's invitation to gloss and interpret." R. Howard Bloch, on the other hand, suggests that, in "translating" and "transmitting" the oral tradition ("traire," l. 28 of the *Lais*'s General Prologue), Marie necessarily "transforms" and "betrays" her material: in Bloch's perspective, "traire" means "to entomb the living voice in the dead letter of a text, to silence it": "The Lay and the Law," *Stanford French Review* 14 (1990): 181–210, here 207–10.

Along with Marie de France's *Lais*, many of the vernacular texts I will examine in the course of this study are standard "canonical" works within the Old French literary tradition. Hence a plethora of seminal scholarly analyses, among which I will cite only those which directly deal with the soundscape of that tradition.

The cognitive value assigned to hearing in Marie's prologue, which replicates the cognitive value of seeing in medieval theology, serves as a reminder that non-visual senses were once an important "part of our sensory and symbolic consciousness, and, in certain significant cases, [were] even believed to be superior to sight."[36] Their eventual supersession went hand in hand with a decline of myth and community as provoked by the rise of empiricism and individualism. In this connection, the "mythical" and "imaginative" artifacts that I propose to explore refer, not only to a collectively shared body of beliefs and practices, but also to a stage of symbolic consciousness which still adhered to a cross-sensory approach to cognition. Visual metaphors could thus be expressed in sonorous terms (as is the case in many prologues of courtly romances, including Marie de France's), while the experience of communal identity could be conveyed by means of sonorous images, as witness the many battle cries registered in the epic tradition. To a degree, therefore, the sensorium transcribed in secular literature resembles the sensorium of Christian thought in that knowledge is in both cases attained through the agency of synesthesia.[37] However, a major difference between the religious and the secular perspectives is the fact that, by mixing various sensory modalities, the secular perspective appears to subvert both the "ordered structure of perception" and the "basic perceptual logic of ordinary language" (to quote Chidester's remark in describing the religious experience according to Augustine: *Words and Light*, 56). As I propose to show in the course of this book, the vitality and resonance of French literature in its formative period are intricately connected with an approach to knowledge which qualifies as cross-sensory (synesthesia), and with the use of a language, Old French, whose vocabulary is still closely connected to its sensory roots.[38] Therein arises an assessment of the world

---

[36] Classen, *World of Sense*, 36.

[37] In contemporary psychology, synesthesia is a crossing of sensory signals in which the stimulation of one sense evokes another. The American Synesthesia Association, which held its first meeting at Princeton University in 2001, analyzes this phenomenon in the hope of thus furthering our knowledge about the inner workings of the human mind. See Richard E. Cytowic, *The Man Who Tasted Shapes* (New York: Putnam, 1993), and Patricia Lynne Duffy, *Blue Cats and Chartreuse Kittens: How Synesthetes Color Their Worlds* (New York: Henry Holt, 2001).

[38] An example is the word "forsené" in combining the realm of the mental (when "forsené" describes a state of madness and irrational behavior), the realm of the sensorial (in reference to the physiological unbalance provoked by madness), and the spatial realm in reference to the movement of propulsion ("for") that throws the mad individual out of normality ("sen"). A similar polysemy characterizes the term "sen," which—especially with the diffusion of Aristotelian thought in the thirteenth century—could refer to any one of the five sensorial perceptions (including smell: "sentir"), thus mirroring at the physical level the five modes of spiritual perceptions explored by medieval theologians: see Georges Matoré, *Le vocabulaire et la société médiévale* (Paris: Presses Universitaires de France, 1985), 130. (Modern science has enlarged the traditionally fivefold approach to the senses by observing the existence "of some

order which contrasts with the rational and stable view articulated by Christian thought in that secular works tend to recognize and reflect the fluid and ever-changing character of the human experience with respect to knowledge and communication. In reproducing the network of contemporary social relations in a manner that at times valorizes the ordered design of Creation, but much more frequently undercuts its hierarchical principles, Old French literature elaborates a cosmology that is more realistic—more truthful and complex—than the one developed by medieval theoreticians and moralists.[39]

This work proposes to show how the acoustic and sonic phenomena transcribed in the early French tradition account for the latter's capacity to depict both the natural world and the human realm in their dynamic reality. The discipline

seventeen different ways in which [animal] organisms can respond to the environment": see Jay, *Downcast Eyes*, 6 n.16; and Robert Rivlin and Karen Gravelle, *Deciphering the Senses* [New York: Simon and Schuster, 1984], 9–28. Still, as Jay notes, science also acknowledges "that humans tend to rely on sight more than any other sense").

"Sen" could also equate with "reason" (as in "sené": reasonable), leading to such variant meanings as wisdom, common sense, wit, or personal opinion. The term then refers to the technical expertise that engages one's rational power, such that, when "sen" appears in literary texts, it combines all of those meanings and epitomizes a concept of artistic creation defined as the ability to produce meaning. See, in the latter part of the twelfth century, the famous distinction established by Chrétien de Troyes among "matere" (subject matter), "sen" (meaning), and "conjointure" (narrative structure), in the prologues of his romances *Erec et Enide*, ll. 13–14, and *Le Chevalier de la Charrette*, l. 26. Both Douglas Kelly (*Sens and Conjointure in the "Chevalier de la Charrette"* [The Hague: Mouton, 1966]) and Michelle Freeman (*The Poetics of Translatio Studii and Conjointure: Chrétien de Troyes's "Cligès"* [Lexington, KY: French Forum Publishers, 1979], 162) have masterfully explored the unifying role of "conjointure" in Chrétien's work. For E. Jane Burns (*Body Talk: When Women Speak in Old French Literature* [Philadelphia: University of Philadelphia Press, 1993], 162), the "bringing together" effected by "conjointure" transfers the act of coupling with a woman into the realm of male literary creation.

Like the Old French "sen," the English word "sense" refers to a variety of "designations [that] include meaning, perception via the body, intellectual cognition, and lust": Margreta de Grazia, "Homonyms Before and After Lexical Standardization," *Deutsche Shakespeare-Gesellschaft West Jahrbuch* (1990): 143–65, here 156. The polyvalence of "sen" as indicative of a rational, but also concrete or sensorial, form of perception stresses the value of the vernacular language as a medium of expression and communication that differs from its modern counterpart in that it does not de-sensualize and abstract the environment.

[39] See for example Georges Duby's masterly analysis of the principle of tripartite society as developed—and manipulated—by medieval theoreticians: *Les trois ordres ou l'imaginaire du féodalisme* (Paris: Gallimard, 1978). The essentially slippery and ambiguous character of the world and language specific to secular artifacts is the reason for their denigration by moralists. Such denigration may also be viewed as a defense mechanism against the novelty of vernacular languages in their cognitive capacity. Consider the superior status traditionally granted to Latin in grammar textbooks: as Russell notes (*Chaucer and the Trivium*, 13), the result was an increased awareness of the perfect yet "chilly" character of Latin, as opposed to a clumsy yet "evocative" vernacular.

of sensorial anthropology is here particularly relevant in that it provides a guideline for conducting such an exploration of textually-transcribed sounds.[40] It is for example important to acknowledge, first, that senses interact with each other and, second, that the act of perceiving often provokes strong affective reactions.[41] Far from a natural given or an invariably historical phenomenon, the order of the senses varies according to the likes and dislikes of a given culture (e.g., the Ongee of the Andaman Islands in the South Pacific live in a world organized by smell while the Tzotzil of Mexico hold that heat constitutes the basic force of the cosmos: Classen, *Word of Sense*, 1). My hope is that this analysis of the sounds registered in Old French literature will help us identify and understand the fears and dreams shared by the listeners thus edified and entertained.

Another source of guidance with regard to the interpretation of orally-transmitted texts is provided by the discipline of chaos theory as it applies, in particular, to information theory.[42] Drawing from a variety of scientific approaches, including thermodynamics, modern biology, and the mathematical formula of probability functions, this theory posits that information results, not from the successful reception of a message, but from the latter's imperfect and incomplete transmission. In thermodynamics, for example, heat functions as a type of noise that opens an initially closed system such that energy is no longer "turned unto itself" (entropy) and can become operative. Modern biology develops a similar definition of the living subject as a complex network of systems and subsystems which avoids entropy by virtue of the energy and information it receives from interaction with its environment. The resulting noise initiates the transmission of information, which each level of the system interprets and converts in ways that produce ambiguity and complexity. According to the mathematical formula of probability functions, which defines information as an inverse function of the ratio of chances, the more improbable the possibility that messages will reach their destination, the more information the receiver will gain. Far from an obstacle to

[40] See Howes, ed., *The Varieties of Sensory Experience*, and Classen, "Creation by Sound/ Creation by Light," 257ff.

[41] This is particularly true of those premodern or non-European cultures which conceive of the senses as active media of communication; witness the late antique and medieval belief in extromission (which holds that eyes send out rays in order to see) and intromission (objects send rays to the eyes). See Cynthia Hahn, "Visio Dei: Changes in Medieval Visuality," in *Visuality Before and Beyond the Renaissance*, ed. Nelson, 169–96, here 174–75; and Michael Camille, "Before the Gaze: The Internal Senses and Late Medieval Practices of Seeing," in *Visuality*, ed. Nelson, 197–223, here 204–8. For late antiquity see L. S. B. MacCoull, "Notes on Philoponus' Theory of Vision," *Byzantion* 67 (1997): 558–62.

[42] Cogently explained by Sjoerd L. Bonting from a theological perspective (*Chaos Theology* [Ottawa: St. Paul University, 2002]), and by Ian Stewart from a mathematical perspective: *Does God Play Dice?* (London: Penguin Books, 1989).

communication, noise is here valued as a positive interference that turns disorder into meaning.

If information emerges, not from the successful reception of a message, but from the latter's imperfect and incomplete transmission, then this calls for a revision of the status of a literary text. To cite William Paulson, it may be that literature is not a reservoir of eternal and invariable truths which a civilization sends to itself over time, but a culture of "mortal vocabularies" engaged in a continual elaboration of new meanings and new configurations.[43] Acknowledging his indebtedness to the French philosopher and historian of science Michel Serres,[44] Paulson connects the potential rejuvenation of literary studies with the capacity to "open our texts to the new codes and messages and noises of science" (*Noise of Culture*, 52). Paulson's assessment of literary texts as "paradoxical objects [that] both complicate information with noise and bring meaning and order out of disorder and play" (50) leads to a definition of the literary scholar as a "navigator" who rereads the texts of the past on the basis of the language of science or, more precisely, on the basis of what science tells us about the workings of language and communication. Such a navigator would dissolve the current division of knowledge by being equally at ease in the realm of letters and that of science, for only then will we succeed in fully recognizing and exploring the function of literature as "the noise of culture."

The literary scholar as navigator entails the presence of a truly interdisciplinary expertise, a claim that will nowhere be made in the course of the present exploration. How, then, does information theory relate to the "acoustemological" journey on which we propose to embark? It provides, first, a definition of noise in terms of a dynamic perturbation that guarantees the vitality and complexity of literature by triggering new meanings and a type of information from the one contained in the initial message. Although this definition contradicts the ocularcentric perspective according to which sonic excesses endanger the rational principle of understanding, it also coheres with recent attempts in the areas of cognition theory and psychology to restore the realm of the senses and recognize the value of synesthesia.[45] Of special interest with respect to the discipline of literary analysis is Wai Chee Dimock's claim that noise is not distracting, distorting, or disruptive but, to the contrary, a generative process that "enriches

---

[43] William R. Paulson, *The Noise of Culture: Literary Texts in a World of Information* (Ithaca and London: Cornell University Press, 1988), 35.

[44] For a cogent summary of Serres' philosophy of noise, see Kenneth Gross, *Shakespeare's Noise* (Chicago and London: University of Chicago Press, 2001), 210–11.

[45] See, in a scientific perspective, Erwin Strauss, *The Primary World of the Senses: A Vindication of Sensory Experience* (London: Collier Macmillan, 1993); and in a psychological perspective, Lawrence E. Marks, *The Unity of the Senses: Interrelation Among the Modalities* (New York: Academic Press, 1978).

the dynamics for interpretation."[46] At the basis of her argument is the infinite hermeneutic horizon of literary texts as objects that travel across space and time and acquire in the process new semantic networks. Much as random noise enables the detectability of otherwise inaudible sounds,[47] literature as an object the tonality of which is heard differently by each "reader" allows for the continual emergence of otherwise undetectable meanings. Linking literary endurance to the lasting elasticity of a text, Dimock thus questions the canonical view à la Harold Bloom—according to which literary texts acquire their immortality from a "competitive and triumphant" struggle against the burden of time.[48] The drawback of canonicity is to place in privileged positions those works that perdure on account of both the originality and the universality of their authors. This would in itself eliminate all literary texts that are anonymous either because their authors are unknown or, when they are known, because their voices function primarily as the echo of a collective voice, as is the case with the early French tradition. Although Dimock's theory of resonance addresses works from the written tradition, this theory also applies to the culture of literate orality, whose value—or "semantic democracy"—lies both in its capacity to sharpen more and more ears and in "its knack for vibrating on issues that matter" (Dimock, "A Theory of Resonance," 1068).

Secondly, the pertinence of information theory to my analysis lies in a definition of noise as a type of positive interference that is often, but not exclusively, sonic, such that any one of our sensory perceptions can act as a trigger whence information emerges. Adhering to this investment of noise as a perturbation that guarantees the vitality of a system, I will also consider the severing effect of noise as a trickster that may separate the two end terms of the communication process. Noise will therefore have a dual function, reflected in my reliance on a specific terminology for the purpose of distinguishing, first, between the various types of interference transcribed in early French literature and, second, between the various types of "language" thus produced. By *logos*, I refer to the systems of conventions that are integral to the vehicle chosen to convey a given story, be it the language of devotion, of courtly romance, or of chivalric romance. Each of these

---

[46] Wai Chee Dimock, "A Theory of Resonance," *PMLA* 112 (1997): 1060–71, here 1063. Dimock's positive view on noise coheres with Paulson's argument (*The Noise of Culture*, 153) that literary texts, especially those of the past, are "noisy" precisely because of their marginality and strangeness in the perspective of today's culture, the values of which they thus help to define.

[47] Known as stochastic resonance, random noise is an activation phenomenon that occurs when "a weak signal is boosted by background noise and becomes newly and complexely audible" (Dimock, "A Theory of Resonance," 1063).

[48] Dimock, "A Theory of Resonance," 1061, citing Harold Bloom, *The Western Canon* (New York: Harcourt, 1994), 36.

systems of conventions adopts a hierarchical stance, in reference to the relation between creature and Creator, lover and beloved, or knight and ideal. Within this structure, *logos* articulates an idealized rendition of social order, consistent with the qualities of submission, obedience, and outstanding conformity, among other elements, which contribute to the presentation of the protagonist as an admirable or heroic character. I define *logos*, then, as an often euphemistic language that beautifies and idealizes its subject matter for the purpose of confirming the victory of order over chaos.[49] In this logocentric context, *noise* refers to all the manifestations, sonic or otherwise, which undercut the *logos* of narration by recording either unwittingly (hence a language of noise hereafter designated as *paralogos*[50]) or intentionally (hence a language of noise hereafter designated as *diabolos*[51]) the often chaotic character of human interaction. The language produced by these interferences, which I designate as the *soundscape* of narration,[52] alters or even subverts the rational discourse of a given text in ways which disclose the significance of noise as gloss.

[49] The fact that euphemism creates the risk of distorting the truth points to the potentially noisy character of language itself, when *logos* takes the form of argumentative discourse or self-serving eloquence or when it generates linguistic confusion and dialectal chaos. The ideal vehicle would be silence, in reference to Paulson's first definition of noise as the interruption of a signal, rather than its sonorous manifestation (*The Noise of Culture*, 67).

[50] *Paralogos* in its interfering function corresponds to Paulson's second definition of noise as "the introduction of elements that are purely random" (*The Noise of Culture*, 67). In this context, *paralogos* does not equate with what Jean-François Lyotard calls "paralogy," in reference to the need for a mode of literary practices that would enable the humanist scholar to participate in society's symbolic transactions (Paulson, *The Noise of Culture*, 179–80). It is closer to the patristic use of παραλογίζομαι as meaning "leave out of the reckoning": G. W. H. Lampe, *Patristic Greek Lexicon* (Oxford: Clarendon Press, 1984), 1021.

[51] *Diabolos* (from "slander, calumny") would loosely correspond to Paulson's third definition of noise as "the introduction of elements of an extraneous message" (*The Noise of Culture*, 76). I shall use the term to describe any production of sounds which seeks to destabilize the language of reason. *Diabolos* will thus refer to the "violent and disorderly forms of speaking" (such as slander, defamation, malediction, rumor, and gossip) analyzed by Gross (*Shakespeare's Noise*) and, more generally, to any sounds whose effect is to "fissure meaning" (Gross, *Shakespeare's Noise*, 1).

[52] In my terminology, a "soundscape" constitutes a language of an often prelinguistic or nonlinguistic character, which as such evokes both Garrett Stewart's "phonotext" (*Reading Voices: Literature and the Phonotext* [Berkeley and Los Angeles: University of California Press, 1990]), Bruce R. Smith's "O factor" (*The Acoustic World of Early Modern England: Attending the O-Factor* [Chicago: University of Chicago Press, 1999], esp. 3–29), and Wes Folkerth's analysis of Shakespeare's sounds (*The Sound of Shakespeare*, esp. 7, 15–26). (On the distinction between articulate and inarticulate sounds in the classical and medieval traditions, see Blair Sullivan, "The Unwritable Sound of Music," *Viator* 30 [1999]: 1–13.) At the same time, my use of the term differs from its sociohistorical function in the perspective of R. Murray Schafer, *The Soundscape* (Rochester, VT: Inner Traditions, 1993), 3–67, and Barry Truax, *Acoustic*

Given the central role of noise in this study, we must at this point consider the history of the word and attempt to specify its significance. In its modern definition, noise generally describes any auditory sensation that is experienced as either "disagreeable" or "undesirable" (Gutton, *Bruits et sons*, 17), but may also, surprisingly, equate with harmony.[53] According to the Larousse dictionary, contemporary French usage has an even more restricted approach inasmuch as the word appears solely in an expression—"chercher noise"—which evokes an inconsequential, albeit noisy, kind of pursuit or quarrel. In striking contrast with its modern counterpart, the Old French "noise" is marked by polyvalence and designates a production of sounds whose origin may be human (shouts and clamors), animal (roars and barks), technical (blares and rings), and natural as well (thunders and blasts).[54] Correspondingly, its occurrence in the soundscape of early French literature evokes a synesthesic type of perturbation which tends to have a noxious effect, consistent with the origin of a word whose possible roots include the Latin *nausea* (seasickness; French "nausée"), *nocere* (to harm; French "nuire"),

---

Communication (Norwood, NJ: Ablax, 1984), 19–20, 57–58, wherein a soundscape refers to the collectivity of sounds that distinguish a given community. For Schafer, these sonorous landscapes vary according to location and evolve in time, leading to the superabundance of sounds that characterizes noisy industrial cities.

The threefold character of the "language" produced by the *logos* of narration and its textually-transcribed sounds (*diabolos* and *paralogos*) corresponds loosely to the three main tonalities characterizing the documents of the early French tradition, that is, "Christian, Bawdy, and Courtly": see Jacques Merceron, "Obscenity and Hagiography in Three Anonymous *Sermons Joyeux* and in Jean Molinet's *Saint Billouart*," in *Obscenity: Social Control and Artistic Creation in the European Middle Ages*, ed. Jan M. Ziolkowski (Leiden: Brill, 1998), 332–44, here 344.

[53] Early modern English (through circa 1650) provides an illustration of the possibly harmonious quality of noise in that the word could refer to a group of professional musicians (Smith, *The Acoustic World of Early Modern England*, 220; there is a present-day early music group called "The King's Noyse"). Noise may also have a lyrical value, as when Coleridge alludes to "a noise like of a hidden brook."

[54] Compare Clément Jannequin's (1485–ca. 1558) famous programmatic choral chansons "Le chant des oiseaux," "La chasse," and "La bataille" / "La guerre"): see Howard Mayer Brown and Richard Freeman, "Jannequin, Clément," in *New Grove Dictionary of Music and Musicians*, 29 vols. (London: Macmillan, 2001), 12: 795–99, esp. 795–96.

[55] As de Grazia remarks ("Homonyms," 151), the polyvalence of vernacular languages in premodern Europe constitutes "a lexicographer's nightmare precisely because its usage is too sprawling to submit to any tidy taxonomy." Like the Larousse dictionary, the OED shows a tendency to resist polyvalence in favor of a "scientific" (here, monolithic) definition. It thus states that, while *nausea* and *noxia* have each been proposed as being the possible origin of *noise*, "the *sense* of the word is against both suggestions." Another example of scientific resistance in the OED is the dual rubrics inspired by *nose*: the first rubric dismisses the term as an "obsolete form of noise," while the second lists its various meanings in reference to the *sense* of smell. It appears in this context that sentience cannot and should not equate with sensation.

and *noxia* (nuisance).[55] It may be that noise, nausea, nuisance, and nose have nothing in common etymologically. The fact nonetheless remains that seasickness endangers one's balance precisely because this phenomenon affects not only audition but, in reality, each of our senses. In this connection, the Old French "noise" illustrates the cross-sensory character of perception by referring to a variety of interferences as these may affect one's entire physiological body as well as the body social in its totality.

The encompassing capacity of the Old French "noise" to resonate high and low throughout the cosmos coheres with medieval theories about the interconnection between macrocosm and microcosm, wherein the universal substances, the natural elements, the physiological elements, the five senses, and the "internal" senses combine harmoniously and, if not, engage in a war among themselves (Vinge, *The Five Senses*, 45–70). Such potential hostility between elements and senses predicts a sonorous ending to the history of mankind, a paradigm of which is the soundscape of Revelation. Forecasting the advent of Judgment Day, Revelation chronicles the fate of God's creatures in terms of a prosecution whose conclusion will either grant them to sing eternally the bliss of heaven, or condemn them to endure forever the realm of weeping and gnashing of teeth. The specifically medieval understanding of history adopts the eschatological perspective developed in the book of Revelation. In Latin or in vernacular, in verse or in prose, devotional or not, texts composed during the medieval period delineate this history between the two end terms of Genesis and Judgment Day. Organizing the analysis of my literary documents in a loosely similar eschatological sequence, I examine a variety of texts which I have selected on the basis of their pertinence with regard to the sonorous character of interaction in the postlapsarian realm, Genesis and Revelation serving as the two metaphoric extremes within which this textuality of noise is located.[56]

Chapter One ("The Big Bang") focuses on the emergence of noise in human history, beginning with the non-Christian tradition (including a number of Egyptian, Micronesian, and Jicarilla myths) wherein the Creator is often a

---

Against the monolithic effect of such "scientific" classifications, however, practical experience as articulated by the early French literary tradition demonstrates that we *make sense of* the world to the extent that we *sense* the world.

[56] Although the main source of documentation comes from the early Old French tradition, I intend to use that tradition as a test case that should, optimistically, also apply to any of the pre- or postmodern stages of Western culture. My hope is also that this incursion into the realm of noise responds, to a degree, to the call by Jean-Marie Fritz ("L'horizon sonore de la poésie de François Villon," in *L'Hostellerie de Pensée. Etudes sur l'art littéraire au Moyen Age offerts à Daniel Poirion par ses anciens élèves*, ed. Michel Zink and Danielle Bohler [Paris: Presses de l'Université de Paris-Sorbonne, 1995], 173–85, here 173) for a study of the sonorous landscape of medieval literature, a study all the more pertinent as this textual tradition seems to give priority to the visual over the auditory.

producer of delight, and his human creatures a sounding board of divine joy. By contrast, the Judeo-Christian tradition develops what seems to be a more doleful account of Creation in which speaking, shouting, and laughing are the threefold stages of humankind's entry into the tumultuous realm of postlapsarian history. My textual exhibits, which include the story of the Fall in Genesis, its rendition into a vernacular play, and a variety of verse saints' lives, reveal a figure of the deity on the model of His creature in that the Maker manifests Himself as a destructive force more often than as a creative energy.

The ensuing soundscape resonates a frequently discordant mode of interaction which is further explored in two subsequent chapters. Chapter Two ("The Blares of Power") considers the noxious effect of noise and exploits the possible etymology of the word (from "nocere," to harm) in inferring the use of sounds as a source of military empowerment. Classical mythology links the disappearance of the peace and harmony of the Golden Age with the advent of a spirit of domination which henceforth marks all human transactions with the brand of violence. The result is a notion of divine justice which focuses on revenge and retribution as the main if not sole means of maintaining order. Although many examples from epic songs and chivalric romances glorify the recourse to aggression when it contributes to the triumph of divine justice, here, too, the key word is domination, achieved through a reliance on sonorous belligerence whose goal is to silence, by overpowering, the martial din of the opponents. Chapter Three ("The White Noise of Perfection") examines the role of "ekphrasis" (the textual description of an art object) in the Grail textual corpus and in other chivalric romances. In my analysis, the "white noise" of knightly superiority functions as a background noise, or trickster factor, wherein whiteness equates with incommunicability and intransitivity. The blinding rather than illuminating effect of light in such texts undercuts the claim that visual imagery necessarily guarantees the transparency of language. My suggestion is that, in reality, language signifies by virtue of its resonance rather than its "transparency." Such is the thesis developed in Chapter Four ("Parasitic Homophones"), which examines the deliberate manner in which Old French works cultivate semantic ambiguity. Focusing on a series of words with similar sounds but vastly different meanings, I show how each term in the pairing contradicts the other in ways that end by eliminating any distinction among the realms of chivalry, courtliness, emotion, alimentation, and sexuality—among other categories. The resulting soundscape represents a subversive approach to the dominant visual paradigm through a narration that amplifies the equivalence between gnawing and knowing.

Chapter Five ("Sonus Mortis") brings to a close this essay on audition by investigating a number of accounts that evoke the end of time. In the moralistic perspective, the artifacts of mythical and imaginative literature qualify as noisy inasmuch as their language blurs the distinction between flesh and spirit.

Because they cultivate a cross-sensory approach to cognition at the expense of the visual paradigm and thus subvert the established order, secular authors and their listeners endanger their very souls and risk the fate of eternal damnation. Many "Visions of Hell" develop a sonoscopic rather than visionary assessment of the result of transgression in affecting one's visual acuity, of the infernal Trickster in interrupting the channel of communication between creature and Creator, and of damnation as a racket of sundering intensity (as brilliantly shown by C. S. Lewis in *The Screwtape Letters* [1942]). Such a world view assigns to damnation a sonorous character, while describing redemption in visual terms. At the opposite of this antagonistic investment of perception stands, I argue, the cross-sensory wisdom of the Old French tradition. In the Conclusion, I suggest that the interest of this tradition consists in acknowledging the connection between sensory consciousness, symbolic consciousness, and the network of social relations. Revisiting the central questions that govern this inquiry of the language of noise, I interpret the significance of that language as a warning against any authoritarian organization of the sensorium that grants preeminence to one specific modality, the danger of which is loss of perspective and undue simplification. As the soundscape of French literature in its early stage reminds us, comprehension equates with inclusion understood as the capacity to combine and connect, for it is through the radar-net of our senses that the world begins to make sense.

I

THE BIG BANG

> "Od grand travail, od grant hahan
> Toi covendra manger ton pan."
> ("You will earn your bread at the
> price of great pain and great moaning.")
> (*Jeu d'Adam*, ll. 435–436)

At the origin of the universe according to John's Gospel (1:1–4) is the Word (*Logos*) understood as God, life, and light. As a symbol of vitality and revelation, the divine *Verbum* stands at the antipodes of the irremediably imperfect language by means of which humans reflect and communicate in postlapsarian history. Under certain conditions, however, human elocution may become a vehicle of enlightenment, as is the case with exegesis in enabling one to speak "the self in terms of the language of the Logos."[1] Language, whether Latin or vernacular, acquires a "scientific" quality when it serves to instruct or edify. Conversely, any work that undermines the harmony of God's creation either accidentally (by *paralogos*) or intentionally (by *diabolos*) is declared nonscientific or outright "evil."[2]

Pace medieval theologians and moralists, however, "scientific" *logos* does not always imply an objective and impartial type of elocution.[3] Logic may thus serve

---

[1] Stephen G. Nichols, "The Light of the Word: Narrative, Image, and Truth," *New Literary History* II (1989): 535–44, here 543. According to Augustine, exegesis helps to decipher the obscure meaning of the Scriptures: "by following certain traces [one] may come to the hidden sense without any error, or at least will not fall into the absurdity of wicked meanings": *On Christian Doctrine*, trans. D. W. Robertson (Indianapolis: Library of Liberal Arts, 1981), 7. For late antique Byzantine philological-exegetical treatment of Creation, see Ludwig Fladerer, *Johannes Philoponos, De Opificio Mundi: Spätantikes Sprachdenken und christliche Exegese* (Stuttgart and Leipzig: Teubner, 1999).

[2] The sonic terminology employed in this essay is defined in the Introduction, which also provides a summary of the distinction, articulated by medieval theologians and moralists, between a 'good' and an 'evil' form of vernacularity. In the moralistic perspective, a "scientific" language refers to those modes of elocution which contribute to the transmission of sacred and secular knowledge. (Roughly speaking, *paralogos* refers to the language at work in the soundscapes of texts marked by a courtly tonality, and *diabolos* to the language at work in the soundscapes of texts marked by a bawdy tonality.)

[3] To quote David Townsend and Andrew Taylor (*The Tongue of the Fathers: Gender and Ideology in Twelfth-Century Latin* [Philadelphia: University of Pennsylvania Press, 1998], 2), Latin derived its authoritative status from the fact that it "was the ideal instrument for the great

to support an impassioned mode of reasoning,[4] while science may manipulate the world's natural resources for violent if not lethal purposes.[5] Scientific or not, rational language is in reality rarely neutral: at the service of fiction, for example, *logos* often bespeaks a turbulent mode of interaction among humans, nature, and the deity. In such cases, as we will see in this chapter, the "noisy" character of the story conveyed through the narration combines and coheres with the language of its soundscape,[6] the result of which is a resounding account of the origin of humankind.

Consistent with the eschatological model that loosely governs the presentation of my textual exhibits, I begin with an examination of those mythological and imaginative artifacts which narrate the creation of the universe. In salient contrast with many non-western myths, which develop a benevolent depiction of both the Creator and his creatures, the Judeo-Christian tradition enunciates a more doleful view of the emergence and evolution of humankind. Explored in the first section of this chapter ("The Fall as Phonic Drama"), such a view links the origin of human history with the sin committed by the primordial couple. According to both Genesis 2–3 and the Old French play of the *Jeu d'Adam* (twelfth century), a consequence of Eve's transgression is that the human voice tends henceforth to be a cry of anguish (Abel) or a production of discord (Cain). After Cain, any human

medieval systematizations, the encyclopedic codifications of the arts and sciences, theology, canon law, and pastoralia, by which theological and social orthodoxy was imposed upon society as a whole. In contrast to the fluidity and free play of the vernacular, Latin preserved the judgments of the past in a language ostensibly frozen in time." My suggestion (stated in the Introduction) is that the language of fiction is "truer" than the discourse of science whenever the latter glorifies the order of the universe in terms of a stable and immutable hierarchy.

[4] An example is sophistry as a type of logical reasoning the function of which is to persuade at all costs, regardless of authenticity or sincerity. In contrast to the pure and disinterested character of the Socratic method, sophistry "is a variety, monetarily advantageous, of the art of disputing, contending, contesting, combating, an art similar to the art of fighting in that its goal is acquisition" (Plato, *Sophist*, 226a). The language of sophistry deserves in this respect to be described as "eristic" *logos*, in reference to the aggressive character of an argumentation the sole function of which is to win over one's interlocutor.

[5] Violence is, indeed, a central concern in contemporary philosophy, as expressed in Michel Serres' warning (*Hermès IV: La distribution* [Paris: Minuit, 1977], 89–104) against the current connection of natural science with power, wealth, and arms. A comparable example is the role of violence in ensuring social order during the Middle Ages: as Christine Raynaud observes in her analysis of the manuscripts containing vernacular texts of a historical nature ("chronicles"), thirteenth-century illustrators used violence as their means to praise (French) aristocratic society, while in the fourteenth and fifteenth centuries this praise of violence via iconography served to celebrate the king in his peace-making function: *La Violence au Moyen Âge, XIIIe–XVe Siècle, d'après les livres d'histoire en français* (Paris: Le Léopard d'Or, 1990), 111, 238.

[6] In my view (summarized in the Introduction), textually-transcribed sounds allow us to hear a story that is frequently—but not always—at odds with the story conveyed through the narration of a given literary work.

being—like the persecutors of the early Christian martyrs—who attempts to interrupt the channel of communication between God and His creatures is eventually punished and condemned by means of a destructive type of sonority, which I analyze in a second section ("After the Fall: The Noise of Sin").

Irremediably weakened by original sin, human nature is correspondingly disempowered in the face of evil. The result is moral blindness, an example of which is the mother of the eponymous hero commemorated in the verse *Vie de Saint Alexis* (ca. 1040). By contrast, Alexis himself emblematizes spiritual insight, enabling him to reflect the transparency of God's *Verbum* through silence and contemplation. Once Alexis' holiness becomes known to the people of Rome, the citizens gather together around his body and sonorously express their elation in a manner which demonstrates the saint's impact in generating unanimity. Yet, as we shall see in this chapter's third and final section ("Noise in the Foundation of Christian Rome"), the saint's devotees are eventually reduced to silence and forced to disperse when the Pope, taking charge of the saint's cult, gives voice to his prerogative as leader and sole orchestrator of order (as actual popes were taking over the canonization process in the late twelfth and early thirteenth centuries). Power, it appears, is proportional to the capacity to make oneself heard by stifling and controlling all rival forms of sonic production. In the institutional setting of the *Vie de Saint Alexis*, the emphasis is therefore placed, not on the saint's value in confirming the generative value of God's Word, so much as on the empowering effect of noise in ensuring one's preeminence in postlapsarian history.

1. The Fall as Phonic Drama

That the deity's creative power may manifest itself through noise is attested by a number of mythological traditions. Ancient Egyptians, for example, appeared to connect life and the power to create life with a specific sound, which some accounts identify as the honking of a wild goose (the sun god Atun) over the vast primeval sea (Nun).[7] Micronesian mythology also links the creation of the universe with an acoustic manifestation:

> Long ago when all was water, Lowa, the uncreated, was alone in the sea. "*Mmmmmm*," he said, and islands rose out of water. "*Mmmmmm*," he said, and reefs and sandbanks were created. "*Mmmmmm*," he said, and plants

[7] For ancient Egyptians, evidence of the life force as a sonorous manifestation is the cry that every species emits at the moment of birth: see Maria Leach, *The Beginning: Creation Myths Around the World* (New York: Funk and Wagnalls, 1956), 217–20. What is noteworthy in the story of Atun as a honking wild goose is the manner in which it translates *aurally* the visual imagery associated with this and the other sun gods venerated in many mythological traditions.

> appeared. Again he uttered the creative word, and birds came into being (Leach, *The Beginning*, 185).

Lowa's creative power takes the form of an utterance that reverberates throughout the aquatic silence, with the result that islands, rocks, plants, and birds successively emerge and become visible.[8] Much like the effect of noise in information theory, Lowa's hum triggers the appearance of new beings by generating a disturbance that transforms the liquid mass into concrete objects. After creating four gods entrusted with the task of presiding over the four directions, Lowa sends a man into the world. This primordial man proceeds to put all the islands in a basket and then places them in their proper order. As for the island of Ebon, it is said that its people are under the special protection of the god of the west, Iroijdrilik, because the name of this god's country is Eb. Thus, when the black tern flies over Ebon, crying out, the people of Ebon believe that this is a promise of plenty and that the god will provide them with an abundance of food. Whether manifested by Lowa's initial utterance or by the cries of the black tern, noise is here assigned a positive effect. The myth makes no mention of discordance, nor of any dispute among the deities or between the deities and men. In that respect, Micronesian mythology stands in striking contrast with the Greek tradition,[9] wherein the creation of the world is soon followed by strife. Hesiod thus mentions that men of the silver race, second in the series of the five ages of man, were "quarrelsome and ignorant, and never sacrificed to the gods," to such an extent that Zeus eventually "destroyed them all."[10]

Another mythological tradition, that of the Jicarilla Apache Indians of New Mexico, proposes a much more benevolent view of the deity's interaction with his

[8] In C. S. Lewis's *The Magician's Nephew* (1955), Aslan creates Narnia by *singing* it into existence.

[9] According to Marie-Louise von Franz, *Patterns of Creativity Mirrored in Creation Myths* (Dallas: Spring Publications, 1972), 129, mythological traditions develop two essential conceptions of creation. One qualifies as extroverted, consistent with a view of creation as an act that exteriorizes the principle of consciousness. The other, which focuses on creation as an inner process ("creation by thought"), is the mark of such "introverted civilizations" as those of the Gnostics, the North American Indians, and some East Indians. This distinction might account for the often benevolent view of the deity in those mythological traditions which betoken an introverted approach to creation (not, however, in Gnosticism, where the creator-deity or demiurge is regarded as evil).

[10] See Robert Graves, *The Greek Myths* (Harmondsworth: Penguin Books, 1960), 1:36: Hesiod, *Works and Days*, 134–140. It should be noted that, at each stage of Hesiod's account, the successive destruction of humankind is followed by a process of re-creation. Whereas my perspective focuses on the effect of strife in provoking discordance and death, that of Bruce Lincoln stresses the regenerative quality of death as a cosmological act wherein "the bodies of the dead replenish, sustain, and even re-create the universe at large": *Myth, Cosmos, and Society: Indo-European Themes of Creation and Destruction* (Cambridge, MA: Harvard University Press, 1986), 127.

creatures. Having made the first man, Creator shows him how to walk, then how to run. But Creator has a more difficult time in teaching man how to talk, for it takes four attempts before man finally "said words"; then,

> "Now shout," said Creator. He gave a big yell himself and showed the man how. The man shouted [. . .]. Creator thought a minute. "Laugh," he said. "Laugh, laugh, laugh, laugh." Then the man laughed [. . .]. The man laughed and laughed. "Now you are fit to live," said Creator (Leach, *The Beginning*, 74).

A noteworthy element in this Jicarilla creation myth is the progression, from speaking to shouting and laughing, which describes the emergence of "homo sapiens." The Creator is here presented as a producer of delight, and his human creature, as the sounding board of divine joy,[11] whence arises a mode of communication between deity and creature which gives priority to sounds over words.[12] Not only does Micronesian or Jicarilla mythology stand in striking contrast with its Greek counterpart, it also provides a portrayal of the Creator which has little in common with God's severe and commanding image in the Judeo-Christian tradition. It is for example significant that the First Laugh recorded in

---

[11] Another example comes from the Hindu Upanishads in a myth which describes the creation of Aditya, the Sun: "When it was born shouts of 'Hurrah' arose [. . .]. Therefore, at its rise and its every turn, shouts of 'Hurrah' together with all beings and all objects of desire arise": Marcelo Gleiser, *The Dancing Universe* (New York: Dutton/Penguin Putnam, 1997), 16. A text from late antiquity, probably from Hellenized Egypt, also sustains that the world was created by God's laughter: von Franz, *Patterns of Creativity*, 135–37. The first time God laughs, light appears; the second time, everything is water; and with God's seventh and final laughter, the soul comes into being. (Strangely, in view of our Jicarilla story, von Franz concludes that "this is the one and only creation myth where God laughs.")

[12] The preeminence of shouting and laughing in this Jicarilla creation myth brings to mind the theory according to which language developed as a modulation of the "call," that is, of a production of sounds (cries ranging from joy to anguish) by means of which a human being audibly translates his interiority: Jean Brun, *L'homme et le langage* (Paris: Presses Universitaires de France, 1985), 15–16. Yet, as Brun remarks, the call is not a specifically human experience, considering that it also serves as a means of communication among animals. A second theory thus posits that language derives, not from the call, but from the complex and organized development of primitive onomatopoeias. Seen against the first theory, which focuses on the auditory aspect characterizing communication among all living creatures, the second theory delineates the origin of language as a mode of exchange that becomes the essential distinction of the human species. Cf. Augustine, *City of God* 16. 31; or John Chrysostom, "Homily 41 on Genesis," in *Homilies on Genesis*, trans. Robert C. Hill, Fathers of the Church 82 (Washington, DC: Catholic University of America Press, 1990), 415.

In the perspective of our Jicarilla creation myth, laughter is superior to articulate language because, as a direct and unmediated mode of communication, it succeeds in conveying the sum total of the intended message.

the Old Testament is not concomitant with the completion of man's creation, but occurs well after the events of the downfall of the human species:

> "And, lo, Sarah thy wife shall have a son." And Sarah heard it in the tent door, which was behind him. Now Abraham and Sarah were old and were stricken in age; and it ceased to be with Sarah after the manner of women. Therefore Sarah laughed within herself, saying, "After I am waxed old shall I have pleasure, my lord being old too?" (Genesis 18:11–12).

Just as significant is the function of Sarah's laughter in questioning the wisdom of God's saying.[13] Rather than a sonorous expression of delight, Sarah's laugh is a noise that endangers the channel of communication between Creator and creature.[14]

Seen against the exhilarating rendition of man's origin in Jicarilla mythology, the first book of the Old Testament provides a grim account of the emergence of humankind. Genesis is, indeed, first and foremost a story of sin and retaliation, which sets the origin of humankind in a soundscape of fury and fear.[15] This calls attention to the founding role of Genesis in informing the turbulent and noisy character of postlapsarian history.

---

[13] To quote the vernacular gloss which interprets this episode in a thirteenth-century prose version of Genesis: "Sara rist por le doute qu'ele en avoit" ("Sarah laughed [at God's prediction] because she did not believe in it"): *La Bible française du XIIIe siècle: Edition critique de la Genèse*, ed. Michel Quereuil (Geneva: Droz, 1988), 189. The gloss also alludes to a similar reaction on Abraham's part; in his case, however, laughing expresses his wonder in the face of God's power ("Abraham rist por la merveille"). (The prophesied child is subsequently named Isaac, meaning "laughter.") The distinction between Sarah's laughter and Abraham's evokes Guillaume Peyraut's classification in his *Summa virtutum ac vitiorum* (mid-thirteenth century). Citing the four types of bad laughter (laughter of envy, perfidy, madness, and vanity), Guillaume then states that the only good laughter is the laugh of prudence, which is both rare and silent: cited by Carla Casagrande and Silvana Vecchio, *Les Péchés de la langue* (Paris: Cerf, 1991), 285.

[14] Echoing my assessment of the sundering and discordant effect of Sarah's laugh, Paul Johnson describes it as "bitter-sweet, sad, ironic, even cynical, a foretaste of so much Jewish laughter through the ages." Only with the birth of her son Isaac does Sarah's laughter become "joyful and triumphant, communicating her delight to us over the distance of four millenia": *A History of the Jews* (New York: Harper & Row, 1987), 15.

[15] A possible explanation for the negative tonality of Genesis lies in the focus it places on the creation of man. In contrast with other mythological narratives like many American Indian myths, wherein man—to quote David Maclagan (*Creation Myths* [London: Thames and Hudson, 1977], 10)—"is only one part in the whole of creation," in Genesis "man is the apex," leading to the ambivalence of the Christian attitude toward the material world.

Genesis 2–3

In the world according to Genesis,[16] the origin of the universe is a sound, that of God's voice in its creative capacity. At the moment when God's voice is heard ("God *says*"),[17] one by one the four elements emerge from the void ("ex nihilo") of silence.[18] Whether this void was nothingness or whether the elements awaited the breaking of silence to exist is not entirely clear (and was variously interpreted by patristic exegetes). What is clear is a presentation of God's power grounded in the audible: the act of creation is a word (*Verbum*)[19] or summons that brings

[16] *Pace* an uncle of mine, the biblical scholar Henri Cazelles, I am no exegete and will approach this and other passages of the Bible from a decidedly literary viewpoint. A primary exegetical approach to the first book of the Old Testament for Westeners is of course Augustine's *De Genesi ad litteram*, which informs the following analysis of Genesis 2–3. For an overall view of medieval (as opposed to patristic) interpretations of Genesis 3, see Eric Jager, *The Tempter's Voice: Language and the Fall in Medieval Literature* (Ithaca and London: Cornell University Press, 1993).

[17] The verb "to say" (Hebrew *amar*, which can mean to declare, name, designate, answer, call, admonish, praise, and command) has for its basic idea "the uttering of some type of spoken word." However, its eight uses in the first book of Genesis focus on "the creative character of God's word" at the moment when He "speaks the world into existence" (*King James Bible*, comp. Spiros Zodhiates [Grand Rapids, MI: Baker, 1984], 1579). It should be noted that Western patristic and medieval exegetes based their interpretations of the Biblical story of the Fall on a Latin translation (from a Greek Septuagint version of the Hebrew original) which became available around 400 A. D. English-language quotations here are from the King James version.

[18] Although the idea that God created "ex nihilo" (a concept of creation introduced by Theophilus of Antioch, ca. 185) has been part of official Christian dogma since 1215 (if not long before), the nature of this creation has also inspired two different views. The first is the notion of continuous creation, according to a "steady-state" model wherein the universe keeps expanding by a continuous creation of matter. The second is the "big bang" or evolutionary model (promoted by the Alexandrian Christian polymath John Philoponus in the sixth century), according to which the universe had an explosive beginning and will have an equally definite, but this time implosive, end. As David Maclagan remarks (*Creation Myths*, 13), since a papal encyclical of 1951 the Roman Catholic Church has supported the big bang model because it shows that "creation took place in time. Therefore, there is a creator; therefore God exists." On the other hand, as Bonting notes (*Chaos Theology*, 16), at issue with the concept of "creatio ex nihilo" is what is today seen as the fact that it conflicts not only with physical science, but also with "both creation accounts in Genesis." For his part, John Philoponus in the sixth century promoted his "Big Bang" exegesis against the pagan eternal-continuous universe on the grounds that it agreed better with the physical science of his time.

[19] God's *Verbum*, his generative saying, has the quality of a command, as in Genesis 2:16–17: "And the Lord God commanded the man, saying, Of every tree of the garden thou mayest freely eat: But of the tree of the knowledge of good and evil, thou shalt not eat of it." The verb "command" (Hebrew *tsâvâh*) "means to constitute, to make firm, to establish [. . .]. When God commands, it happens" (*King James Bible*, comp. Zodhiates, 1631 [the parallel being Psalm 148:5]).

forth the universe and gives it a syntactical coherence. Although Adam, by "giving names" and by "saying" (Genesis 2: 20 and 2:23), contributes vocally to the emergence of the world out of its confusion, his participation is strictly that of a recorder and taxonomist.[20]

In the inaugural scene of Genesis, words as divine syntax or as human dictionary resonate without evoking a reply, for, indeed, there is no need of a response in the harmonious universe that is taking shape. Linguistic interaction begins when the talking serpent arrives at center stage: "And he *said* unto the woman, Yea, hath God *said*, Ye shall not eat of every tree of the garden?" (3:1, emphasis added). His expertise in the art of argumentation enables the serpent to reproduce, and thus interfere with, God's creative utterance. Just as God "said" (1:3) and both the natural and human realms complied, now the serpent "says," the result of which is a systematic de-creation of the universe. Eve's response reiterates in its turn God's command to Adam (2:16–17): "And the woman *said* unto the serpent, We may eat of the fruit of the trees of the garden: But of the fruit of the tree which is in the midst of the garden, God hath *said*, Ye *shall not eat of it*, neither shall ye touch it, lest ye die" (3:2–3, emphasis added). Whereas Eve repeats faithfully the words of her Maker, the serpent alters God's saying through a quotation which is, in reality, neither correct nor complete ("Ye shall not eat *of every tree*"). After having deliberately amplified the arbitrary and prohibitive character of God's command, the serpent proceeds to question its truthfulness: "And the serpent said unto the woman, Ye shall not surely die" (3:4). Significantly, here his response to Eve no longer quotes God's saying. God as the sole source of verbal creativity momentarily disappears and is replaced by the serpent himself (he "*said*"); whence the latter's imperative tone ("Ye shall *not surely* die") as the new master and the initiator of a new order.

Temptation as presented in Genesis is linguistic in nature, enticing Eve to analyze God's words rather than to repeat them verbatim.[21] Thus introduced to the art of interpretation, Eve metamorphoses from a non-sentient to a sentient being through a process of acculturation which calls upon the successive agency

---

[20] From the Hebrew *adamah* (red dirt), the name of "Adam" in itself indicates a material rather than mental form of existence. Also noteworthy is the *kaleō* employed in the Greek version to designate Adam's nominating activity, for the verb has here a clearly vocal, rather than scribal, character. Whereas God's language is verbal, and its effect substantial, Adam's language is adjectival and functions as an appendage.

[21] Thus Ambrose of Milan concludes that Eve's "error lay in the report of the command" (*De Paradiso*, trans. Savage, 12:56).

of hearing, seeing,[22] and tasting.[23] Yet once she digests Satan's words, Eve realizes that, contrary to his promise, the tree is a source not of suavity but of bitterness, instability, and fluctuation.[24] Experiencing the first action of God as Disassembler rather than Creator, the Primordial Couple is taken out of the Garden and cast into the postlapsarian realm. There, they and their lineage will either fear or attempt to rival God's power, henceforth understood as a severing rather than generative force.

The "Jeu d'Adam"

> "Escote, Adam, e entent ma raison!
> Je t'ai formé, or te dorrai itel don" (ll. 49–50).
> ("Listen, Adam, and hear my saying; I made you, and shall now make you the following gift.")

Thus begins the Garden scene of Genesis as recounted in the earliest extant religious play of the Old French tradition: the *Jeu d'Adam* (*Ordo representationis Adae*). A short (1305 verses) tripartite play composed in Normandy around the end of the twelfth century,[25] the Old French text presents successively the story of the Fall, that of Abel's murder, and prophecies announcing Judgment Day. In the lines quoted above, which are taken from the first part of the play, God (Figura) tells Adam that he is about to receive a gift (the Garden) ensuring that he will never have to endure hunger, thirst, cold, or heat. The meaning of God's saying is embedded in a physiological assessment of earthly paradise

---

[22] Eve "*saw* that the tree was good [. . .], a tree to be desired to make one wise" (3:6; emphasis added).

[23] Following suit, Eve's voice induces Adam to discover and savor the realm of sensory perception: in *La Bible française du XIIIe siècle: Genèse*, ed. Quereuil, 116, God admonishes Adam for having listened to his wife's voice, which caused him to eat the forbidden fruit ("tu oïs la voiz de ta fame et manjas du fruit que je t'avoie comandé que tu n'en manjasses pas"). For an overview of the Gnostic version of the story see Elaine Pagels, *Adam, Eve, and the Serpent* (New York: Random House, 1988).

[24] Evidence of the "noisy" confusion that characterizes the postlapsarian realm is the lethal effect of the four natural elements. Water puts the survival of mankind in jeopardy (the Flood: Genesis 7); air turns foul (the Tower of Babel, 11); earthly matter plagues Egypt (12:17); and fire destroys Sodom (19:24). That noise acts against stability and clarity is suggested by the possible etymology of the world (Latin *nausea*, Greek *nautia*) as "that which makes one seasick."

[25] According to Alfred Jeanroy, "Le théâtre religieux en langue française jusqu'à la fin du XIVe siècle," *Histoire Littéraire de la France* 39 (1962): 169–258, here 171. In his edition of the play (Geneva: Droz, 1969), Paul Aebischer (19) proposes an earlier date (mid-twelfth century).

which suggests an equivalence between the realm of sentiment ("raison," l. 49) and the realm of the senses.

In contrast to Genesis, therefore, sensorial perception pre-exists the event of the Fall and is in reality an essential aspect of bliss in the Garden. A second contrast is, in the play, the centrality of language as a medium of communication used indifferently by God, His creatures, and Satan. In the opening scene, for example, interaction between Adam and Figura is expressed vocally, in such a way that listening ("escote," l. 49) leads to understanding ("entent"). The Old French text nonetheless develops a hierarchical perspective on language which distinguishes among the noble tone of Figura's speech, the prosaic character of His creatures', and the parasitic effect of Satan's.[26] Another important distinction between creature and Creator is Adam's deferential attitude as vassal in the face of his Lord ("seignor," l. 112). Eating the forbidden fruit would in that context constitute a transgression contravening the rules of feudal exchange, as Adam readily acknowledges when he promises never to forswear himself and betray his Lord. Reason ("sens") dictates that one prefer bliss over pain, for only a fool ("folor") would choose to eat of the tree that makes one smell and taste death ("sentir mort," l. 112).[27] However, as Adam ends his oath, secure in his allegiance to God, "folor" is about to triumph over "sens." For, as the Latin script indicates, now enter demons running throughout the stage, followed by Satan (Diabolus). Diabolus asks Adam—and not Eve, as in the case of Genesis—to repeat God's command, and Adam complies by summarizing the core of God's

[26] Whereas Figura uses the decasyllabic line characteristic of the elevated style, Adam resorts to a more secular form of expression (the octosyllabic line typical of romance). On the combination of *sermo humilis* and *sermo sublimis* in the *Jeu d'Adam*, see Erich Auerbach, *Mimésis* (Paris: Gallimard, 1968), chap. 7. On the play as performance, see Maurice Accarie, "La mise en scène du Jeu d'Adam," *Senefiance* 7 (1979): 3–16; and Robin F. Jones, "A Medieval Prescription for Performance: *Le Jeu d'Adam*," in *Performing Texts*, ed. Michael Issacharoff and idem (Philadelphia: University of Pennsylvania Press, 1988), 101–15. See also John Stevens and Richard Rastall, "Medieval Drama III.2 (ii): Vernacular Drama: Early and Miscellaneous Plays," in *New Grove* 16: 247–49. Satan's name in the play, Diabolus, is an eloquent indictment of evil language (*diabolos*: "that which disassembles") as opposed to Figura's Word in its unifying quality (*symbolos*: "that which brings together"). As Eugene Vance notes, "the devil's equivocal poetic images subvert God's image in man, not to speak of man's image in woman; Satan seeks thus to disjoin the first couple and to deny the goodness of the creation": *Mervelous Signals: Poetics and Sign Theory in the Middle Ages* (Lincoln, NE, and London: University of Nebraska Press, 1986), 202.

[27] The original reads: "Por une pome, se jo gerpis t'amor, / Que ja en ma vie, par *sens* ne par *folor*, / Jugiez doit estre a loi de traïtor / Que si parjure e traïst son seignor!" ("If for an apple I ever forsake your love, rationally or foolishly, may I be brought to justice and condemned as one who forswears oneself and betrays his lord!", ll. 109–12). ("Taste death" is a biblical locution, as in Matthew 16:28, Mark 9:1, Luke 9:27, John 8:52.)

command.[28] But he refuses to act on Diabolus' advice and eat the forbidden fruit, provoking the Enemy's remark that it is folly on Adam's part not to taste the fruit that would make him equal to God in every respect. Unaware of the fact that Diabolus here inverts the opposition between wisdom and folly as articulated in Adam's oath to Figura, the Primordial Man persists in his "folly" by twice opposing Diabolus' "wise" saying.

This initial failure to persuade Adam does not discourage Diabolus, whose mirthful attitude ("hylaris et gaudens") as he reappears on stage indicates that his scheme is soon to succeed; not with Adam, however, who resists anew and orders his interlocutor away. As in the narration of Genesis, it is Eva, whom Diabolus describes as "a feeble and soft thing" (l. 227), who initiates man's Fall. Relying on a strategy of persuasion grounded in aural[29] and gustatory[30] arguments, Diabolus convinces Eva to take and eat the apple, the result of which is an acuity of vision which enables her to see her resemblance to Figura. Compared to Eve's downfall in Genesis (from seeing, to understanding, down to tasting), the play describes it as the result of a reverse, and twofold, sequence (from tasting to seeing [cf. Psalm 33:8]). Yet Eva's vision produces blindness and not enlightenment; language itself disintegrates, giving way to utterances that signal the degradation of the human species. In Figura's phonic account of the consequences of the Fall, Adam will earn his bread—and Eva will give birth—at the price of great pain and moaning (as recorded by the onomatopoeic Old French word *hahan*: see the quotation that opens this chapter). Dialogue itself turns into discord (*tençon*: a dispute or contest in the troubadours' lyrical tradition), as emblematized by Cain's murder of Abel, whose blood casts out so profound a "clamor" that its "rumor" reaches heaven (ll. 733–34).[31] The voice of humankind tends henceforth to lose its revelatory

[28] In Adam's words, "De tuit le fruit de paradis / Puis jo manger—ço m'a apris— / Fors de sul un: cil m'est defens" ("I may eat of all the fruit trees in paradise, God taught me, except one: that one is forbidden to me", ll. 147–49).

[29] See line 235: "Parler to voil" ("I want to talk to you"); and line 239: "Or te dirrai, e tu m'ascute" ("I will now tell you, and you, listen to me carefully"), in which Diabolus reiterates God's previous exhortation to Adam, "escote" (l. 49, quoted above).

[30] See line 252: "(Eva) -Quel savor a? (Diabolus) -Celestial!" ("-How does [this fruit] taste? -Heavenly!"). Noting the recurring conflation of *savoir* and *savor* throughout the play, Burns interprets the pun as a demonstration that, for Eva, "knowledge can be pleasurable" such "that one can taste with the mind or think with the body" (*Bodytalk*, 29). This conflation of the sensory with the rational suggests that "knowledge might exist side by side with pleasure, that obedience might be mixed with disobedience, and order with disorder." Many of the Old French works I consider in Chapter Four bring to mind Eva's challenge of "God's plenary word" in that they, too, substitute for His hierarchical and univocal perspective "the vision of a world where opposites might coexist in a dialogic and relational dynamics" (Burns, *Bodytalk*, 102).

[31] According to *La Bible française du XIIIe siècle: Genèse*, ed. Quereuil, 115, 122, God learns of Cain's crime when He hears the "voice" of Abel's blood ("la voiz du sanc de ton frere"). (The Latin Vulgate of Genesis 4:10 is "vox sanguinis fratris tui clamat ad me de terra,"

capability, either because it resounds as a strictly physiological phenomenon (*ha-han*), or because it deliberately short-circuits the relation between signifier and signified, as when Cain denies ever having harmed his brother.

A Realm of "Babblers"

The consequences of the Fall as recounted in the Old Testament amplify the characteristic of human *logos* in producing parasitic noise and confusion. Babel (Genesis 11:1–9) is here last in the process of degradation—from the Fall, to the first murder, to the Flood, down to the generation of the sons of Shem—whence the realm of "babblers" originates.[32] Before Babel, when "the whole earth was of one language, and of one speech" (Genesis 11:1),[33] language served to differentiate humankind from the other species that inhabit the earth, while serving at the same time as a link uniting "the families of the sons of Noah" (Genesis 10:32) into a single nation of speakers. However, the human community is about to lose its uniform mode of communication when Nimrod and his followers decide to build a city, along with a tower "whose top may reach unto heaven."[34] Similar to Adam and Eve's dream of becoming "as gods" (Genesis 3:5), Nimrod and his people seek thus to rival God and impose their authority on the rest of Noah's descendants: "let us make us a name, lest we be scattered abroad upon the face of the whole earth" (Genesis 11:4).[35] God punishes the transgressors through a

---

so that is a literal rendering.) Whereas Cain and his lineage will henceforth be reduced to silence, Eve and her lineage will endure a sonorous type of punishment, in reference to the suffering involved in giving birth ("Je monteplieré tes souspirs en ton concevement").

[32] The word Babel may be at the root of *babble*, which is itself connected with the Old French verb *baver* (to gurgle; see J. J. Shipley, *Dictionary of Word Origins* [Totowa, NJ: Littlefield, Adams & Co., 1967], 37, 42). Hubert Bost, *Babel: Du texte au symbole* (Geneva: Labor et Fides, 1985), 75 thus proposes a translation of Genesis 11:9 which amplifies the babbling result of the Babel episode: there, Yahveh "fit balbutier les hommes" ("caused men henceforth to stammer").

[33] The distinction in Hebrew between language (margin, border, and edge) and speech (a word; then, answer, decree, counsel, eloquence, judgment, and reason) defines the former in spatial terms, in reference to the limit that delineates the realm of the human species, while the latter appears to refer to the practice of language as elocution. I have taken this notion from the "Hebrew and Chaldee Dictionary" in the *King James Bible*, comp. Zodhiates, 129, 29.

[34] It is Josephus who names Nimrod as the builder of the tower (*Antiq. Jud.* 1.113, 115). Considering that the Babel episode derives from a Babylonian myth and that Nimrod was the national hero of the Assyrians, Hugo Gressman, *The Tower of Babel* (New York: Jewish Institute of Religion Press, 1928), 6 thus concluded that the Biblical narrative "originated in Babylonia, was taken over by the Assyrians, and then through the Arameans came to the Israelites."

[35] In the gloss provided by *La Bible française du XIIIe siècle: Genèse*, ed. Quereuil, 157, the tower signifies, in tried-and-true patristic fashion (e.g. Augustine, *Tract. in Joh.* 6.10; *Enarr. in Ps.* 54.11), "l'orgueil du monde" ("the pride of the terrestrial world"). Here as in many other passages of the commentary, the moral lesson takes the form of a warning against vainglory,

disassembling decree: "Go to, let us go down, and there confound their language, that they may not understand one another's speech" (Genesis 11:7).[36] The effect of the Babel episode in terms of a linguistic Fall ("lapsus linguae") is both discord and discordance, which Augustine connects with the tendency, characteristic of post-Babelian language, to sever the connection between what we would now term signified and signifiers. To recover some form of linguistic coherence, one must venerate those divinely-instituted signs whose "signifying force" help us attain revelation (*On Christian Doctrine*, trans. Robertson, 87). For whoever uses or worships the signifier at the expense of the signified ("idolatry") condemns himself to ignorance or, worse, to linguistic perversion.

Augustine's warning against the seduction of semiotic mendacity finds its echo in many medieval interpretations of the Babel episode. An example is provided in one of the surviving manuscripts known as *Bibles Moralisées*, the Bible of Codex Vindobonensis 2554 (ca. 1230–1250).[37] The Babel episode is illustrated by two images (fol. 3v), the first of which focuses on the tower proper and depicts the downfall of its builders. According to the accompanying Old French caption, "Here the pagans make the Tower of Babel, against the commandment of God,

consistent with the values of the monastic community (Dominican nuns) for whose edification this prose translation may have been undertaken (as suggested by Quereuil, 11).

Babel as the petrified manifestation of linguistic confusion has inspired a multiplicity of perspectives: see for example Roger Caillois, *Babel* (Paris: Gallimard, 1948), and George Steiner, *After Babel* (New York and London: Oxford University Press, 1975). The motif is just as pervasively represented in art (see the illustrations collected by Helmut Minkowski, *Aus dem Nebel der Vergangenheit steigt der Turm zu Babel* [Berlin: Rembrandt-Verlag, 1960]): in November 1997, there took place in Paris the opening of an exhibit focusing on Ignatio Rabado's work, entitled "The Library of Babel." Reminiscent of Borges' imaginary library of the same title as a locus of disconnected and fragmented works, the exhibit consisted of isolated books, each one hanging from the ceiling.

[36] The Hebrew meaning of Babel is "mixture" and "confusion" (*King James Bible*, comp. Zodhiates, 18, 21). Another meaning of Babel is "gate of God," in reference to the Babylonian "Bâbilu." In the Babylonian tradition, therefore, Babel takes on a positive significance, for, as Hugo Gressmann observes (*The Tower of Babel*, 5, 15), the construction of the tower is a myth about the creation of the world wherein "the temple tower is an imitation of the earth," which "was conceived as a multi-staged mountain with three or four or seven stage-formed terraces." In the anti-Babylonian perspective developed in the Biblical text, Babel is by contrast the first skyscraper whose significance is to concretize the people's desire to found an empire (Bost, *Babel*, 56).

[37] *Bibles Moralisées* are essentially picture books that contain a detailed illustration of sacred scripture. Produced in Paris probably for members of the Capetian court, the *Bible* of Codex Vindobonensis 2554 alternates biblical text and commentary, each of which inspires a number of illustrations (ed. Gerald B. Guest [London: Harvey Miller, 1995]). According to John Lowden (*The Making of "Bibles Moralisées"* [University Park, PA: Pennsylvania State University Press, 2000]), who dates the codex in the early 1220s, this *Bible* was commissioned by or for Blanche of Castile.

and God strikes them down and turns their work to nothing."[38] Among the discrepancies between text and image, which reoccur throughout the codex, is the cryptic allusion to "the commandment of God," considering that the eleventh chapter of Genesis makes no mention of any taboo regarding the building of a tower. Also interesting is the codex's emphasis on the material aspect of Babel and its consequences. The second image thus includes the figures of three clerics, whose respective postures illustrate the downgrading effect of the episode, from the standing position of the central figure to the bent position of the right-hand figure down to the prostrate position of the left-hand figure. It is only with the *Bible*'s following caption that the episode takes on a linguistic significance: "That the pagans began the tower of Babel against God's commandment signifies the astronomers and the dialecticians who make false proofs against the will of Jesus Christ, and He turns their work to nothing and blinds them and strikes them." Perverse eloquence leads to mental and spiritual blindness, as amplified in a subsequent image wherein a series of arrows come down to pierce the three clerics, one of whom is struck in his right eye.

That pride and arrogance have a severing effect and remove one from the transparency of the divine *Verbum* is reiterated in the roundels and captions that gloss one of the plagues of Egypt (fol. 19r). The first sequence recounts how Moses struck the water in such a way that frogs covered Pharaoh and his people and made a "grant noise." Contemporary application of this event is presented in the second sequence, the commentary which provides the following exegesis: "That Moses struck the water and frogs came out, the frogs that scream and cry ('braent' and 'crient'), signifies the flatterers (*losengiers*) and jongleurs (*gengleors*) of the courts of kings and princes who constantly cry into the ears of kings and barons and princes and counsel them to do ill with their power." Modernizing the Egyptian setting of Exodus, the *Bible* here posits a disparaging equivalence between the noisy frogs of the plague and all those individuals who jam the channel of proper communication.

2. After the Fall: The Noise of Sin

The emergence of Eve as a speaking subject also signals the emergence of human language in its imperfect character. As we saw, Genesis illustrates this degradation through the soundscapes of anger and lament respectively produced by Cain and Abel. Postlapsarian history is henceforth a noisy affair, in the sense that humans, animals, and nature itself manufacture a type of sounds the effect of which is often noxious. These sounds, however, are not necessarily loud, nor are they necessarily inarticulate. My analysis of the noise of sin will thus examine a variety of phonic phenomena which I propose to consider decrescendo, according to a descending scale of resonance.

[38] Each citation from the vernacular original reproduces Guest's translation.

Pagan *diabolos*

At the top of the scale is the stridency of pagan language as a mode of elocution the goal of which is to interrupt the saint's interaction with God. Old French Passions of the martyrs provide a resonant illustration of this mode in the threats used by the persecutors to force the saint to recant.[39] Yet pagan menaces never succeed in persuading the martyr-to-be, so that the tyrant, acknowledging the inefficacy of his language, abandons the realm of words for that of action. Verbal debate is then replaced by a confrontation—between the "beauty" and the "beast"—in the course of which the tyrant often regresses to a primitive stage. For example, when Olybrius sees Margaret emerging unharmed from one of her many ordeals, the pagan is so overwhelmed by rage that he gnashes his teeth in a manner prefiguring his eventual condemnation to Hell.[40] As for the saints, they treat pagan noise as inconsequential: witness the way Christina ignores the wailing emitted by her mother ("braie et crie," l. 1232) and by the women who witness her tortures ("le hals brais et les cris," l. 3602) as well as the yelling of Julian, one of her many tormentors.[41] The saint's composure enrages Julian, who denounces her verbal exchange with God as a "diabolical" attempt to "dupe" and "deceive" his people.[42] Pagan language takes here the form of a semantic inversion, for it is of course Julian's words and not Christina's which are "diabolical." Just as sinful is Julian's irate reaction to holy *logos*, inducing him to ordering that Christina's tongue be cut out during one of the most famous episodes of her legend.[43]

[39] E.g.: if the eponymous heroine of the verse *Passion de Sainte Agnès* (ca. 1250; ed. A. J. Denomy, in *The Old French Lives of Saint Agnes and Other Vernacular Versions of the Middle Ages* [Cambridge, MA: Harvard University Press, 1938], 65–98) persists in refusing to honor the idols, she will be made a prostitute and "we will then see," her tormentor warns her, "how feeble is the power of this Jesus in whom you believe" (ll. 331–32). (This is a topos in late antique hagiography.)

[40] See "les dens estraint" at l. 125 of the verse *Passion de Sainte Marguerite* (thirteenth century; ed. A. Joly, *La Vie de Sainte Marguerite* [Caen and Rouen: Mémoires de la Société des Antiquaires de Normandie, 1878], 215–22). The same animal imagery serves to describe the reaction of Faith's tormentor, Dacian, in the verse *Passion de Sainte Foy* (early thirteenth century; ed. A. T. Baker, *Romania* 66 [1940–1941]: 49–89): realizing that he will never break the resistance of his victim, Dacian begins twisting and turning "as a snake does when its venom reaches its heart and makes it swell" (ll. 803–806).

[41] These citations refer to Gautier de Coinci's verse *Passion de Sainte Christine* (ca. 1214–1221); ed. O. Collet (Geneva: Droz, 1999). The loudness of Julian's voice is expressed at l. 3682: "a halte vois s'escrie."

[42] See in Gautier's text, l. 3544 ("diable parole") and l. 3545 ("ghille" and "decevance").

[43] The saint reacts in her turn by throwing the severed organ at Julian such that his right eye is pierced. Gautier de Coinci's *Passion de Sainte Christine* is to a degree a Christian transformation of the Philomela myth: in some versions, Tereus raped Philomela and cut out her tongue; unable to identify her persecutor, Philomela wove her story into the designs of a tapestry. She was eventually transformed into a nightingale, the emblem of love song in the lyrical tradition. See Ovid, *Metamorphoses* 6.426–674.

Old French Passions vilify the martyr's persecutor through a process of degradation which transforms him from a relatively sentient being as speaking subject, to a bestial creature producing inarticulate sounds, down to a body of pain absorbed by the realm of darkness and stench.[44] The downward motion that accompanies the unfolding of the tyrant's story evokes Babel in terms of an architecture of decadence wherein the sinner is gradually deprived of sense and reason. Instead of empowering the tyrants at the level of verbal persuasion, their reliance on *diabolos* causes their eventual downfall. For having attempted to break, though noise, the communication between saint and deity, they are in their turn "silenced" when God avenges His saints by means of a sonorous destruction.[45]

Senseless Moaning

Another manifestation of pagan noise is the reactions of pity sometimes expressed by the characters who witness the saint's ordeal. In the verse *Passion de Sainte Catherine* (thirteenth century), the crowd wails noisily ("noise," l. 1470) as carpenters are fabricating the wheel on which the saint is about to be bound. It is also through loud moans ("firent pleinte tres grant," l. 735) that, in the verse *Passion de Sainte Foy* (early thirteenth century), the onlookers react to the tortures imposed on Capraise, Faith's companion in martyrdom. In the hagiological

[44] As Hell is described in Gautier's version of the *Passion de Sainte Christine*: "es tenebres d'infer, en la püant santine" (l. 3565).

[45] When Agnès is thrown into the fire, God avenges the maiden so that the flames spare her and burn, instead, many of the pagan onlookers (ll. 705–708). In the *Passion de Sainte Catherine*, Jesus sends his vengeance through an angel who hurls a tempest so violent that the wheel of torture is destroyed into fragments, which fall upon those present such that brains are split open and four thousand pagans die (ll. 1511–1528). In the *Passion de Sainte Agnès*, a cataclysmic event comes to eradicate pagan authority, for there occurs a tempest and a storm so violent that much of the city is destroyed along with a vast number of pagans (ll. 784–788). And it is an earthquake which, in the *Passion de Sainte Marguerite* (ll. 426–428), concludes the heroine's confrontation with Beelzebub. As Raynaud remarks (*La Violence au Moyen Age*, 21, 261), acts of violence as represented in medieval texts and manuscripts are legitimate whenever they support the established order, but condemned whenever they endanger it. The latter is obviously the case with the pagan tormentors of the hagiographic tradition, whence the extreme brutality characterizing the illustrations of the manuscripts (until the end of the thirteenth century) which contain this tradition. On violence in early verse Passions of the martyrs, see Shmuel Shepkaru, "To Die for God: Martyr's Heaven in Hebrew and Latin Crusade Narratives," *Speculum* 77 (2002): 311–41; Cynthia Jean Hahn, *Portrayed on the Heart: Narrative Effect in Pictorial Lives of Saints from the Tenth through the Thirteenth Century* (Berkeley: University of California Press, 2001), esp. chap. 4, "The Virgin as Corpus: Bodily Offering," 90–128; Sarah Kay, "The Sublime Body of the Martyr: Violence in Early Romance Saints' Lives," in *Violence in Medieval Society*, ed. Richard W. Kaueper (Woodbridge, UK, and Rochester, NY: Boydell Press, 2000), 3–20); and cf. Susan Ashbrook Harvey, *Holy Women of the Syrian Orient* (Berkeley: University of California Press, 1987).

context, these displays of compassion are comparable to the tyrant's verbal abuse in that the resulting noise could affect, if not interrupt, the saint's communion with the divine. Pagan noise, however, proves to be totally ineffective to the extent that the saint turns a deaf ear to the soundscape of either threat or compassion.[46]

Noise is similarly at work in the stories of nonmartyr saints inasmuch as, here too, sounds serve to differentiate between holy protagonists and ordinary humanity. In this connection, the fact that the Lives of nonmartyr saints take place in a now Christianized society does not radically alter the type of reactions inspired by the protagonist. Whether expressing contempt, fear, or sadness, these reactions are often indicative of moral blindness as expressed by inappropriate displays of emotion. A salient example, in the verse *Vie de Saint Alexis* (ca. 1040), is the anguish manifested by the hero's parents in the face of their son's achievement. Resolved to devote his life to God, Alexis departs from Rome on the eve of his wedding night and settles in the city of Alsis, where he spends seventeen years in silent meditation. Although Alexis does in time return to Rome and lives seventeen more years under the roof of his father, Eufemien, he also never identifies himself to his parents. Silence is therefore integral to Alexis' spiritual journey: the rare manifestations of the saint as a speaking entity, which in the main express his interaction with God, have a noticeably non-dialogic character and corroborate the hero's desire to avoid the noise of earthly communication. This noise has to do, first and foremost, with the sounds of parental sorrow induced by Alexis' disappearance and, after his death, by the discovery of his identity. The noise of the hero's grieving father ("Grant fut la noise," l. 421) elicits the equally sonorous anguish of his mother. The *Vie* thus develops a running contrast between, on the one hand, the gradually more resonant expression of parental grief and, on the other hand, the saint's progressive transformation into a silent and spiritual being. In Alexandre Leupin's view, Alexis ("a" + "lexis", "without speech") as a wordless entity stands in that respect at the opposite of his father *Eufemien* ("well-speaking"): by making himself "a *lexis* of the Divine," the function of the saint would be to redress "the rhetorical deviance inherent [in] terrestrial discourse, especially [in] his father's speech."[47]

However, against Leupin and despite the name of Alexis' father, it appears that the linguistic antithesis of Alexis' non-verbal perfection is not Eufemien as an emblem of perverse eloquence, so much as it is the hero's mother. For it is she, indeed, who emblematizes the type of inversion evoked in the rhetorical figure of euphemism (or its equivalent, antiphrasis) wherein good is put in the place of

---

[46] Thus, when Margaret hears the noise and shouts made by the onlookers ("La noise et le cri de la gent," l. 202), she disparages these aural signs as an ill-conceived form of advice ("mal conseiller," l. 205).

[47] Alexandre Leupin, *Barbarolexis: Medieval Writing and Sexuality* (Cambridge, MA: Harvard University Press, 1989), 48.

evil. Her behavior when she hears of the servants' failure to find her son is in that respect exemplary. She proceeds to strip his chamber and replaces what used to be tapestries and decorations ("palie" and "ornement," l. 138) with sacks and tattered curtains. Although this action coheres with the hero's ascetic achievement, it is also a reverse investment of austerity inasmuch as she is thus expressing human grief instead of cultivating spiritual happiness. Whereas the protagonist, by escaping from the burdens of earthly existence, enjoys a corresponding lightness of being (Alexis as "alegié"?), stripping the room of its ornaments brings no relief to his mother. To the contrary, she experiences sadness as a kind of gravity both external and internal: witness the way she now sits down on the ground. The downward direction of her story is punctuated by a soundscape the resonance of which is reprehensibly doleful. Nowhere is the poet's indictment better expressed than in the scene that depicts her displays of raw anguish at seeing dead the flesh of her flesh. In what Rachel Bullington aptly describes as an animated Pietà,[48] the maternal character initiates an impassioned one-sided dialogue with her son whose only response is the silence of the dead.

Undoubtedly poignant from a terrestrial perspective, the encounter between mother and son has a primarily didactic function and amplifies the moral lesson of the poem regarding the blinding effect of possessive love. Whereas sorrow prevents Alexis' mother from transcending the realm of the flesh, joy as experienced by Alexis' silent communion with God is what enables him ultimately to savor the bliss of paradise.

Perverse Eloquence

Adhering to the stabilizing world view enunciated by the discourse of orthodoxy, Old French hagiography opposes the suavity of holy *logos* to any production of sounds which has a parasitic intent or effect. Vernacular hagiographers also show their awareness of the complexity of human language and thus assign to *diabolos*, for example, the power to deceive through seduction rather than threat. Pagan interference may thus take the form of a falsely affable eloquence, as when the tyrant Dacian, in the verse *Passion de Sainte Foy*, attempts to lure Faith away from her religion through deceptively sweet words ("en losengant," l. 657). The term (*losenge*) employed by the Old French hagiographer to indict Dacian's mode of elocution brings to mind the commentary of the *Bible Moralisée*, quoted above, according to which frogs that scream and cry signify the court flatterers (*losengiers*) and jongleurs. In the moralists' view, we recall, works marked by a courtly tonality are irremediably perverse in that they glorify the flesh at the expense

[48] Rachel Bullington, *The Alexis in the Saint Albans Psalter* (New York: Garland, 1991), 152.

of the spirit. Even worse is the fact that courtly literature pretends to meditate on matters of the heart, although its primary care is in reality the body. Despite its condemnation at the hands of contemporary moralists—and fortunately for medieval audiences and modern readers—courtly literature expanded and flourished in a multiplicity of ways.

A noteworthy aspect of this literary production is the concern it manifests for the problematics of communication as experienced at the courts of aristocratic society and at their fictional counterparts.[49] The verse *Roman de Silence* (thirteenth century) is here an emblematic example in that its author, Heldris of Cornwall, revolves his story around issues of both a rhetorical and a hermeneutic nature. Heldris thus introduces his romance by claiming that, even though *Losenge* (False Praise) reigns supreme at court, his will be a straightforward narration, without any gloss ("metre de glose") or sophistry ("jo n'i fas nule sofime"; ll. 68–71). As the romance's title indicates, the focus of Heldris' story is therefore "silence" understood here as an unadorned and hence transparent type of language. It is in this connection remarkable that, although the concept of silence as absence of speech is abundantly represented in twelfth- and thirteenth-century romances, the word "silence" rarely appears. That courtly literature of the period is marked by a profusion of acoustic phenomena would suggest, then, that interaction in aristocratic society was essentially noisy.[50] Heldris' *Roman de Silence* might in that sense be viewed as an attempt on the author's part to support a "noiseless"—as opposed to parasitic—mode of communication. The language of Silence, the romance's heroine, would stand at the opposite of ornamental elocution as emblematized by Eufeme (the wife of Evan, the king of the realm; note the name again), who represents eristic reasoning.[51]

---

[49] I further analyze the tradition of courtly romance in Chapters Three and Four.

[50] An example is the context in which the word "silence" appears as a hapax in Béroul's rendition of the Tristan myth (ca. 1165; series of fragments of 4,485 octosyllabic lines), in reference to Tristan's dog, Husdent, which the hero trains not to bark ("Quë il laisast cri por silence"). See Danièle James-Raoul's study of imperfect communication ("hindered speech") in courtly literature: *La parole empêchée dans la littérature arthurienne* (Paris: Champion, 1997), esp. 101, 105–8.

[51] Most readers today see the romance as an allegory about the indeterminacy of either gender (an arbitrary social construct) or narrativity (an arbitrary system of signs). See the critical studies listed in Sarah Roche-Mahdi, ed., *Silence: A Thirteenth-Century French Romance* (East Lansing, MI: Colleagues Press, 1992), 341–42; and more recently Catherine L. White, "Women and Their Fathers in Three French Medieval Literary Works (*Le Roman de Silence*, *Erec et Enide*, and *Le Livre de la Cité des Dames*)," *Medieval Feminist Newsletter* 21 (1997): 42–45; Burns, *Bodytalk*, 243–45; Roberta L. Krueger, *Women Readers and the Ideology of Gender in Old French Verse Romance* (Cambridge: Cambridge University Press, 1993), 101–27, and "Questions of Gender in Old French Courtly Romance," in *The Cambridge Companion to Medieval Romance*, ed. eadem (Cambridge: Cambridge University Press, 2000), 132–49; Peggy

Heldris begins his bipartite narrative with a love story between Cador and Eufemie, which leads to marriage and to the birth of an only daughter, Silence, who is the focus of the romance's second section. At the heart of Silence's drama is a decree, pronounced by King Evan, that inheritance will no longer pass through and to women. Evan's new law compels Cador and Eufemie to raise their daughter as a boy ("Silentius") in order thus to ensure that their land remain in the possession of their lineage. When Silence (as Heldris keeps naming his protagonist) is twelve years old, Nature appears to blame her for behaving like a man, instead of joining the ladies in their chamber and learning how to sew. Thereupon Nurture arrives on stage and engages in a lengthy dispute with Nature on the argument that gender is a social construct and not a "natural" given. The dispute between the two allegories brings no relief to Silence,[52] who continues to keep her true identity hidden. Four years later, the youth joins the court of King Evan in the guise of Silentius, where "his" handsome countenance arouses the lust of Queen Eufeme. The latter attempts, in vain, to satisfy her desire by resorting to all kinds of trickery, including linguistic deception (*losenge*, l. 4260). Seen against the queen's wicked use of language, it seems that Silence speaks the unadorned language of truth, thus representing a mode of elocution which is neither parasitic nor eristic ("Sans noise faire et sans tenchier," l. 106). Yet the fact remains that "Silentius" is herself a living lie. Heldris' heroine contradicts in that sense the author's own definition of truth as that which should not be concealed or kept quiet ("car la verté ne doi taisir," l. 1669). Moreover, Heldris himself resorts to mendacious language inasmuch as, by his own admission, he adorns the truth of his story with lies and for the sake of poetic embellishment ("Avoic le voir sovent mençoigne / Por le conte miols acesmer," ll. 1663–1665).

McCracken, "'The Boy Who Was a Girl': Reading Gender in the *Roman de Silence*," *Romanic Review* 85 (1994): 517–36; Sharon Kinoshita "Heldris de Cornuälle's *Roman de Silence* and the Feudal Politics of Lineage," *PMLA* 110 (1995): 397–409; Barbara Newman, *From Virile Woman to WomanChrist* (Philadelphia: University of Pennsylvania Press, 1995), 165–66; and Monica Brzezinski Potkay and Regula Meyer Evitt, *Minding the Body: Women and Literature in the Middle Ages, 800–1500* (New York: Twayne, 1997), 64–65, as well as the two issues of *Arthuriana* (1997 and 2002) devoted to the *Roman de Silence*. My own focus is the interest of Heldris' romance with respect to the ambivalence of language in its parasitic or connecting capacity. (As evidenced by the five Scottish ladies analyzed by Elizabeth Sutherland, *Five Euphemias* [New York: St. Martin's Press, 1999], medieval aristocratic women were occasionally named "Euphemia", probably after the saint.)

[52] The similarly eristic character of the language used by both Nurture and Nature indicates that, far from being the emblem of a "natural" expression, Nature herself resorts to impassioned reasoning. This is corroborated by the heroine's silent remark that, in indicting her shameful behavior, Nature is using the language of sophistry ("Dont se porpense en lui meïsme / Que Nature li fait sofime": ll. 2539–2540).

Heldris' attempt to "speak about silence" is of course a contradiction in terms, and there lies, I suggest, the interest of his romance. At the heart of the author's indictment is eloquence in its eristic rather than euphemistic character. What Heldris the romance-writer criticizes is obviously not the deliciously mendacious language of fiction; rather, it is a mode of elocution used for the purpose of harming and alienating, which is exactly Eufeme's intention in attempting to seduce Silentius and, when rejected, in attempting to avenge herself against the youth (as in the biblical story of Joseph and Potiphar's wife). As a seed of discord and violence, the queen needs to be silenced, which is effected by King Evan's order that she be drawn and quartered, whereupon the king marries Silence. The realistic character of the romance's ending is noteworthy: the "truth" of fiction consists here of an awareness that life on earth is not black or white, such that white lies are at times necessary to ensure peace,[53] just as violence is at times necessary for the protection of social order.

3. Noise in the Foundation of Christian Rome

Contemporary moralists would undoubtedly condemn Heldris' romance as a work bereft of any instructive value. In this perspective, although the mendacious language of fiction does not have the stridence of pagan noise, it has nonetheless the same parasitic effect in terms of an interference which tends to jam the channel of communication between creatures and Creator. Conversely, vernacular hagiography is a useful form of orality in that it induces its listeners to turn their attention to spiritual matters. An example is the *Vie de Saint Alexis*, whose value lies in the ability, shared by both the poet and his hero, to "say God" with a minimum of noise. What justifies the hagiographer's transcription of Alexis' silence is the edifying quality of his text, which invites its listeners to admire and commemorate the saint's wordless communion with God. The revelation of divine truth thus assumes an acoustic manifestation, indicating that the realm of oral transmission can obtain the same enlightening quality as that of the visual.

This didactic investment of audition varies, however, according to the manuscript tradition that preserves the story of Alexis.[54] In the case of the earliest extant version, that contained in the St. Albans Psalter (Ms. L), we are dealing

[53] Eufeme is from the start so wicked and eager to generate disputes ("de noise faire") that King Evan often resorts to lies in order to control his wife (ll. 4267–4270).

[54] This tradition comprises some seventeen extant manuscripts (described in Christopher Storey, ed., *La Vie de Saint Alexis* [Oxford: Blackwell, 1968], x–xiii) in which the text survives in whole or fragmentary form. Four of those manuscripts remain of major importance and formed the basis of Gaston Paris' 1872 edition of the poem; among them are the St. Albans Psalter (Ms. L, now the property of St. Godehard's Church in Hildesheim) and a manuscript

with a codex the peculiarity of which is that the Old French poem is inserted in the midst of a Latin Psalter. Probably brought together for Christina, anchoress and eventually prioress of Markyate, Ms. L combines languages, art, and music in a manner that calls into question the status of this version of the Alexis story as a text to be communicated orally or to be read privately.

"Alexis": Scripture or Script?

According to Michael Camille, who deplores the effect of modern printing in reducing sensations to a purely optical distance, the Psalter is a paradigmatic example of a mode of "rapturous reading" that was rooted "in a somatic and sensuous experience." This richly illustrated manuscript provides an experience that is "predominantly visual rather than verbal," leading to an investment of speech ("locutus") as place ("locus"): the Psalter is "a place where image, voice, and text were enunciated for a particular gaze," Christina of Markyate's, who could thus project herself into the life of her alter-ego as she, like Alexis, opted to "leave the bonds of family and the safety of civilization."[55]

The pictorial frontispiece of the poem summarizes the hero's achievement through a sequence of images which, read from left to right, contrasts Alexis' choice of an unadorned mode of existence (as he is about to embark on the boat that will take him away from home) with the realm of material ease (represented by the rich textiles and architecture that here characterize both his spouse and Eufemien's abode). For Camille, therefore, Ms. L invites its reader, Christina, to a mental performance that gives priority to the visual as her means to find consolation in the midst of her misfortunes and ordeals. This interpretation also gives priority to silence by fostering the reader's meditation, silence being the distinctive attribute of both Alexis and Christina as exceptional and holy individuals. Camille's argument that the Alexis text was to be read privately focuses on an additional peculiarity of Ms. L in introducing the Old French *Vie* with a prologue, in vernacular prose, which states that "Here begins a pleasing song and a spiritual account" ("Ici cumencet amiable cancun e spiritel raisun"). This statement seems to valorize the text in terms of an aurally and aesthetically pleasing experience ("amiable cancun"), over and above the religiously significant value

---

now at the Bibliothèque Nationale, Paris, f. fr. 4503 (Ms. A). Both L and A appear to be of twelfth-century English provenance, Ms. L being the earliest extant version (ca. 1120) of a poem the prototype of which, in the view of most literary scholars, "would have been composed in eleventh-century France" (Bullington, *The Alexis in the Saint Albans Psalter*, 1).

[55] Michael Camille, "Philological Iconoclasm: Edition and Image in the *Vie de Saint Alexis*," in *Medievalism and the Modernist Temper*, ed. R. Howard Bloch and Stephen G. Nichols (Baltimore: Johns Hopkins University Press, 1996), 371–401, here 382–94.

of its transcription ("spiritel raisun"). According to Camille, however, it is the latter function that prevails, an evidence of which is the specific text that ends the Psalter: indeed, for the last line of the Alexis poem is immediately followed by a long quotation from a famous passage of Pope Gregory the Great, first in Latin and then in French, on the "raison des paintures."[56] Although Gregory praises the value of pictures as a mode of reading beneficial for the illiterate (*Ep.* 9.105 [*PL* 77.1027C–1028A]), the passage here amplifies the visual character of Ms. L in terms of a story to be both read and contemplated. In Camille's view, the prologue's initial allusion to an "amiable cancun" invents the existence of an anterior version of the *Vie*; but "there is no poem of the eleventh century, of course, the Hildesheim version [Ms. L] being the oldest extant one" ("Philological Iconoclasm," 387).

Camille's denial of a prior and older version of the *Vie* is opposed to that of Rachel Bullington (*The Alexis in the Saint Albans Psalter*, 9–12), who argues (against the view developed by Otto Pächt and others)[57] that the poem's prologue in Ms. L is of a different period and author from the text proper. As it functions in the Psalter, the "amiable cancun" nonetheless takes on a specific significance that directly addresses Christina's religious community. A careful examination of the manuscript's features thus induced Bullington to conclude that the codex was designed for a cloister of nuns for whom the non-scriptural, vernacular, and aesthetic specificity of the Alexis poem may well have offered an opportunity to enact his story in the course of a dramatic reading. One indication is the element of pathos which distinguishes the poem from the other texts included in the Psalter and which is also the core of the emerging genre of para-liturgical dramas. Citing the prevalence of the Emoting Female within that dramatic tradition (like the three weeping women presented in the St. Gall *Quem quaeritis*), Bullington interprets the character of Alexis' mother as an example of the "laïcization of the sacred matter" which is at work in those early dramas (*The Alexis in the Saint Albans Psalter*, 211). The "planctus" of Alexis' mother would echo that of the women on stage and share their function in humanizing the divine.[58]

Another specificity of Ms. L is the burial scene, which occurs in an amplification (by twenty strophes: ll. 551–625) of the version of the *Vie* as contained, for

---

[56] On Gregory the Great's famous text about images, see Peter Brown, "Images as a Substitute for Writing," in *East and West: Modes of Communication*, ed. Evangelos Chrysos and Ian Wood (Leiden: Brill, 1999), 15–34.

[57] Otto Pächt, C. R. Dodwell, and Francis Wormald, *The St. Albans Psalter* (London: The Warburg Institute, 1960).

[58] Alexis's spouse could have a similar role, considering her depiction, in the pictorial frontispiece of the poem, which visualizes her with "a hand on her cheek in the 'pathos formula' of dejection and sorrow" (Camille, "Philological Iconoclasm," 391).

example, in Ms. A.[59] While the latter codex ends with the mention that Alexis' soul is now in Heaven as a just reward for the life of outstanding humility he led on earth, Ms. L prolongs the story and proceeds to enumerate the various healing miracles operated through the saint's body, until his remains are laid to rest in the course of a majestic funeral ceremony. Although this visual splendor to a degree contradicts the unadorned character of Alexis' achievement, it also augments the textile quality of the *Vie*, thereby corroborating Bullington's contention that the codex was designed for a community of women. In this view, what mattered for the codex's female receivers was its emphasis on both the material (including the rich textiles worn by Alexis' spouse in the poem's initial illustration and the lavish objects mentioned in the burial scene) and the maternal, in reference to the *cancun*'s specific language (Old French as "mother tongue": Bullington, *The Alexis in the Saint Albans Psalter*, 207) and to the centrality of Alexis' mother as an embodiment of the Emoting Female motif. The codex would appeal not so much to Christina the saintly recluse by offering her visually a model exemplar of meditation, so much as it would appeal to Christina the hapless woman by offering her aurally a number of model exemplars of suffering women.[60]

"Alexis": Song or Noise?

That the Psalter (Ms. L) is at the basis of two diverging assessments of the Alexis poem testifies to the richness of the manuscript tradition in inspiring approaches to the text which vary in accordance with the values, concerns, and modes of transmission characterizing each codex. Subscribing to Bullington's view that the version of Ms. L derives from a previous "cancun," my suggestion is that the soundscape of the poem as preserved in the Psalter may well help us to retrieve the message that this lost "cancun" intended to convey to its listeners.

While inducing sonorous grief on the part of his parents, the posthumous revelation of Alexis' sanctity also provokes elation throughout the city. Regardless of their station in life, the great and the humble gather around the saint's body and joyfully celebrate the discovery of the Man of God (*ledece*, ll. 533 and 536). To this earthy expression of delight corresponds that of Alexis now that his soul enjoys (*liez*, l. 545) both the pleasure of heaven and the company of his spouse after the latter's death (in the amplification of the *Vie* as contained in Ms.

[59] On the contrast between Ms. A and Ms. L in developing a different interpretation of Alexis's story, see Donald Maddox, "Pilgrimage Narrative and Meaning in Manuscripts L and A of the *Vie de Saint Alexis*," *Romance Philology* 27 (1973): 143–57.

[60] My view, expressed in the preceding section, is that the "planctus" of Alexis' mother is a clear inversion of her son's achievement in rejecting the safety and comfort of aristocratic life. For Christina, a better model, it would seem, is Alexis' wife as a lamenting "sponsa" who will eventually entrust herself to the Eternal Bridegroom.

L: "lur *ledece* est grande," l. 610). Although the text relies on a similar terminology to describe joy in heaven and on earth, it is nonetheless clear that those feelings of happiness are radically different in terms of experience and motivation. In Alexis' perspective, the bliss of paradise consists of a plenitude that enables him to contemplate God face to face: "A/*lexis*" finds in Heaven the *lexical* complement that is lacking in the human realm. In contrast with the spiritual investment of the pleasures enjoyed in paradise, the kind of elation expressed through the "vox populi" ("ad une voiz," l. 531) focuses on the tangible benefits that are generated by Alexis' body. A first type of benefit is the body's effect in curing the sick: everyone who comes to the holy body is restored to health (*sanctét*, l. 557), in such a manner that whoever arrives in tears goes away rejoicing (Psalm 125:6). A second type of blessing is the function of Alexis as their petitioner before God, indicating that Alexis has now acquired full expertise in God's silent and transparent lexis. Third, the poet evokes Alexis' mediative power in ensuring the salvation of the soul (*salvedes*, l. 605). Behind an apparently gradual assessment of those benefits—from the corporeal (health) to the moral (purity of the soul) up to the spiritual (redemption)—emerges a glorification of Alexis' sanctity that focuses on its tangible value with regard to the people of Rome. Because he is a *sainz*, they obtain safety on earth (*sanctét*) and, at the hour of death, safety in heaven (*salvedes*): whence the people's unanimous elation (*ledece*) in witnessing the power of Alexis as a miracle-worker.

The effect of the saint in generating harmony brings to mind the possible etymology of "religion" as that which unites and assembles. However, institutionalized religion as represented by the Pope appears to have a severing effect. An example is the Pope's attempt to regain control over the saint's body by offering gold and silver to Alexis' numerous devotees in the hope that they will then disperse. The Pope does eventually succeed in taking hold of Alexis' corpse, when, seven days after Alexis' death, he orders that the funeral take place. There ensues much weeping and wailing throughout the city, a collective grieving that blends into a single clamor ("lor voiz," l. 593). What the people laments is not only the entombment of Alexis' body, but also, if implicitly, its appropriation by the dignitaries of Rome. Ultimately, the Pope's authoritative voice dominates the "vox populi" in a manner that reasserts his prerogative as leader of the community. Not only does this appropriation run counter to Alexis' value as the sounding board of divine bliss; it also transforms the story of Saint Alexis into a founding myth wherein the emergence and maintenance of order require the sacrifice of a victim.

Consider the violent origin of Rome as recounted by Livy's *Ab urbe condita*, an example of which is the desire, equally shared by the twin brothers, Romulus and Remus, to found a city. As Livy notes, this desire reflects an "hereditary passion—the thirst for power—whence results a criminal conflict" between

Romulus and Remus (1:6). They and their respective factions argue among themselves; then debate turns into combat, in the course of which Remus meets with his death. However, according to a more popular tradition, to which Livy's text appears to give credence, Remus died directly at the hands of his brother. Compared to the collective and, hence, anonymous character of Remus' death in the less popular tradition, the second version of the story situates the "criminal conflict" in the context of brotherly rivalry. If Romulus killed his twin brother, the reason is that he wanted to affirm his identity as an autonomous and distinct individual. His crime (Latin *crimen*) consists of a desire to separate himself (Greek *krinein*) from his twin brother, whence sprang his decision (Latin *decidere*) to murder (Latin *caedere*) Remus and thus emerge as the one and only leader of the city. That the origin of Rome requires the murder of a victim is corroborated by the circumstances of its founder's death. One day, as Romulus is holding an assembly with the city's fathers, a storm struck him and he disappeared forever. Momentarily struck dumb, the fathers then proceed to invoke the name of Romulus and implore his protection (1:16). There exists here again a second version of the event according to which Romulus died at the hands of the fathers themselves, who tore him to pieces.[61] Yet the first version eventually prevailed, leading to the apotheosis of Romulus as an immortal deity and, henceforth, to the emergence of the Roman empire.

The key word here is empire, articulating the resemblance between the Romulus story and the Alexis story in terms of a founding myth wherein a body serves as the cornerstone of social order. At a time (ca. 1040) when the Church of Rome is determined to defend its preeminence as a temporal power, the function of Alexis as the founding hero of the Christian Rome[62] has a highly

[61] Lincoln, *Myth, Cosmos, and Society*, 43 discerns two principal functions in the script of Rome's founding myth (according to Plutarch, *Life of Romulus*, chap. 27). The first focuses on its cosmogonic value: after having torn Romulus's body into pieces, each senator hid a fragment of Romulus' dismembered body and proceeded to place it in the earth; the performance of sacrifice here consists in dispersing material substance from its microcosmic form to the macrocosm, thus sustaining creation. The second function is sociogonic: imitating Romulus as the primordial father of Rome, the senators as *patres* will henceforth assume his role and incarnate Rome in its totality. The distribution of "Romulus' bodily parts is thus a mythic sociogony, describing the creation of a differentiated social order in which no *gens* could claim totality or absolute supremacy, but in which each had a role to play in the functioning of the city": Lincoln, *Myth, Cosmos, and Society*, 43.

[62] As Peter Brown notes (*The Cult of the Saints* [Chicago: University of Chicago Press, 1981], 97), the festival of a saint functions like the reenactment of a foundation myth for the Christian community. In Lincoln's observation (*Myth, Cosmos, and Society*, 164–65), the priestly class (i. e., the medieval First Order of "those who pray") is an elite intelligentsia devoted, not only to speculation on man and cosmos (and to the rituals attending that speculation), but also to "the propagation of a social ideology encoded in sociogonic and regiogonic myths"; for myth is "the mode of ideology most characteristic of the preindustrial world."

political—rather than spiritual—significance. We are provided with a myth whose primary benefit is Rome as the center of institutionalized religion (cf. Richard Krautheimer, *Rome: Profile of a City, 312–1308*, 2nd ed. [Princeton: Princeton University Press, 2000], 41–42, 255).

Noise as Political Empowerment

The *Vie de Saint Alexis* introduces a number of "voices" each of which receives a specific value according to the speaker's social standing.[63] At the top of this sonorous hierarchy is God's voice, which resonates twice (once before and once after Alexis' death) in the narration. In its first occurrence, God's voice is heard by the sacristan of the church of Alsis, a miracle which prompts everyone in the city to rush toward the saint in order to honor him. Alexis reacts by fleeing Alsis so as to avoid the burden of collective admiration. In this perspective, the poet's transcription of God's voice acts as parasitic interference in that such "noise" creates the risk of propelling Alexis back to the type of earthly existence from which he is so determined to distance himself. For the protagonist to be recognized as saint, however, necessitates a process of revelation which Leupin characterizes as the "publication of sainthood" (*Barbarolexis*, 50). Such is the role of the Pope's voice in his capacity to interpret holy *logos*: as the official spokesman of both God and His saint, the Pope stands second in the sonorous hierarchy elaborated by the *Vie*. Next is the hagiographer's own voice in reproducing and transmitting the divine truth as embodied by Alexis and elucidated by the Pope. On the model of God, the Pope and the *Alexis* poet share in speaking an harmonious and enlightening language, the opposite of which is, for example, the noise of family mourning in its senseless character. The poet's attempt to resort to the language of transparency is not, however, altogether successful to the extent that the voices of both God and the Pope as well as his own resound in an authoritative rather than spiritual manner. Such an authoritative stance is directed primarily at those members of society whose access to knowledge is both indirect (via public recitations like that of *Alexis* as *cancun*) and nonscriptural by virtue of their illiterate status. In that sense, the poem's sonorous hierarchy distinguishes between meaningful sounds and nonsensical ones, that is, between the language of science and the gibberish produced by Rome's *vox populi*.[64] Despite the hagiographer's implicit disparagement

---

[63] The various meanings of the Old French *voiz* include "sound," "word," "rumor," as well as "authority": see Asdis R. Magnúsdóttir, *La Voix du cor* (Amsterdam and Atlanta: Rodopi, 1998), 369, n. 5.

[64] One of Alcuin's letters to Charlemagne (in 798?; *Epistula* 166, PL 100: 437–38) describes the voice of the people as nonsensical noise: "Nec audiendi, qui solent dicere: 'Vox populi, vox Dei,' cum tumultuositas vulgi semper insaniae proxima est" ("One should not listen to those who say that the voice of the people is the voice of God, for the noisiness of

of the citizens of Rome, it is nonetheless clear that the latter know what they want (Alexis' body) and why (as their protector). Just as clear is the Pope's goal in taking hold of the saint's body as a means to reinforce his authority. Orchestrating the cult of a saint, as does the Pope, is indeed integral to the status of the Church dignitaries in Western Europe, whose power tended to coalesce with the power of a saint's shrine (Brown, *The Cult of the Saints*, 9).

The soundscape of the *Vie de Saint Alexis* echoes this political investment of the cult of the saint, considering the manner in which the Pope gains prominence by gradually subduing Rome's *vox populi*. Then and now, it appears, institutional power is connected with the capacity to control and legislate noise. This is the core of Jacques Attali's thesis regarding the containment of violence by the State: in Attali's terminology, "noise" is the sonorous expression of the disorder and violence of society; the control of noise by the State is thus a powerful way to maintain order.[65] Because of its political focus, Attali's study does not elaborate on the function of noise as a production of meaning, nor does it consider the grounds on the basis of which a society qualifies as noisy. One wonders, for example, whether the noises of modern and postmodern culture are stronger and louder than those which characterize the non-industrialized collectivities depicted in the artifacts of premodern Europe.[66] Noise may, in reality, be just as disturbing when it resonates in a relatively silent mode of existence or in the natural background of nature. An example is the pre-industrial urban setting of the *Vie de Saint Alexis*, where wailing, rejoicing, praying, and speaking out are heard

---

the masses is always very close to madness"). (Cf. Timothy E. Gregory, *Vox Populi: Popular Opinion and Violence in the Religious Controversies of the Fifth Century A.D.* [Columbus: Ohio State University Press, 1979], esp. 3–39.) In Latin Christianity, the cult of the saints was an "explicitly aristocratic" phenomenon through which the upper-class culture could gain and retain control over the masses (*rusticitas*): see Brown, *The Cult of the Saints*, 124. Regarding the inferior status of the illiterate (as "sounding bodies") vis-à-vis the learned elite (as "inscribed bodies "), Smith notes that "the latter are much more susceptible to political control than the former" (*The Acoustic World of Early Modern England*, 167). Power also derives from the capacity to resort to "speech barriers" for purposes of confusing rather than enlightening the interlocutor. Analyzing spoken and written language in areas such as the hospital, courtroom, and governmental guidelines, Ruth Wodak thus illustrates how power relations are maintained through the use of intimidating discourse: *Disorders of Discourse* (White Plains, NY: Addison Wesley Longman, 1996).

[65] Jacques Attali, *Bruits: essai sur l'économie politique de la musique* (Paris: Presses Universitaires de France, 1977); *Noise: The Political Economy of Music*, trans. Brian Massumi (Minneapolis: University of Minnesota Press, 1985).

[66] According to Smith (*The Acoustic World of Early Modern England*, 49), such is indeed the case, for, even "the loudest sounds that a sixteenth- or seventeenth-century listener might encounter [. . .] fall within a range of decibel intensities that would nowadays almost rate as normal events." Each sound was clearly heard in what Schafer (*Soundscape*) designates as the "hi-fi" soundscapes of premodern Europe.

all the more distinctly as the saint himself adheres to linguistic abstinence and communes with God in silence. Dominating all other phonic manifestations, the Pope reaffirms his authority on the ground that, as a virtually perfect replica of God's voice, his own voice is the best if not sole source of signification.

The *Vie*'s allusion to the cataclysm that threatens to disintegrate the city of Rome and engulf its inhabitants (ll. 298–299) is noteworthy, for the text provides no reason that could explain and justify such danger. Listeners are left to assume that the city is in some fashion guilty and thus doomed to destruction, were it not for the existence of the Man of God as Rome's shield and redeemer. Therein results a figure of the deity that evokes the vengeful character of the Maker in the Old Testament. Rather than adhering to the view that it is on earth as it is in heaven (Matthew 6:10), the founding myths of the Christian tradition construct a cosmology where it is in heaven as it is on earth. In this decidedly human assessment of Creation, the emphasis is placed, not on the vital effect of the initial sound whence God's universe originated, so much as on the lethal consequences of this explosive origin. From Genesis down to the narration of postlapsarian discordance in vernacular hagiography, the soundscape of humankind resonates a mode of interaction that is essentially a power struggle, as chronicled with equal force in accounts that tell a story of warfare and belligerence—to which we will now turn.

II

THE BLARES OF POWER

> "Devers Espaigne vei venir tel bruur,
> Tanz blancs osbercs, tanz elmes flambius!
> Icist ferunt nos Franceis grant irur."
> ("I see, coming from Spain, such noise,
> So many bright hauberks, so many shining helms!
> Those will cause here a great pain to our Franks.")
> (*Chanson de Roland*, ll. 1021–1023)

In the beginning was noise: such at least is the message that appears to emerge from the creation and foundation myths explored in the preceding chapter. Compared to the opening verse of John's Gospel, these accounts of the origin of humankind amplify the sonorous rather than the scriptural value of God's Word. Holy *Logos* manifests itself as a resounding force that is initially creative, thus leading to the emergence of the universe. After the Fall, however, God's voice acquires a frequently punitive and even lethal character, as reflected in stories wherein interaction between Creator and creatures—as well as among humans—takes the form of a power struggle. Challenging God's authority is of course doomed to failure, whence the significance of verse hagiography as an indictment of those humans who act as parasitic interferers. In the hagiologic perspective, listeners will develop an understanding of the divine *Logos* to the extent that they strive to imitate the saint's harmonious mode of communication with the deity. It is on account of its instructive merit in providing listeners with admirable models of behavior that, we recall, Old French hagiography figures among the forms of vernacularity which contemporary moralists deemed worthy. Just as useful, in the latter's perspective, are the narrative chants (epic songs) commemorating those secular heroes who actively defended the Christian faith. The result is a tendency to praise verse Saints' Lives and epic songs as equally good forms of vernacular orality with respect to their ethical worth and historical authenticity.

Narrative chants of the type praised in moralistic discourse inform the core of this chapter, which examines the function of the Christian epic hero in fighting on behalf of God's truth. I begin ("The Nemesis Principle") with an analysis of the concept of divine justice as articulated in non-Christian mythology, where violence and retribution appear to be the main if not sole means of maintaining order. Whether epic songs of the Christian tradition enunciate a similar notion of divine justice is the central issue considered in the remaining sections. My exploration considers those phonic manifestations which exploit an understanding of "noise" as strife and contention, consistent with a possible etymology of the word (from Latin "nocere," to harm). Paying specific attention to the trumpet and the horn, I examine their significance as sonorous signals that God is to triumph over His enemies. From the trumpets heard in the Jericho episode (section 2) to the battle cries of the first extant French epic (the *Chanson de Roland*), textual soundscapes seek to glorify the martial excellence of God's soldiers. In the latter case, the battle owes its epic quality to an encounter that pits together two equally sonorous opponents. This would create the risk of eliminating any distinction between Christian and Saracen warriors, were it not for the fact that each camp is also assigned a specific production of sounds (section 3). The question, ultimately (section 4: "Sundering Horns"), is to determine whether textual soundscapes here cohere with the *logos* of narration: does the noise of martial excellence confirm the hero's moral rectitude? or is the noise of trumpets and horns primarily a sign of human aggression?

1. The Nemesis Principle

Non-Christian mythology articulates a frequently violent concept of the deity, as reflected in the aggressive mode through which gods communicate among themselves as well as with humans. An example is Indra, the storm god of Hinduism and a master warrior, who (like Zeus) kills his father (Varuna) to assume the latter's leadership. Some traditions also say that Indra took his wife (Indrani) by force. In acknowledgment of Indra's potency, humans invoke him in the hope of turning his martial expertise into a source of protection. One such exploit is Indra's victory over the demon Vritra, who had reduced humans to starvation through drought by imprisoning the cloud-cattle. Sustained by a potent drink (soma) as well as by the hymns of priests and the sacrifices offered him by humans, Indra stormed Vritra's fortresses and succeeded in releasing the cloud-cattle.[1]

The Indra story illustrates a tendency in creation myths to connect the emergence of the universe with a struggle between two antagonistic forces. Comparable to the conflict between Indra and Vritra is, according to Empedocles, the fight between Eros and Neikos ("strife") (frag. 17) in accounting for the successive failures of the creation of beings. Whereas Eros fights in order to reconstitute the original oneness of Sphairos (a spherical god), Neikos fights in order to dissolve that oneness. As a result, in von Franz's words (*Patterns of Creativity*, 176), "all the limbs of the god were whirled about and then met, as if by chance,

[1] Veronica Ions, *Indian Mythology* (New York: Peter Bedrick Books, 1984), 17–20.

and so there were at first completely monstrous creations." Those abortive attempts at creation cluster around the creation of man, as if this represents a specially difficult chapter for the creative deity, requiring that he try several times before achieving approximately what he has in mind. Sometimes the created beings are failed attempts because they are too close to the animals, clumsy, unable to talk, and creeping on all fours. At other times, the creatures are too good, that is, too powerful, thus constituting a source of potential rivalry for their creator. Consider the ten-year-long conflict between the Titans and the Olympian gods as recounted by Hesiod (*Theogony*, trans. Evelyn-White, ll. 678–721), until Zeus decides to show his force by "hurling perpetual lightning" such that "the bolts with flashes and thunder flew in succession from his stout hand." The resulting blast engulfs the Titans, who are "sent down far beneath the broad ways of the earth to Tartarus." The monstrous beings who result from these failed creations are not destroyed, but survive as animals or nefarious demons: thus the subterranean Titans produce earthquakes and all sorts of mischief.

Zeus is offered another opportunity to use his power in a punitive manner when the Giants in their turn endeavor to challenge the Olympian realm. Evoking the action of Nimrod and his followers in defying the deity (Genesis 11), the Giants Otus and Ephialtes attempt to storm heaven by piling the mountains Olympus, Ossa, and Pelion upon one another. Zeus responds by striking them with his bolt and by throwing down their mountainous edifice (in Ovid's version of the myth, *Metamorphoses* 1). Like the preceding war between Titans and Olympian gods, the latter's conflict with the Giants has a cosmological dimension which opposes heaven and earth. It is in this connection noteworthy that Earth engenders each of the sixfold series of monstrous creatures who endeavor successively to challenge the Olympian realm. That Earth manufactures generations of beings who prove to be defective suggests that only Zeus and his cohort possess the capacity to fashion rational creatures. Thus some traditions relate that, after the Giants' defeat, the gods undertake to create man.

As Hesiod recounts it, however, the resulting five ages went from bad to worse. In the Bronze Age, for example, "the race was terrible and strong. They loved the lamentable works of Ares and deeds of violence [. . .]. They were destroyed by their own hands and passed to the dank house of chill Hades, and left no name" (*Works and Days*, trans. Evelyn-White, ll. 143–155). In the current fifth generation (the Iron Age), the state of affairs is not much better and, although men "have some good mingled with their evils," nonetheless "Zeus will destroy this race of mortal men" inasmuch as, ineluctably,

> The father will not agree with his children, nor the children with their father, nor guest with his host, nor comrade with comrade [. . .]. Men will praise the evil-doer and his violent dealing. Strength will be right and reverence will cease to be; and the wicked will hurt the worthy man, speaking false words against him [. . .]. And then Aidos and Nemesis, with their

> sweet forms wrapped in white robes, will go from the wide-pathed earth and forsake mankind to join the company of the deathless gods; and bitter sorrows will be left for mortal men, and there will be no help against evil (*Works and Days*, trans. Evelyn-White, ll. 180–201).

In Hesiod's pessimistic chronicle, the human species is irremediably marked by the brand of violence. In the Bronze Age, they venerate the war god Ares—who is typically accompanied by a group of assistants that includes his sister Eris ("discord"), Deimos ("terror"), and Phobos ("fear")—over and beyond any other deity. Discord and strife are again the core of human interaction during the Iron Age, considering the hostility that characterizes relations between fathers and sons, the spirit of possessiveness causing one man to "sack another's city," and the eristic use of eloquence by this "foul-mouthed" race. Expectedly, Aidos ("modesty") and Nemesis ("righteous indignation") will arise and condemn humankind to the realm of eternal evil.

Nemesis (from "nemō," to distribute) here embodies distributive justice in the sense that she punishes all those whose prosperity is undeserved or acquired by wicked means. In addition, she condemns those who, like many of the evil men in the Iron Age, are guilty of hubris ("pride" and "violence"). But the polyvalence of Nemesis in Greek mythology also leads to a rather complex picture wherein she is at times Leda, the nymph-goddess pursued by Zeus; or at times Adrasteia ("the inescapable"), which happens to be the name of Zeus' foster-nurse, an ash-nymph. And since ash-nymphs and the Furies were sisters, Nemesis is also associated with the Eumenides (the Furies as "kindly ones"), a euphemism used as a means to escape from the Furies' wrath (Graves, *The Greek Myths*, 1: 122, 126, 206–8). It is not incidental that the race of Iron sprang from ash trees (*Works and Days*, l. 144), for this suggests that the evil of humankind—its cruelty as well as its tendency to speak "false words"—is none other than a reflection of its maker(s). Also significant is the fact that meanings of "nemesis" include jealousy and envy, for this suggests that the deity will cause reversal of fortune regardless of her victim's moral worth. Taken as a whole, the semantic field of Nemesis as both deity and concept brings forward a notion of divine justice grounded in a retributive rather than distributive type of judgment. Order in the human realm is maintained through disturbing and often destructive manifestations of power such as the ones generated by each of the storm gods of the mythological tradition and, following suit, by the members of the corresponding collectivity of creatures.[2]

[2] The resemblance between the divine realm and the human realm is integral to the very phrase "creation myth," in combining a cosmogonic type of creation and an imaginative one. As Maclagan observes (*Creation Myths*, 6), those two senses of the word creation "may somehow have got confused, so that what we, like Narcissus, take to be something quite other turns out to be our own image in reflection."

What is here designated as the "nemesis principle" refers, then, to a view of the deities which emphasizes their violent disposition. Humans respond by covering up this threatening aspect of the divine realm and glorifying instead the gods' respective contribution with regard to the containment of violence. Thus Zeus (or Jupiter) is no longer the emblem of arbitrary retribution but becomes a figure of impartial justice, as either king, priest, or judge. Instead of symbolizing strife, Ares (or Mars) is now assigned the capacity to declare wars in due form. As for Mars Quirinus, his expertise in inciting division and dispute is transformed into an expertise ensuring fairness in commercial exchange and transaction. Reproducing this functional trinity, order in the human realm consists of a traditionally tripartite society that distinguishes between those who pray ("oratores"), those who fight ("bellatores"), and those who work ("laboratores").[3] Hidden behind this apparently stabilizing classification, however, lurks the presence of a hierarchical construct wherein the key word is domination. Those who work do so for the benefit of the first two orders, while those who fight are supposed to devote their martial expertise to the protection of those who pray and work. There results a discourse focusing on the appropriation of power by a few, rather than on a fair repartition for the benefit of all. The trinity of deities evoked above reveals itself to be just as unilateral, considering that Jupiter, by presiding over quarrel and strife, associates himself with war-related matters, while Mars, by determining the proper rules of wars, associates himself with legal-related matters. In his capacity of regulating all commercial operations, Mars Quirinus assesses the value of a commodity on the basis of its rarity (the stock), and it is not incidental that the "stock" refers initially to that piece of wood on which scapegoats were attached and sacrificed.[4] All things considered, therefore, the trinity of Jupiter, Mars, and Mars Quirinus refers to a single embodiment of power as obtained by the appropriation of the control of justice, war, and exchange. Also noteworthy is the pyramidal structure of order reflected in both Greco-Roman mythology and medieval society, for this points to the effect of monopolization in ensuring the domination of a select few.[5] Whether divine or human, tri-functionality relies on a method—the nemesis principle—which qualifies as reductive

[3] See Duby, *Les trois ordres*. The resulting pyramidal structure exemplifies what Jesse M. Gellrich qualifies as "mythological thought," that is, the reliance on forms and space "to close gaps and stabilize uncertainty within culture": *The Idea of the Book in the Middle Ages* (Ithaca and London: Cornell University Press, 1985), 138.

[4] This interpretation of the "stock" and, more generally, of the sacrificial strategy of order at work in tri-functionality refers to Michel Serres' hypothesis on the topic (*Le parasite* [Paris: Grasset, 1980], 131, 297).

[5] The very term "monopoly" evokes the privilege that grants a single unit ("monon") the right to regulate all forms of exchange and transaction ("pōlein," to sell). On the role of the "law of monopoly" as the socio-genesis of central government, see Norbert Elias, *La dynamique de l'Occident*, trans. Pierre Kammitzer (Paris: Calmann-Lévy, 1975), 29–45.

to the extent that the containment of violence, which is left in the hands of a select few, requires the sacrifice of a select few. In Hesiod's account, for example, the Olympian gods who emerge as winners do so at the expense of rival deities (the Titans and the Giants) who are downgraded or subdued, as in the case of Prometheus once this Titan accepts becoming allied with Zeus. That Zeus' exercise of justice is arbitrary rather than impartial is demonstrated by the fate awaiting Prometheus once the latter endeavors to aid and protect the human species. Fearing that humans would become too powerful and independent, Zeus retaliates by ordering that Prometheus be chained naked to a pillar in the Caucasus mountains. The Prometheus story illustrates eloquently the significance of divine justice in combining dominance, wrath, and jealousy, as emblematized in the figure and concept of nemesis.

Cosmogonic creation thus reflects the working of the human imagination in attempting to fight against the threat of entropy, which in Hesiod's Bronze Age occurred when men "were destroyed by their own hands." Parallel to the Darwinian concept of natural selection, its societal embodiment in the nemesis principle provides a definition of culture as a collective effort to contain violence through remedies that are themselves violent. It comes as no surprise, therefore, that the creation of the human species as recounted in the mythological tradition tends to be a mixed blessing, consistent with an image of the creatures that reflects the ambivalent nature of their creator(s). To quote Hesiod anew, men in the Iron Age "have some good mingled with their evils," which creates the hope that good will prevail, were it not for the pessimistic prediction that entropy will again be their fate. Wrapping her "sweet form" in a white robe, Nemesis will thus ensure, surreptitiously, the triumph of evil. Hesiod's story is a mastery of half-statements and understatements, leaving obscure or hidden the actual source of strife among men. An unspecified calamity weighs upon the human race, whose discordance merits that it be punished. Instead of joining "the company of deathless gods," humans are condemned to suffer the "bitter sorrows" of mortal existence and endure the tempests and storms that relentlessly come down from heaven.

2. The Trumpets of Jericho

While non-Christian mythology contains a plethora of deities governed by violence, Exodus points to the responsibility of Moses' people for the emergence of the forceful and, at times, vengeful God of the Old Testament. Initially, the Creator expresses His power by means of sounds that are solemn but not punitive. At Mount Sinai, for example, Moses is told that a trumpet (a word that makes here its first occurrence in the Old Testament: Exodus 19:13) will announce God's appearance to His people. On the third day, "there were thunders and lightnings, and a thick cloud upon the mount, and the voice of the trumpet exceeding loud;

so that all the people that was in the camp trembled [. . .]. And when the voice of the trumpet sounded long, and waxed louder and louder, Moses spake, and God answered him by a voice" (19:16–19). The sonorous sign that the Creator is about to appear, which causes man to tremble and the mount to shake (19:18), generates so great a fright in Moses' people that, when they perceived it, "they removed, and stood afar off. And they said unto Moses, Speak thou with us, and we will hear: But let not God speak to us, lest we die" (20:18–19). Moses took their message, and God agreed not to speak to the people any more, complying with His creatures' request henceforth to maintain distance. The people's wish not to frequent God's sacred groves had for its primary consequences that nature became silent for them[6] and that God's sonorous manifestation lost its vocal quality to become a noise of might and potency.

Still largely unrecognized, the value of noise as a potential source of energy has nonetheless generated a certain measure of interest among scientists. Certain research centers—for example, the Georgia Institute of Technology—have begun to develop a process capable of transforming noise into power.[7] While the scientific exploration of sonorous energy is a relatively recent phenomenon, by contrast literature has long acknowledged the power of noise:

> And the Lord said unto Joshua, See, I have given into thine hand Jericho [. . .]. Ye shall compass the city, all ye men of war, and go round about the city once. Thus shalt thou do six days. And seven priests shall bear before the ark seven trumpets of ram's horns: and the seventh day ye shall compass the city seven times, and the priests shall blow with the trumpets (Joshua 6:2–4).

God's command at this moment of Joshua's story confirms and complements the announcement made earlier by the "captain of the host of the Lord," who appears to Joshua with a drawn sword in his hand and predicts his upcoming victory over the Canaanites of Jericho (5:13). Significantly, the weapon held by God's messenger has a symbolic rather than military significance, as made clear by the fact that the destruction of Jericho does not occur through the sword, but through

[6] Meditating on this passage of Exodus, Annie Dillard notes that "silence is not our heritage but our destiny: we live where we want to live": Moses' people initiated a process whose end result was that nature itself (pantheism) became silent (pan-atheism): "Teaching a Stone to Talk," in *This Sacred Earth*, ed. Roger S. Gottlieb (New York and London: Routledge, 1996), 32–36, here 33.

[7] Implemented by a cement factory (belonging to the German company Polysius) in Colorado, the system consists of a machine resembling a huge slide trombone, the sound waves from which are regulated so as to vibrate in rhythmic pattern with those produced by a combustion chamber. The vibrating effect of the machine forces the noise of the combustion chamber to circle back on itself and turn into energy. Also, extra-low-frequency (ELF) sound waves are the basis of military submarine communications.

noise. For six consecutive days, the only sound that resonates from Joshua's host is the blowing of the priests' trumpets; for Joshua has commanded his people: "Ye shall not shout, nor make any noise with your voice, neither shall any word proceed out of your mouth" (6:10). On the seventh day, however, Joshua's people follow his order to "shout with a great shout." And thus it came that, under the combined noise produced by the priests' trumpets and by the people's shout, Jericho's "wall fell down flat" (6:20). Here as in the Sinai episode, man is made to hear first, and then to witness, the might of his Maker. However, unlike the sonorous appearance of God at Mount Sinai—which serves as a solemn prelude to the covenant concluded with His people—the trumpets of Jericho have a severing effect, distinguishing the good (Joshua's people) from the bad (the Canaanites). As in the case of the Babel episode, the event that takes place at Jericho is a resounding demonstration of the Lord's value as the source of all energy. Any attempt to resist and rival the Creator or to oppose the settlement of His chosen people deserves disintegration. Acting like the slide trombone developed in recent scientific research, the noise produced by the trumpets of Jericho turns the product of human engineering back against itself, thereby effecting the destruction of man's artifact and the downfall of the city.

The *Bible Moralisée* produced in Paris (ca. 1230–1250) for members of the Capetian court summarizes the Jericho episode in a manner that emphasizes, both textually and visually, the pulverizing effect of the trumpets (ed. Guest, fol. 34r). Dominating the roundel, two trumpeters stand in the left corner of the picture and sound their instruments, which are elongated and directed upward. At the opposite side of the roundel, blocks of stones fly off the walls of the city. The accompanying Old French text states that "Here Joshua comes and has his trumpets (*boisines*) sound and the ark carried to the city of Jericho such that the walls fall and are completely destroyed." The pictorial gloss of the episode is in parallel with the preceding image, with the apostles standing on the left side of the roundel, and on the right, pieces of pagan idols flying about, over a group of fleeing unbelievers. According to the commentary, the sounding of the trumpets signifies "the Apostles who spread their preaching through the world" (Psalm 19:4), while the falling of the walls signifies "that the idols of the Jews and the miscreants fell and came to nothing."[8] Although the text and the depiction of the Apostles stress the latter's eloquence, the consequence of their preaching nonetheless discloses the force of their words as speech acts with lethal resonance. In

[8] "Ici vient iosue et fet corner ses boisines et fet porteir l'arche entor la citei de iericho et li mur chairent et fondirent tuit ius"; and, "Et que li fill israel cornerent lors boisines et porterent l'arche et li mur chaierent senefie les apostles qui espanderent lor predication par le monde et porterent sainte eglise et li gieu et li mescreant et lors ydols chairent et vindrent a noient": trans. Guest (in text).

the *Bible*'s context, violence is justified inasmuch as the Apostles are here presented as the righteous agents of divine vengeance.

Against the *Bible*'s interpretation, however, it may be that the Jericho episode is not an anecdote in praise of God's "chosen" people, but a story of tribal rivalry. This is at least the reading that Gil Bailie proposed[9] on the basis of a pivotal phrase—"The people crossed opposite Jericho"—which narrates the crossing of the Jordan river by Joshua and his followers (Joshua 3:16). In the King James version ("the people passed over right *against* Jericho") as in Bailie's translation ("opposite"), the emphasis is placed on the adversarial stance of this crossing, indicating on the part of Joshua's people a fixation on their historical enemies. Instead of crossing the Jordan "in the sight of" Yahweh, Joshua's people cross the river "opposite" Jericho as a site of enmity. Marking Israel's entry into history, in Bailie's view the crossing of the Jordan by Joshua's people also marks the emergence of two institutions: that of holy war, along with "the new form of cultural organization that accompanies it," that is, tribal confederacy. And thus we are back to the nemesis principle according to which social order works for the empowerment of a select few. Postlapsarian history as narrated by both the Jericho episode and the *Bible*'s gloss depicts God as an equivalent of Jupiter in the latter's capacity to rule over matters of religion, war, and justice, while turning His power into a weapon used against the enemies of the true faith and, occasionally, against God's Chosen People as well.[10]

It is of course facile to indict archaic societies, like that of the Israelites in the Book of Joshua, for their reliance on sacred violence. That centuries later the *Bible Moralisée* could still develop a similarly adversarial perspective vis-à-vis the Jews and other "miscreants" is more problematic.[11] In this connection, another vernacular adaptation of the Jericho episode (in the verse *Bible* by Macé de la Charité-sur-Loire, late thirteenth century) appears to provide a more benevolent interpretation of the story to the extent that the text stresses the nonmilitary character of the

[9] Gil Bailie, "Crossing the Jordan 'Opposite Jericho': Ethnocentrism as a Response to the Sacrificial Crisis," lecture at the colloquium *Violence and Religion*, Stanford University, Spring 1992. As Bailie observes, the Hebrew word *neged* expresses a form of proximity that may evoke openness ("in the sight of") but may also evoke confrontation ("in front of," "in the presence of").

[10] See for example Jeremiah 19:3: "Thus saith the Lord of hosts, the God of Israel; Behold, I will bring evil upon this place, the which whosoever heareth, his ears shall tingle."

[11] Beginning with Pope Urban II in 1095, the development of the Crusades betokens a still more violent understanding and appropriation of divine justice. As Bailie remarked, the "distortion of the cross of suffering love into a sword of righteous hate and sacred violence is so blatant and so obvious a perversion of the Christian revelation that it becomes part of that revelation": "Crossing the Jordan." This has remained the fashionable view in recent years, but has its critics: see Christopher Tyerman, "Proteus Unbound: Crusading Historiography," in idem, *The Invention of the Crusades* (Toronto and Buffalo: University of Toronto Press, 1998), 99–126.

conquest of Jericho. In Macé's rendition of the episode, the most remarkable element of the battle is the fact that Joshua's people emerge as winners even though they possess neither lance nor javelin, neither hauberk nor sword (ll. 8759–8760): "But when the trumpets began to resound, the walls of Jericho—which was protected by seven walls—came crumbling down."[12] Numeric symbolism in Macé's poem serves to describe, not the repeated action of Joshua's priests (whom the text does not mention), but the impregnable aspect of the city. Yet man's technical expertise (the sevenfold fortification of Jericho) is about to disintegrate under the action of God's voice as vibrated by the bugles ("buisygnes") of Joshua's host.[13] Particularly noteworthy, in the context of this chapter, is Macé's implicit indictment of human engineering in the hands of the "bellatores" as evoked by the knightly weapons mentioned at ll. 8759–8760. In equating evil with the art of warfare, Macé's verse rendition reinscribes the Jericho episode in ways which criticize any and all warmongers of medieval society.

3. Battle Cries

Contemporary clerical opinions regarding the order of the "bellatores" were diverse, ranging from praise of the nobility (knightly *militia*) in its protective function to condemnation of knightly violence (knightly *malitia*).[14] It is in view of the latter aspect that moralists at times use the figure of the tournament knight ("miles") as a metaphor for the seven deadly sins. In a sermon addressed to "the

[12] "Mes quant les buisygnes sonnaint, / Li mur de Jerico versaint / Qui de .vij. murs estoit ensaincte" (ll. 8765–8767). From Latin *bucina* (the cornet used by those who tend bovines—from Latin *bos*), a *buisygne* (*buisine*) is properly speaking a bugle.

[13] The folkloric tradition tends to develop a human rather than sacred interpretation of resonance as a natural phenomenon that may have a disassembling effect. Thus many legends connect the destruction of bridges with some moral or social transgression, as evoked in the French song "Sur le pont du Nord." The phenomenon in question has to do with the resonance of building materials: on 16 April 1850 the Basse-Chaîne bridge at Angers collapsed under the pressure of marching soldiers, when the waves created by their steps disrupted those of the bridge material, provoking the death by drowning of two hundred soldiers.

[14] See Richard W. Kaeuper, *Chivalry and Violence in Medieval Europe* (Oxford: Oxford University Press, 1999), 64–81. For some (like Peter the Chanter and his cohort of disciples; see Page, *The Owl and the Nightingale*, 19–33), the reciting of epic poems is worthy inasmuch as these works support the principles of the Christian faith. At the same time, many sermons condemn those listeners who prefer hearing about the battles of Roland and Olivier to hearing about Jesus' fight against the Devil. A vernacular example thus states that "plus uolentiers oroit tos tens parler des batailles Rolant et d'Olivier qu'il ne feroit de Nostre Seignor Jhesu Crist": Zink, *La Prédication en langue romane*, 383.

An issue (raised by Bernard of Clairvaux and Alan of Lille, among others) was the way chivalric culture venerated honor and prestige, because these values fostered a spirit of competition among knights who were thus motivated to test their knightly expertise through acts

Magnates and the Knights,"[15] Jacques de Vitry (early thirteenth century) cites pride as the reason that knights engage in tourneys in the hope of "eliciting the praise of men and attaining inane glory." Pride leads to envy, causing the bad knight to prove his military superiority over rival knights; and envy leads to hatred and violence, through tourneys in the course of which the knight often wounds or even kills his opponent. A comparable criticism of warriors and warmongers is found in a verse adaptation of the *Passion de Sainte Barbara* (late thirteenth century), which opens with a reminder of the moral benefit that listeners will reap from its recitation: "I want to tell you a new kind of story, such as you never heard before. Know that it is not about Ogier, neither Roland nor Olivier, but about a holy maiden, who was most courteous and fair."[16] What is "novel" in the story of "courteous and fair" Barbara is that it will not concern any hero of the first extant French epic (the *Chanson de Roland*, ca. 1100), including Roland himself, who is here deprived of the epithet—"li proz" ("the brave")—which is habitually his textual mark and his most prominent characteristic.[17] Yet, as we have seen, moralistic discourse at times praises the tradition of epic songs in providing the public with admirable models of behavior, and so do many secular romance writers. In his *Roman de Rou* (ca. 1160), Wace evokes the role of the *Chanson de Roland*, as sung by the poet Taillefer, in sustaining the Norman host's military ardor during the Battle of Hastings. From the military incident that took place

---

of unchecked and selfish violence. In chivalric literature, Kaeuper notes (*Violence in Medieval Society* [Woodbridge, UK, and Rochester, NY: Boydell Press, 2000], 34), "honor is tirelessly portrayed as won by thoroughly physical acts of prowess." The centrality of honor and prestige accounts for the popularity of the tournament and explains the Church's indictment of this and other "detestable games" where knights "come together to demonstrate their strength and rashness" (from the 1130 decree of Pope Innocent cited by Bumke, *Courtly Culture*, 271). Yet the Church's efforts to control the tournament were not altogether successful for, as Bumke notes (*Courtly Culture*, 271), "not even threats of draconian punishment could dissuade" the nobility from one of its favorite occupations.

[15] "Ad potentes et milites": in Jacques Le Goff, *L'imaginaire médiéval* (Paris: Gallimard, 1985), 258–59.

[16] "Histore voel conter nouvelle, / Piecha n'oïstes la pareille. / Sachies que ce n'est pas d'Ogier, / Ne de Rolant ne d'Olivier, / Mais d'une sainte damoisielle / Qui par tant fu courtoise et belle" (ll. 3–8).

[17] In elaborating this contrast between Saint Barbara and the *Chanson*'s heroes, the poet also acknowledges, albeit tacitly, the fact that audiences were more inclined to listen to secular songs than to devotional works. The characteristic of Roland as a superlatively performative warrior is reflected in the iconographic programs of manuscripts that contain vernacular chronicles, wherein the two most depicted motifs are Roland's story and the Crusades: Raynaud, *La Violence au Moyen Âge*, 243. The *Chanson* has inspired a plethora of commentaries, many of which acknowledge the violent component of its hero: see, among others, Jean-Charles Payen, "Une Poétique du génocide joyeux: Devoir de violence et plaisir de tuer dans la *Chanson de Roland*," *Olifant* 6 (1979): 226–36, and Peter Haidu, *The Subject of Violence: The "Song of Roland" and the Birth of the State* (Bloomington: Indiana University Press, 1993).

at Roncevaux (in the year 778) to its heroic amplification in the *Chanson* down to Wace's *Rou* and beyond, the spread of Roland's fame transforms him into an emblem of knightly perfection.

The *Chanson*'s soundscape seems to corroborate the exalted status of both Roland and his companions through sonorous manifestations that seek to equate the Franks' military excellence with moral superiority.[18] To all appearances, however, nothing distinguishes Franks from Saracens at the level of military equipment, language, or social organization. Each of the two armies prepares for battle to the sounds of the trumpets ("grailles") that resonate throughout the mountains.[19] It is the great noise (l. 1005) produced by the pagans' thousand trumpets which alerts Olivier that the Saracens are about to attack Charles' rear guard; to which echoes the great noise made by the trumpets of Charles' host when they undertake to return to Roncevaux in order to avenge the rear guard (ll. 2150–2151). Regardless of allegiance, fighting is noisy: the encounter between French and Saracen soldiers makes the hauberks groan ("fremir," l. 3484), the swords grate on top of helmets ("cruisir," l. 3485), and the dying men scream ("braire," l. 3487). The sonorous resemblance between the two opposing armies creates the risk of obfuscating the ideological argument according to which, in Roland's words, "Paien unt tort e chrestïens unt dreit" ("Pagans are wrong, the Christians are right," l. 1015). It is at this level that the epic's soundscape becomes fully operational to the extent that it assigns a specific type of sounds to each camp. On the Saracens' side, only their trumpets are designated as "buisines" when the pagan leader Marsile (l. 1468) and his ally, the pagan emperor Baligant (l. 3138), summon their soldiers for the upcoming battle against the Franks. Although the "buisines" are not in themselves evil, considering their solemn role in the Jericho episode as adapted by Macé's *Bible*, their exclusively pagan usage in the *Chanson* is charged with significance and suggests a connection between the pagan realm and the animal realm. Consider the effect of Baligant's bugle-horn in rallying his divisions: "Come the men of Occian, *braying* and *neighing*, and the men of Arguille, *yelping* like dogs; they charge the Franks with such overwhelming force that they break their ranks and scatter them away, killing seven thousand in this attack."[20] Under the commanding figures of worthy opponents lurks the bestial

---

[18] As Kaeuper observes (*Chivalry and Violence in Medieval Europe*, 130–31), the *Chanson* develops an unmitigated praise of knightly *militia*: "Even a great cleric such as Archbishop Turpin must fight as a knight (contrary to prohibitions by Church reformers) and is valued accordingly."

[19] See for example ll. 700, 738, 2110, 2116, 2150, 2443, and 3118 for what concerns the "grailles" of Charles' host; and ll. 1004, 1454, and 3136 for what concerns the "grailles" of the pagan army.

[20] "Cil d'Occiant i braient e henissent, / Arguille si cume chen i glatissent; / Requerent Franc par si grant estultie, / El plus espés ses rumpent e partissent. / A icest colp en jetent mort .VII. milie" (ll. 3526–3530). It is tempting, albeit unverifiable, to associate Baligant's bugle-

reality of Baligant's host. The only soldiers who are caught in the act of neighing and yelping are the Saracens, whose aggression is presented as being caused by the Devil himself, to whose realm they will in time be condemned.[21]

Seen against the demonic noise of the pagan host, the Christian army reflects the brightness of God's light. The suggestion made by Anne Lombard-Jourdan that Charles' sword "Joyeuse" may derive from "Jovis"[22] is here noteworthy, for it elaborates a link between the imperial figure of the *Song* and the Roman deity (Jupiter) as the emblem of rational knowledge and justice. That Charles is God's representative is attested by the text's allusion to the origin of his imperial pennon: "Geoffroy of Anjou carries the *oriflamme* (golden-red banner): it was Saint Peter's, and was then called Romaine. But there the Franks changed its name into Monjoie" (ll. 3093–95).[23] As a symbol of the radiance of the Christian faith, the luminous quality of Charles' pennon predicates the downfall of his pagan enemies on account of their moral blindness.[24] That divine justice is about to triumph is confirmed at the moment when Ogier attacks Amborre, Baligant's standard-bearer, and strikes him with such force that Amborre crashes to the

horn, not with the ox ("boeuf"), but with the goat ("bouc"; from Celtic/Germanic "buccho"). The French word "boucan" ("din") may result from a contamination between "bouc" (as a symbol of debauchery) and "Bacchanalia" (the occasion of noisy orgies).

[21] Illustrated manuscripts that contain vernacular chronicles provide a similarly diabolical depiction of pagan soldiers. An example, in the *Grandes Chroniques de France* (of Charles V), is their resemblance with the Devil ("resemblant a diable") on account of, first, the hairy masks they wear and, second, the drums on which they beat savagely. Both the text (Ms. Paris, Bibl. nat. fr. 2813, fol. 119 [A.D. 1379]) and its accompanying image connect this use of masks and drums with the Saracens' desire thus to frighten Christian soldiers and their horses (Raynaud, *La Violence au Moyen Âge*, 136, and fig. 61). Manuscript illustrators also rely on other distinctions to characterize the pagan army, among others: Saracens are never depicted with a straight sword, which is an exclusively Christian weapon; their shield is always round, as opposed to the oval-shape Christian shield (Raynaud, *La Violence au Moyen Âge*, 80, 118). They are condemned to eternal damnation, like Marsile, whose soul is taken away by two devils and thrown into Hell (in Ms. Paris, Bibl. nat. fr. 2813, fol. 123v). Hell is here represented in traditional fashion as a dragon's open mouth, which is symbolically located on the lower left corner of the image: see Raynaud, *La Violence au Moyen Âge*, plate 20.

[22] Anne Lombard-Jourdan, *"Montjoie et saint Denis!": Le centre de la Gaule aux origines de Paris et de Saint-Denis* (Paris: CNRS, 1989), 60–61.

[23] "Gefreid d'Anjou portet l'*orie flambe*: / Seint Piere fut, si aveit num Romaine; / Mais de Munjoie iloec out pris eschange." The interpretation of Charles' oriflamme as a golden-red banner is contested by Anne Lombard-Jourdan, *Fleur de Lis et Oriflamme* (Paris: CNRS, 1991), whose hypothesis is explored later in this section.

[24] The epic's claim that pagans are morally blind finds a vivid confirmation in the visual expurgation of a fourteenth-century copy of Charlemagne's *Conquest of Spain*, "where the turbaned infidels have been blinded in each miniature [by a fifteenth-century reader] and only the Christian figures can 'see'": Michael Camille, "Obscenity under Erasure: Censorship in Medieval Illuminated Manuscripts," in *Obscenity: Social Control and Artistic Creation in the European Middle Ages*, ed. Ziolkowski, 139–54, here 143.

ground. Seeing the fall of his banner, the pagan emir begins to realize, too late, that he is wrong and that Charlemagne is right (ll. 3549–3554). Nowhere is the righteousness of Charles' war against the Infidels better demonstrated than is the effect of Ogier's aggression in revealing the truth of God's Word.

Along with the above-mentioned "buisines," another specifically pagan type of sounds are the "hues" and "cries" (l. 2064) they shout when charging the rear guard. Yet the Franks are far from silent, and while shouting as a substantive ("cri") is applied only to the Saracen host, both armies encourage themselves through yells ("s'escrier") and other battle cries. The *Song*'s soundscape is in that respect particularly rich, so much so that we will limit the exploration of rallying cries to considering the emblematic role of "enseigne" and "Monjoie."

At times associated with the pennon, at times used as a weapon, and at times a war cry indifferently shouted by pagans and Christians, the word "enseigne" counts among the *Song*'s numerous examples of semantic ambivalence. An attractive hypothesis has been recently proposed by Anne Lombard-Jourdan (*Fleur de Lis et Oriflamme*), wherein Charles' pennon would be a lance of Celtic origin, eventually adopted by French kings in the course of the twelfth century as the emblem of their royal prerogative. A number of pseudo-historical chronicles thus claim that Philip Augustus owed his victory at the battle of Bouvines (1214) to the effect of his sacred pennon in "being thirsty for human blood" (158–59). A fictional precedent of this royal oriflamme is Charles' "enseigne": in the hands of the emperor's standard-bearer, Guineman, it is clearly a lance, considering the manner in which Guineman pierces one of Baligant's counts (l. 3363). That Charles' ensign is a sacred lance leads Lombard-Jourdan to question the validity of interpreting the expression "orie flambe" (l. 3093) in terms of a golden-red banner. For according to her "orie flambe" derives neither from "aura flamma" (golden flame) nor from "laurea flammula" (golden banner) but from "aura flans" (blowing breeze), an expression used by moralists and chroniclers to describe God's voice in its either harmonious or thundering manifestation (220–24). The merit of this interpretation is that it gives full weight to the triple significance of "enseigne" as pennon, lance, and battle cry. At the top of the lance stands a flag that flaps in the wind, enabling Charles' host to hear God's commanding voice and inspiring them in turn to shout their war cry. It is the latter meaning that appears to predominate, the risk of which, as we noted, is to create a uniform soundscape of aggression.[25] From "insigna" (sign), the word "enseigne" refers to a mark of distinction that is here expressed aurally: the signified (pagan

[25] To cite an example from the Christian side: Naimes exhorts Charles to arm himself and rally his army by "shouting your battle cry" ("si criez vostre enseigne"; see ll. 1790–1794); and from the pagan side: "si escriet l'enseigne paienor" ("he shouts the pagan battle cry," l. 1221). For other occurrences of the pagan battle cry, see ll. 1921, 3146, and 3297.

or Christian allegiance) is thus supplanted by its corresponding signifier and becomes the sonorous signature of both Charles and his pagan opponents.

However, the *Song* once again circumvents the danger of indistinction by means of another aural manifestation that is specific to the Frank camp: *Monjoie*. The best-known of Charles' battle cries,[26] Monjoie emblematizes the emperor's authority, while functioning as the joyous expression of Christian right. It is not fortuitous, we are told, that the name of Charles' sword is *Joyeuse*, for it is in honor of their emperor's weapon that French barons came to choose Monjoie as their battle cry: "Because of this cry, no one can resist them" (l. 2511).[27] Through Charles as His representative, Christian soldiers fight in the name of God, and this is the reason that their war cries are cheerful, in anticipation of both the bliss that Roland and his rear guard will enjoy in Paradise and the victory of Charles'host against Baligant's. Therein lies what distinguishes Charles from his enemy, in a battle cry, Monjoie, that has no pagan equivalent. This is what transpires from the ultimate confrontation between the two opponents in the course of which the emir invokes "Precieuse" (Precious) and Charles "Monjoie" (ll. 3564–3565). Because Baligant's war cry refers to his sword, one would expect on Charles' part a similar conjuration of Joyeuse. Yet the emperor prefers to use his most famous battle cry, as if Monjoie were somehow more suited than Joyeuse to express his adherence to the Christian faith. Although the symbolic value of Joyeuse is not in question, it is also a personal weapon, in contrast with Monjoie as a collective and disembodied expression of Christian legitimacy. In that perspective, it may be that Baligant is destined to be defeated to the extent that he relies on an object, Precieuse, which lacks transcendence and emblematizes pagan venality. The fact is that the exact origin and significance of either Monjoie or Joyeuse remains to this day a mystery. An intriguing occurrence, in that connection, is the manner in which the *Chanson* twice links Monjoie and Joyeuse to another textual challenge: AOI, a three-lettered enigma which reoccurs 180 times and appears

[26] In exhorting his companions to fight long and hard, Olivier reminds them of Charles' war cry ('L'enseigne Carle n'i devum ublïer'): "A icest mot sunt Franceis escrïet. / Ki dunc oïst Munjoie demander, / De vasselage li poüst remembrer" ("At these words, all the Franks cry out. Whoever could hear them shout Monjoie would never forget their worth and bravery": ll. 1179–1182).

[27] Mentioned by the *Chanson* (ll. 2501–2511), the resemblance between Charles' sword and the Franks' battle cry in terms of a joyous resonance is accredited by Orderic Vitalis in his *Ecclesiastical History* (ca. 1135), cited by Lombard-Jourdan, *"Montjoie et saint Denis!,"* 55. For some scholars, however, Monjoie refers to the "Monte Gaudii" where Saint Denis was martyred; for others, the word derives from the Frankish "mund-gawi" (protected place; see Lombard-Jourdan's review of the scholarship pertaining to Monjoie/Montjoie, in *"Montjoie et saint Denis!,"* 325–30). Calling into question the habitual view that "Joyeuse" is connected with joy, Lombard-Jourdan opines that the word combines two Germanic expressions of sacerdotal dignity (*gau* and *-itia*).

in the main at the end of a stanza.[28] Such a correlation between the three-lettered word and the two battle cries *enseigne* and *Monjoie* suggests that AOI is itself a shout of martial encouragement, much like the "ahoï" of German march songs. Although any attempt to decipher the enigmatic AOI may be unwise, it is also somewhat irresistible. In the realm of interpretative hypothesis, everything is possible and no conjecture is in itself harmful. Clearly harmful is, by contrast, the effect of the Christians' battle cries in energizing Charles' soldiers. Their march appears to be relentless and points inexorably to the destruction of Baligant as the Frank emperor's nemesis.

The symptomatic opening of this event occurs when Ogier causes Baligant's standard-bearer to crash to the ground, for, as we saw, the downfall of the emir's ensign signals visually the pagans' imminent defeat. The stanza concludes with an AOI which resonates like a battle cry designed to electrify Charles' soldiers and muster the maximum of their energy; and indeed, there follows a combat that strikes the final hour for the pagan force. What this episode of the *Chanson* demonstrates, therefore, is the centrality of noise as the primary tool used by the Franks to silence pagan "bruur."[29]

4. Sundering Horns

Roland's "olifant" remains to this day the best-known sonorous mark identifying Charles' army. Among the particularities of Roland's horn is the fact that its sound dominates the "cors" and "grailles" used by the other soldiers (l. 3119); that its distinct voice is immediately recognizable, enabling Charles to realize that his nephew is calling for help and has not long to live (ll. 1768, 2108); and that it is entrusted to the noblest soldier of Charles' army—first Roland, and, after his death, Charles' standard-bearer, Guineman. Also noteworthy is the thunderous

[28] The first instance occurs when Olivier concludes his fiery speech to a pagan opponent by shouting Charles' battle cry: "*Munjoie* escriet, ço est l'*enseigne* Carlun. *AOI*" (l. 1234). As for the second example, here is how the epic describes Turpin's praise of the rear guard: "Dist l'arcevesque: 'Ben ait nostre barnage!' / *Munjoie* escriet, ço est l'*enseigne* Carle. *AOI*" ("The archbishop says: 'May our barons be blessed!' He shouts Monjoie, which is Charles' battle cry. AOI," ll. 1349–1350). The vast number of hypotheses inspired by those three letters include: AOI as a musical refrain; a performing device ("adaudi" as an invitation to listen and pay attention); the abbreviation of the *Chanson*'s repeated formula, "Halt sunt li pui"; the abbreviation of Amen, or Alleluia; or an exclamation denoting enthusiasm (evoking the *ahoï* of German march songs): see *Chanson de Roland*, ed. Gérard Moignet (Paris: Bordas, 1969), 31.

[29] In his assessment of the might of Marsile's soldiers, Olivier mentions the din they produce through a term, *bruur* (l. 1021), which applies exclusively to the Saracen army. Pagan "bruur" is thus opposed to Christian "noise" as a dual use of sonorous energy which is legitimate only in the second case.

quality of Roland's olifant, which thus echoes Charles' function in representing a God of justice and righteous vengeance.[30] In sum, Roland's "olifant" and Charles' "oriflamme" share the same nature (divine energy) and the same root ("aura flans"). There is, therefore, no contradiction in the role of Guineman as standard-bearer and newly-appointed horn-bearer, because *oriflamme* and *olifant* are the both visible and sonorous evidence that Charles' army is destined to win the battle and destroy the enemies of the Christian faith. The eventual success of the imperial host does ensure that, in Roland's words, no bad songs will ever be made on the Franks' account ("que malvaise cançun de nus chantet ne seit," l. 1014). In inciting the rear guard to act in such a manner that only good songs will be told "about *us*" ("de *nus*"), Roland expresses aloud the desire of all of his companions to be recognized and remembered as worthy champions of God's cause.

Yet, although the "nus" of line 1014 seems to stress the collective character of the Franks' claim to legal and moral rectitude, Roland's harangue to the rear guard discloses, in reality, the personal rather than communal motivation that inspires him to invoke fame and glory. As line 1016 indicates ("no bad example will ever be made out of *me*": "de *mei*"), Roland's concern focuses on his personal posterity, which he appears to value over and above his duty as both Christian warrior and Charlemagne's vassal. Wisdom dictates that Roland call upon Charlemagne and thus cause the return of the French host as reinforcement of the rear guard. But Roland prizes prowess over wisdom. Whereas for Olivier the noise of pagan "bruur" (l. 1021) forecasts the toil and pain awaiting the rear guard, it is music to Roland's ears, who sees here an opportunity to translate the noise of the battle into a song insuring the immortality of his name.[31] The song to be sung in the future will incidentally celebrate Charlemagne and his host, but

[30] As Lombard-Jourdan notes (*Fleur de Lis et Oriflamme*, 230), Roland's olifant resonates throughout the mountains as thunder would. In the *Chanson de Troie*, "olifant" rhymes with "tonant" (thundering); in the book of Revelation, God's voice is "as of a trumpet" (1:10). Churches used to contain an ivory trumpet known as "thunder," which replaced the bells when those were silent during the last three days of Holy Week.

[31] Linking the two expressions "malvaise cançun" and "malvaise essample" (ll. 1014 and 1016), Stephen G. Nichols connects Roland's distinction with his capacity to see "the impending battle in terms of textual potential: good song versus bad song": *Romanesque Signs: Early Medieval Narrative and Iconography* (New Haven and London: Yale University Press, 1983), 171. Roland would thus be the only one to acknowledge "the index potential of the battle-as-text." Vance (*Mervelous Signals*, 85) contrasts Charlemagne's "scriptural" world—"a world of opaque letters"—with Roland's as "a world of living, vocal presences." Focusing on the switch of personal pronouns (from *nus* to *me*), I read the passage as evidence of Roland's relentless determination to secure the immortality of his name. Roland's horn in that sense emblematizes the meaning of noise as repute; according to the OED, "to make a noise in the world" means to attain notoriety and renown.

will primarily be the "song of Roland." That the ensuing battle is a bloody affair, leading to the death of Roland's twenty thousand companions, corroborates the self-centered character of Roland's thirst for glory. Only when the rear guard is reduced to sixty does he decide to blow his horn in order to call Charlemagne back to Roncevaux. What resonates throughout the mountains is not Roland's call for help so much as the affirmation that he fought valiantly and thus deserves to have his name inscribed in the register of human greatness. And while Roland's sonorous claim does effect his immortality, it also confirms the centrality of fame as the single fixation governing his behavior—a fixation which has been aptly described as "the frenzy of renown" (Leo Braudy, *The Frenzy of Renown* [New York: Oxford Universty Press, 1986]). Significantly, his death results, not from a blow inflicted on him by pagan weaponry, but from his blowing his horn. Roland's indestructible character in the face of the enemy is a measure of his success in turning pagan "bruur" into a sound that initiates his sonorous preeminence as the true if not sole hero of the *Chanson*.

The sonorous equivalence of Roland's *olifant* and Charles' *oriflamme* brings to mind a rhetorical figure ("similiter desinens"), known as a "figure of sound," wherein poetic discourse places words of similar resonance in a rhyming position.[32] In the case of the olifant/oriflamme pair, "similer desinens" has a harmonious resonance in that the sound of the horns and battle cries which punctuates the Christians' attack on the Saracens coheres with the principle of the holy war. While trumpets and horns can be melodious whenever they serve to glorify and reveal the truth of God's Word,[33] they can also become deadly instruments in the hands of all those who, like Roland, use warfare as their means to obtain fame and glory.

That the sound of Roland's olifant is in that respect dissonant is corroborated by Alan of Lille's definition of music in his *De planctu naturae* (before 1171), 17 metre 9, esp. lines 1–7. The first instrument that Alan mentions as being "paramusical" (to use Magnúsdóttir's expression: *La Voix du cor*, 206) is the trumpet, whose "dreadful" and "blaring" sound hails war and tells of preliminary skirmishes. Next is the horn, which produces a "wandering sound and unregulated tone" that knows "not how to obey the melody of instrumental music."

---

[32] This is the case in vernacular chivalric romance, the structure of which is typically a succession of octosyllabic lines in rhyming couplets. By contrast, the structure of epics like the *Chanson de Roland* is typically a succession of stanzas, each of which comprises a variable number of decasyllabic lines whose ending is similar in sound ("assonance"). At work in words that occupy a terminal position (whether the assonating words of an epic stanza or the rhyming words of romance), "similiter desinens" can also apply to words that are placed elsewhere in the metric line.

[33] Thus Hildegard of Bingen (1098–1179) wanted to drown her voice in the peal of a "trumpet sounded by the Living Light" ("sonus tubae a vivente lumine"), as she related in one of her letters to Elisabeth of Schönau (*Epistolarium*, 2; *PL* 197. 217–18).

Along with the sistra, which has "the voice of a female Mars and prophetess of war," trumpets and horns are evil instruments in that they stir men's pugnacious impulses (trans. Sheridan, 209, 211). Considering that Alan's trumpet evokes the Roman *tuba*, a straight-shaped wind instrument as opposed to the curved appearance of the horn ("cornu"), it is tempting to establish a connection between Roland's olifant and pagan wrong ("tort," l. 1015; from "tordu" as that which is not straight, but curved and bent) on the basis of a "similiter desinens" that would, this time, stress the conceptual similarity of Roland's horn and pagan error in terms of deviance. For Lombard-Jourdan, however, Roland's olifant is a sacred instrument which derives from its Celtic origin the capacity to produce storms, summon legions of heavenly soldiers, and spread natural calamities (*Fleur de Lis et Oriflamme*, 229–33). This would be the reason that Roland refuses at first to blow his horn, because only the gravest of circumstances would justify that one dared thus call upon divine intervention. But this interpretation does not explain why Roland decides ultimately to blow his horn, at the moment when all is lost for the rear guard. A more valid explanation emerges from Roland's primary impulse to secure his renown by fighting and dying as the best possible warrior. Receiving the help of Charles' host would run counter to this quest for fame, which is why Roland rejects Olivier's suggestion that he blow his horn. On the other hand, for his body to be found and his name immortalized necessitates Charles' return, which is why Roland, once most members of the rear guard have been killed, undertakes to sound his olifant with all his strength, so hard that bright drops of blood spring from his mouth and veins in his forehead crack with the strain. Glory is obtained at the price of his life, and it is not incidental that Roland's death is caused by the sound of his olifant, nor that the word is here in assonating position with running blood ("sancs"), bursting brain ("rumpant"), and extreme pain ("ahans," l. 1762). The onomatopoeic character of this soundscape of self-inflicted suffering is an index of the sundering effect of those horns which, like Roland's olifant, serve to blare the repute of its owner, over and above the *Chanson*'s claim thus to translate, loud and clear, the power of God's very voice.

The function of the olifant in ensuring the immortality of Roland's name validates the claim made by those among the moralists who denigrate knightly prowess as a lethal use of force governed by personal ambition. In this perspective, nothing differentiates the epic warrior from the chivalric hero of romance at the level of motivation: although the heroes of romance aspire for glory on earth rather than in Heaven (as is the case with Roland), they share with their epic counterparts a notion of quest that is essentially self-interested.

I propose to conclude this chapter with a brief exploration of those chivalric horns, like the one introduced in Chrétien de Troyes' first extant romance (*Erec et Enide*, ca. 1170), which echo Roland's olifant as instruments sonorously publicizing the martial superiority of their owners. The horn in question is connected with an episode of Chrétien's romance which occurs when the eponymous heroes reach Brandigan, the city of King Evrain. There, Erec learns from his friend, Guivret, the existence of a test, known as "Joie de la Cort" (Joy at Court), which has so far defeated each of its challengers.[34] Despite Guivret's warning that he will gain only shame or even death, and ignoring the sorrow of his wife Enide and the grief of the people of Brandigan, Erec decides to give it a try and thus goes to the orchard where the test is to take place.[35] As a sort of Garden of Eden, the site is redolent with medicinal herbs, flowers, and fruit, and graced by the songs of the most melodious birds under heaven. But this orchard is not entirely harmonious, considering that the stakes of its enclosure are each topped with a man's head. Each, that is, except for the last stake, which carries nothing *as yet* but a horn: whoever dares sound it will be guaranteed fame and honor. At this point, Erec declares to Enide that he will succeed in the test. Although it might look foolish ("fox," l. 5852) on his part thus to boast, his self-confidence is founded not on pride ("orguil," l. 5853), but on his love for her.

The unfolding of the episode discloses that Erec is in reality motivated by pride rather than love. Once in the orchard, Erec sees coming toward him the most formidable of all knights, a foot taller than any man known. They begin to strike each other with their lances and continue fighting until late in the afternoon, until Erec's challenger grows so tired that he concedes failure. Mabonagrain, for such is his name, now recounts how he had fallen in love with the maiden of the orchard, had promised to comply with any one of her requests and, because of his oath, had henceforth found himself under the obligation to stay in the garden until the arrival of a knight strong enough to defeat him. Such an outcome had been postponed by Mabonagrain's very stature, causing his downfall as a knight inasmuch as his exploits could not be publicized and were performed for the maiden's sole benefit. To be complete, Erec's victory needs indeed to be known throughout the land: seizing the horn, he proceeds to sound it with such might that its call reaches everyone in the realm, from King Evrain's court to Arthur's. The hero's ensuing fame and status pose an implicit threat to the

[34] The "Joie de la Cort" episode begins at line 5457 in Chrétien de Troyes, *Erec et Enide*, ed. Jean-Marie Fritz, in *Chrétien de Troyes. Romans* (Paris: Librairie Générale Française, 1994), 234 (from Ms. BN fr. 1376). This episode, which has inspired numerous literary analyses (reviewed by Terence Scully, "The *Sen* of Chrétien de Troyes' *Joie de la cort*," in *The Expansion and Transformation of Courtly Literature*, ed. Nathaniel B. Smith and Joseph T. Snow [Athens, GA: University of Georgia Press, 1980], 71–94), is for Burns proof of Erec's relentless desire to succeed in the test and thus obtain the maximum of honor (*Bodytalk*, 190).

[35] The people of the city express sonorously their sorrow ("Ahi! ahi!," l. 5697) and lament the manner in which the "Joie" test is about to betray Erec: "tu cuides *conquerre*; / Mais ton duel et ta mort vas *querre* ("you think that you will conquer it; but you are in search of that which will be your bereavement and death," ll. 5699–5700; my emphasis).

authority of King Arthur, indicating that rivalry and competition reign supreme in the knightly society of romance as well as in its factual counterpart. Such a realistic assessment of human interaction accounts, I suggest, for the "truthful" character of the language of fiction. At the same time, the pleasure of fiction resides in part in the author's capacity to "solve" the problematics of communication and conclude his romance with the triumph of peace and order. The last episode of Chrétien's romance thus overcomes the potentially sundering effect of Erec's horn by transforming its sound into a call for communal revelry. In response, members of Evrain's court start playing various instruments, including harps, psalteries, and organs. It is in that context interesting to note that Alan de Lille praises stringed instruments for their soothing and civilizing effect and criticizes those pugnacious instruments, like the horn, whose "wandering sound" and "unregulated tone know not to obey"—but "scorn"—"the melody of instrumental music" (*De planctu Naturae*, trans. Sheridan, 209). Chrétien's narrative ending owes its harmonious quality to the substitution of "civilizing" musical instruments for the "pugnacious" horn by means of which his hero had affirmed his preeminence as the best knight of the realm. In the final analysis, the storyteller eliminates from his romance both the "wandering" sound of the horn and the status of his protagonist as a wandering knight.[36]

In the discourse of orthodoxy, the religious clergy (the order of the "oratores") is the symbolic head of the body politic, whereas the warrior class, its upper torso, has for its role ensuring the protection of the more or most vulnerable members of society. This exalted view of knightly *militia* was in time to influence chivalric literature and provoke the emergence of a new concept of heroic behavior. That thirteenth-century romance writers tend to adhere to a notion of the "miles" that amplifies the protagonist's peace-making value suggests a corresponding transformation in the soundscape of fiction, one which should in principle alleviate, if not eliminate, its often strident tonality. If such is the case—an issue that we examine in the following chapter—then this would also suggest that narration and soundscape cohere and combine in a manner that registers a non-aggressive and even harmonious mode of human communication.

[36] The romance concludes with the crowning of Erec as new king of Nantes, suggesting that Erec will now adhere to a sedentary rather than nomadic mode of life.

III

THE WHITE NOISE OF PERFECTION

"El segrei u li abbes fu
E le cors nostre seignur tint
De Charlemeine li sovint;
Al cors piement se demente."
(In the church where the abbot
had stood and held the body of Christ
[Gilles] came to think of Charlemagne;
pious compassion fills his heart.)
(*Vie de Saint Gilles*, ll. 2975–2979)

Jacques de Vitry's use of the tournament "miles" as a metaphor of the seven deadly sins reflects the view, shared by a number of contemporary moralists, that chivalric literature is useless for, or even adverse to, the transmission and revelation of God's truth. Knightly behavior as criticized in de Vitry's sermon (early thirteenth century) finds a positive antithesis in the protagonist of contemporary Grail literature as a sort of "miles Christi" committed to the upholding of God's justice and the protection of innocence.[1] In contradistinction to both the warrior figure celebrated in the epic tradition and the knight-errant of twelfth-century courtly romance, power and renown are, in principle, no longer the goals of the hero's quest, suggesting a shift of emphasis that now focuses on his internal merit rather than on his standing in courtly society.[2]

---

[1] On the religious concept of knighthood in Christian thinking and secular literature, see Bumke, *Courtly Culture*, 290–301, and Maurice Keen, *Chivalry* (New Haven and London: Yale University Press, 1984), 44–63. (One might bear in mind that Jacques de Vitry himself served in the Latin Levant as bishop of Acre [1216–1225] and probably observed such behavior at first hand.)

[2] The textual as well as the scholarly corpus related to Grail fiction is so large that my survey will of necessity be selective. Most critics view the Grail quest as an attempt to regenerate and spiritualize traditional chivalry; I am interested here in the way color symbolism coheres with, but more often contradicts, the revelatory value of both the Grail and its quest. On the transformations of imaginative literature in the thirteenth century, see among others Norris J. Lacy, "The Evolution and Legacy of French Prose Romance," in *The Cambridge Companion to Medieval Romance*, ed. Roberta L. Krueger (Cambridge: Cambridge University Press, 2000), 167–82; Paul Vincent Rockwell, *Rewriting Resemblance in Medieval French Romance: "Ceci n'est pas un graal"* (New York and London: Garland, 1995); E. Jane Burns, *Arthurian Fictions: Rereading the Vulgate Cycle* (Columbus: Ohio State University Press, 1985); and Nancy

I propose in this chapter to evaluate the degree to which Grail fiction succeeds in developing a non-violent mode of chivalric behavior. My selection of textual exhibits adheres to the argument, stated in the Introduction, that the specificity of mythical and imaginative literature—regardless of origin, date, or metric form—lies in a description of society that is much more realistic than the stilted world view of "scientific" discourse. At the same time, the sort of "truth" conveyed by fiction does not necessarily reflect, and may even contradict, the intended meaning of a story, whence the occasional incoherence between what the author means and what he says. The works analyzed in this chapter (which are mostly but not exclusively borrowed from thirteenth-century storytelling) have as their common characteristic that they tend to rely on symbolic synesthesia in order to construct their particular cosmology. As we recall, the mixing of sensory perceptions is integral to Augustine's definition of the religious experience, an example of which is his description of God's truth in terms of "a light that is heard." Cognition of a terrestrial kind should not, by contrast, be experienced or expressed through sensory interpenetration, at the risk of violating the ordered structure of human perception and ordinary language (Chidester, *Word and Light*, 56). However, to the extent that many Grail authors claim to reinscribe traditional romance in ways that bestow on the hero's quest a spiritual orientation, symbolic synesthesia may in this case be a legitimate device used to heighten the transcendental value of their narratives.

Because any one of our senses is capable of generating the same type of "interference" in a text as audition, each mode of perception can thus have a similar function in either reinforcing or subverting the *logos* of narration. The "white noise" explored in this chapter refers in that sense to the combination of visual and auditory marks by means of which chivalric romance seeks to situate its protagonists on the scale of knightly excellence. I begin with an analysis of those knightly characters whose imperfection is expressed through a soundscape and colorscape the openly negative import of which coheres with the moral lesson of the story ("The Hues and Tones of Knightly *Malitia*"). Conversely, what distinguishes a good knight is a trajectory that enables him gradually to perceive the transparency and harmony of God's Word ("*Miles Christi*: A Quest for Revelation"). Many Grail texts assign this illuminating quality to Galahad the "White Knight" as the ultimate hero of the quest. Yet Galahad's twofold attribute also contradicts the hero's revelatory value as a result of its undecidable character: is he perfect in a moral sense (white) or in a military sense (knight)? I submit ("Whiteness as Non-Signification") that Galahad's attribute functions like the

Freeman-Regalado, "La Chevalerie Celestiel: Spiritual Transformations of Secular Romance in *La Queste del Saint Graal*," in *Romance: Generic Transformation from Chrétien de Troyes to Cervantes*, ed. Kevin Brownlee and Marina Scordilis Brownlee (Hanover, NH, and London: University Press of New England, 1985), 91–113.

"white noise" of information theory in terms of a parasitic interference, or static, which generates confusion rather than enlightenment. As a counterpoint to the unreadable character of chivalric whiteness are those characters, like Saint Gilles (whose Life is explored in this chapter's last section: "Whiteness as Communication"), who embody a non-lethal and even life-sustaining mode of interaction. At issue, in the final analysis, is whether the colorscape amplified by thirteenth-century romance—and, in particular, by Grail literature—has an illuminating value and as such succeeds in eliminating the noisy soundscape of traditional chivalry.

1. The Hues and Tones of Knightly "Malitia"

Beginning with Chrétien de Troyes' unfinished *Perceval* (also known as the *Conte du Graal*), the legend of the Grail has inspired a vast number of sequels and amplifications wherein the enigmatic object ("graal") that is integral to the narration of Perceval's adventures becomes the holiest of vessels, thereby requiring, to be attained, a correspondingly sanctified mode of life. Already presented as a sacred serving dish in Chrétien's text, in many of its sequels the Grail becomes an ideal that attracts a plethora of characters, most of whom fail because they ignore or misunderstand the spiritual significance of the quest.

The prose romance known as the *Roman du Graal*[3] (ca. 1205–1210) enunciates a criticism of those impulses, like pride and ambition, which typically govern a knight's behavior. When Perceval sees the empty seat that stands at the Grail Table, his desire to prove himself the best in the realm incites him to dare sit down on it. At once the seat's stone splits open and cries out a sorrowful shout ("braist"),

---

[3] The development of Grail literature after Chrétien is a complex phenomenon (aptly described by Mathilda Tomaryn Bruckner as a "growth industry": "Rewriting Chrétien's *Conte du Graal*—Mothers and Sons: Questions, Contradictions, and Connections," in *The Medieval Opus: Imitation, Rewriting, and Transmission in the French Tradition*, ed. Douglas Kelly [Amsterdam and Atlanta: Rodopi, 1996], 213–44, here 213), which appears to begin with Robert de Boron's tripartite verse romance, *Le Roman de l'Estoire dou Graal* (ca. 1200). Of Robert de Boron's trilogy, which includes the stories of *Joseph of Arimathea*, of *Merlin*, and of *Perceval* (as here the predestined hero of the quest), only the first segment (*Joseph*) has been preserved in its entirety. The *Roman du Graal* which I examine in this section is a prose rendition of the last, and lost, segment (*Perceval*).

Rooting the legend of the Grail in Christian history, Robert de Boron links Chrétien's "graal" to the vessel used by Jesus during the Last Supper (ll. 395–396) and, after His death on the cross, by Joseph of Arimathea to gather Christ's blood (ll. 556–572). The story then focuses on Joseph as the guardian of the Grail: only the good among Joseph's people are allowed to sit at the Grail's table, and only the purest one of all will be able to sit at the empty seat that stands by Joseph's side.

while the world seems to be precipitated into an abyss. From the clamor of the earth emerges such a profound darkness that no one can see beyond a league (ed. Cerquiglini, 204–5). Noise, which serves here to amplify the blinding effect of pride, is not fortuitous but supports the intended meaning of the narration as a sort of sacred scripture. Also noteworthy is the fact that noise does not have a destructive effect, for this reinforces the moral rather than material significance of the passage's soundscape. The most efficient means to condemn traditional chivalry is to avoid all manner of violence, whence the revelatory rather than lethal manner in which Perceval is told to mend his ways. Indeed, each of Perceval's adventures discloses the violent character of interaction among knights as well as between knights and ladies, as is illustrated in the episode of the "Gué Perellos" (236–38). In the course of his journey, Perceval reaches a ford where he meets Urbain de la Noire Espine, who relates to the hero how he became prisoner of the lady of the Gué Perellos by promising her that he would guard her ford and challenge any passing knight. Offered the position of guardian of the ford, Perceval tells Urbain that he has no interest in a task that has already caused the death of so many knights. At this very moment, a great roar ("tumulte," 238) resonates and it seems as if the entire forest is falling into an abyss. From this noise comes a cloud of smoke of such darkness that (again) neither knight is able to see further than a league. As Perceval soon learns, these natural phenomena represent the alienating effect of those women, like Urbain's lady of the Gué Perellos, who monopolize chivalric prowess for their own selfish purposes. Concluding with the restoration of order and harmony, this episode reiterates the moral lesson developed earlier in the episode of the Table's empty seat. In both instances, the soundscape is accompanied by visual manifestations—a darkness or a cloud of smoke—which anticipate a moment of full disclosure. Far from interfering with the *logos* of narration, noise serves as a preliminary stage in the revelation of the text's significance, which the darkness into which Arthur's court is momentarily plunged, or the symbolic cloud of smoke at the Perilous Ford, renders visually explicit.

The revelatory value of the quest for the Grail is again the core of another Old French narrative: the prose *Queste del Saint Graal* (ca. 1220),[4] which links success in the quest to moral purity. Such a requirement predicts the failure of most of the "questers" introduced in this narrative, including Lancelot

[4] For recent studies of the *Queste*, see the bibliography contained in Grace M. Armstrong, "Questions of Inheritance: *Le chevalier au lion* and *La Queste del Saint Graal*," *Yale French Studies* 95(1999): 171–92, here 172, n. 2; Kaeuper, *Chivalry and Violence*, 253–54, n. 3; and Norris J. Lacy, ed., *Medieval Arthurian Literature: A Guide to Recent Research* (New York: Garland, 1996). Colin Manlove, *Christian Fantasy from 1200 to the Present* (Houndmills: Macmillan, 1992), 19–20 singles out the "howls" and "shrieks" of the evil characters.

on account of his adulterous relationship with King Arthur's wife.[5] Indeed, Lancelot repeatedly displays his incapacity to comprehend the intrinsic value of the holy vessel, which he is the first among the questers to encounter (ed. Pauphilet, 57–62). Arriving one night at an ancient chapel, he notices, emerging from the woods, a knight who wonders aloud when he will see the Grail and thus be cured. At this very moment the vessel appears on the altar of the chapel, and once the wounded knight presses his eyes on its table ("la toche a ses euz") he finds himself instantly healed. In contrast with the wounded knight in his capacity to speak and go to the altar to touch its table, Lancelot can neither move nor talk.[6] His gazing ("regarde") at the vessel does not go beyond the literal level and lacks, therefore, the mental acuity needed to understand the mysteries of the Grail. The circumstances of Lancelot's second encounter with the vessel as it occurs later in the *Queste* (253–61) amplify the connection between his imperfect vision and his moral blindness. The scene takes place at a castle through which Lancelot walks until he reaches the door of a room, which opens suddenly. From outside the door, Lancelot catches sight of the vessel, which is covered with a cloth of bright red samite ("vermeil samit") and surrounded with angels holding lighted candles ("cierges ardanz"). Although a voice has warned him not to enter the room, Lancelot proceeds to do just that. As he is about to reach the vessel, however, a force throws him down, hands carry him away, and for twenty-four days Lancelot lies on a bed unable to move, hear, or speak ("a perdu le pooir dou cors, et del oïr et del veoir"). Here, as in the case of his previous encounter with the vessel, Lancelot's unworthiness manifests itself in a sighting of the vessel that brings him no redemption. The story of King Mordrain (82–86) illustrates in a comparable manner the punishment that awaits all those who dare glance at the vessel without adequate internal disposition. Having transgressed a voice's injunction not to approach the vessel, Mordrain is at once surrounded by a dark cloud and deprived of the ability to see and move ("li toli la veue des elz et le pooir dou cors"). He will remain blind and ill for four hundred years, until the arrival of the Good Knight, the ninth descendant of his line.

Predictably, black is often the mark of moral blindness, whereas white characterizes purity. One of the questers, Gauvain, has a dream in which he sees a hundred and fifty bulls feeding in a meadow (*Queste*, ed. Pauphilet, 149): the

---

[5] See Lancelot's confession: "je sui morz de pechié d'une moie dame que je ai amee toute ma vie, et ce est la reine Guenievre, la fame le roi Artus" (*Queste*, ed. Pamphilet, 66; "I have sinned unto death with my lady, she whom I have loved all my life, Queen Guinevere, the wife of King Arthur": trans. Matarasso, 89).

[6] In many Grail fictions, the spectacle of the Grail renders the unworthy quester powerless to move: such is the case of Gauvain in the prose *Perlesvaus*, *Le haut livre du Graal: Perlesvaus*, ed. William A. Nitze and T. Atkinson Jenkins, 2 vols. (Chicago: University of Chicago Press, 1932–1937; repr. New York: Phaeton Press, 1972), 1:119.

flock is in the main black, except for three outstanding bulls, two of which are white and resplendent ("blanc et bel"), while the third bears only faint traces of spots ("signe de tache"). A chance encounter with a monk who happens to be well-versed in the art of dream interpretation provides Gauvain with the following exegesis (155–57). The black bulls represent those questers who have fallen into mortal sin through lechery and pride, as opposed to the three untainted bulls, which represent the three sinless questers. The two bright white bulls in the trio are Galahad and Perceval, and the third bull is Bohors, who bears traces of spots in memory of his lapse when he lost his virginity.[7] The resulting colorscape visually expresses the hierarchy that distinguishes each of the questers, placing Galahad at the top because of his virginal status. At the bottom of the scale stand all those questers who, despite the guidance provided by the many monks and priestly figures whom they encounter during their journey, continue to wander in the forest as in a labyrinth of confusion.[8]

Against the *Queste*'s use of the forest as a symbol of moral blindness, many romances amplify the nurturing quality of the woodland. In Jean Renart's verse romance *L'Escoufle* (1200–1202), for example, the forest is a shelter which contributes to the blossoming of reciprocal love away from the noise of courtly society. Jean begins his bipartite narrative with the story of Richart of Montivilliers, whose marriage to an Italian princess leads to the birth of a son, Guilliaume. The latter's love for Aélis, the daughter of the emperor of Rome, constitutes the second section of Jean's narrative. The union between the two young lovers seems at first secure, as confirmed by the Roman emperor's promise to his friend Richart that he will choose Guilliaume as his heir. After Richart's death, however, evil advisers convince the emperor to break his oath on the argument that the privilege thus granted to Guilliaume would foster strife between the emperor and his barons. The emperor forbids Guilliaume henceforth to be with Aélis, a decree which compels the two lovers to flee his court silently ("sans noise," l. 3358; and "sans faire noise," l. 3861) and take refuge in the forest. During one of the rests they take in the course of their escape, Aélis offers a love ring to Guilliaume and

[7] "Se meffist en sa virginité." Bohors' lapse led to the birth of his son, paradoxically named Elyan le Blanc ("the White"); but Bohors has since atoned so fully by his purity of life that his sin has been forgiven. Although Perceval does not sin in the flesh, he eventually lets himself be tempted by an evil seductress, whence his chaste rather than virginal status.

[8] On the revelatory role of the *Queste*'s various exegetes, see L. De Looze, "A Story of Interpretations: The *Queste del saint graal* as Metaliterature," *Romanic Review 76* (1985): 129–47; Emmanuèle Baumgartner, *L'arbre et le pain: Essai sur la "Queste del saint graal"* (Paris: Sedes, 1981); and Tzvetan Todorov, *Poétique de la prose* (Paris: Seuil, 1971). On the effect of the labyrinthine composition of the *Queste* as "moral maze," see Penelope Reed Doob, *The Idea of the Labyrinth from Classical Antiquity through the Middle Ages* (Ithaca and London: Cornell University Press, 1990), 175–91. On the medieval forest as a site of the worst acts of violence, see Raynaud, *La Violence au Moyen Âge*, 71.

then settles down for a nap. At the moment that Guilliaume places the ring back into its purse, a kite ("un escoufles," l. 4544), mistaking the purse for a piece of meat, picks it up and flies away. Hesitating at length between his desire to stay and protect Aélis and his fear that she might misinterpret his loss of her gift, our hapless hero decides to go in pursuit of the kite. When she awakes, Aélis laments the disappearance of her companion: could it be that the emperor's men came and killed him, or took him as their prisoner? But that could not be, she reasons, because their action would have made so much noise ("tel noise faite," l. 4680) that she surely would have heard it. Aélis comes to the conclusion that Guilliaume has abandoned her for some reason, which leaves her no other alternative than to resume her wandering alone. Having in the meantime recovered the purse (the kite having dropped what was not, after all, a piece of meat), Guilliaume returns to the site of their rest, but there is of course no trace of Aélis.

The momentous episode of the kite's theft of the love ring elucidates the meaning of Jean's entire romance by introducing a bird of prey as the emblem of chivalric behavior in its negative connotations. Not only does the bird's action resemble that of the emperor and his men in provoking the lovers' separation, it also echoes Jacques de Vitry's depiction of chivalry as a metaphor of the deadly sins, considering the motivations (envy and cupidity) that inspire the bird to grasp the love ring, as well as the manner (by attack and theft) in which it seizes the desired object. The title of Jean's romance epitomizes all the components of traditional romance, such as the self-serving reason that typically elicits the knight's quest, and the resulting clashes between rival questers who pursue the same object of desire, which the author intends to reject. This is what transpires from Jean's selection of the *escoufle*—a bird of prey much despised during the period (ed. Sweetser, xi)—as the embodiment of knighthood in its "scavenging" character. To the kite's visual representation of evil chivalry corresponds the noisy soundscape of those knightly forces which forced the two lovers to flee away from court. However, the safety of the forest does not last and the din of aggression causes them to separate, until the moment of mutual recognition, some seven years later. Then the noise that is heard becomes the mark of collective rejoicing, when the bells of Rouen celebrate the arrival of Guilliaume as the new Count of Normandy, and when the "joie de la cort" salutes cheerfully the reunion of the two lovers. Relinquishing Chrétien de Troyes' presentation of his heroes' apotheosis in successfully combining love and chivalry, Jean develops an opposition between those two systems of value which indicts the aggressive character of traditional chivalry in terms of a noise that interferes with and, hence, postpones the love story of Guilliaume and Aélis. Were the Gauvain introduced in Chrétien's *Chevalier au Lion* (*Yvain*) to encounter Jean Renart's hero, as he does Yvain (ed. Hult, ll. 2484–2538), he would undoubtedly admonish Guilliaume for neglecting to act in support of his own glory and renown. What kind of "knight" is he, other than a spineless type, who does not impose his will and retain or regain his lady by feats of arms? Jean Renart responds to this putative accusation by celebrating the noiseless quality of reciprocal love, when it blossoms away from the site (the court) whence chivalric rivalry and aggression originate.

2. "Miles Christi": A Quest for Revelation

That the court is not a site conducive to harmonious interaction is confirmed, in the *Roman du Graal*, by Merlin's prediction that Perceval's ultimate sighting of the Grail will cause the disappearance of the "marvels" of Britain. King Arthur weeps at this news (ed. Cerquiglini, 272), for he understands the significance of this outcome in marking the end of both his chivalry and his reign. At the antipodes of Arthur's court is the domain of Bron, the Fisher King,[9] where Perceval achieves his quest and is entrusted with the vessel whence emanate a melody and a fragrance so wonderful that the hero believes himself to be in Paradise. Three days later, a miracle enables Perceval to see David and hear his harp at the moment when Bron's soul is taken to heaven (271). David's harp stands here symbolically at the opposite of those noisy instruments, like Roland's olifant or Erec's horn, which proclaim the superior power and glory of their owners. Full revelation of the mysteries of the Grail will only be granted to a selfless type of knight, which is the role destined to Galahad in the *Queste del Saint Graal*. The hero's perfection finds its reward in the concluding episode of this Grail text, wherein the vessel takes on a Eucharistic significance. Invited to look into the holy receptacle, Galahad praises its content as a source of unique valor ("granz hardemenz") and prowess (278). Given the anti-Arthurian context of the *Queste*, true valor and prowess do not refer to a self-interested or lethal use of chivalry but serve here to describe the "miles Christi" as a spiritual rather than terrestrial being. In Galahad's experience, divine truth lies beyond sensory perception and requires, to be understood, the capacity to relinquish the realm of the senses and contemplate the Grail as an icon of revelatory value.

However, because ordinary humanity cannot emulate Galahad's degree of purity, it also cannot hope ever to achieve the ethereal quality of his vision. With this in mind, the *Queste*'s author introduces—besides the vessel itself—a variety of sacred objects the chief characteristic of which is their readability. Unlike the Grail, rendered invisible by the cloth of red samite that covers it, those objects expose their splendor and disclose their meaning in a manner that points to their narrative importance as "ekphrasis." A rhetorical figure that combines

---

[9] In this Grail text, the Fisher King, whose name is Bron, is the descendant of Joseph of Arimathea and the father of Perceval's father, Alain le Gros (*Roman du Graal*, ed. Cerquiglini, 225).

description ("phrasis") and amplification ("ek-"), ekphrasis focuses on specific art objects—like Achilles' shield in the *Iliad*—which serve metaphorically to translate the significance of a given story.[10] The use of ekphrasis by the *Queste*'s author establishes a connection between the various questers of his story and specific art objects whose role is to help assess the spiritual value, or lack thereof, of their respective journeys.[11] Each of the objects associated with Galahad is meant to demonstrate his inherent virtue, an example of which is the shield, bearing a red cross on a white ground, which the hero receives in anticipation of the service he will render as Christ's soldier. Even more noteworthy regarding the exegetical function of ekphrasis are those objects which Galahad and his two closest companions, Perceval and Bohors, discover during the episode of the Miraculous Ship (199–228). In their exploration of the sacred vessel, the three friends see, first, a sword of burnished beauty, the pommel of which is formed of a stone combining all the colors found on earth. On this sword lies the richest of cloths, which is embroidered with letters announcing that only the best knight will be able to grip it. The sword's blade also happens to be engraved with letters, red as blood ("vermeilles come sanc"), which tell that only the strongest and most valiant knight will be able to unsheathe it. As for the sword's scabbard, as red as a bright rose, it too is inscribed with letters, gold and blue, predicting that he who wears it shall do greater deeds than any living man.[12] On the basis of those art objects, Perceval and Bohors are now convinced that the predestined holder of the sword is Galahad himself and that with it he will achieve the quest for the

[10] See Richard Crescenzo, *Peintures d'instruction: La postérité littéraire des "Images" de Philostrate en France de Blaise de Vigenère à l'époque classique* (Geneva: Droz, 1999), 19–56. In line with Horace's prescription—"ut pictura poesis"—ekphrasis consists of a verbal reproduction of the realm of plastic art works or, more precisely, "a verbal representation of a fictional visual representation": Murray Krieger, *Ekphrasis* (Baltimore: Johns Hopkins University Press, 1992), xv. Krieger notes that the pictural or sculptural work of art described in ekphrasis may not actually exist, nor might it ordinarily be possible to craft an object on the basis of this verbal representation. (However, there are exceptions.) See also Ruth Webb, "*Ekphrasis* Ancient and Modern: The Invention of a Genre," *Word and Image* 15 (1999): 7–18.

[11] An example is the golden crown which serves as a test of Melyant's resistance to pride and envy ("orgueil et covoitise"), a test which he fails miserably (*Queste*, 41–42, 45–46). The superabundance of objects is such that they predominate over the questers in importance and, as Tzvetan Todorov notes (*Poétique de la prose*, 75), become the primary heroes of the *Queste* as well as the generators of storytelling.

[12] On the emblematic significance of colors, see Michel Stanesco, "Cligès, le Chevalier coloré," in *L'Hostellerie de Pensée*, ed. Zink and Bohler, 391–402; Michel Pastoureau, *Figures et Couleurs: études sur la symbolique et la sensibilité médiévales* (Paris: Le Léopard d'Or, 1986); and Brent Berlin and Paul Kay, *Basic Color Terms* (Berkeley and Los Angeles: University of California Press, 1969); and, for comparison with late antiquity, Liz James, *Light and Colour in Byzantine Art* (Oxford: Clarendon Press, 1996).

Grail.[13] The two friends' confidence results from their having "read" correctly the objects contained in the ship, a reading which entails both a visual and a scriptural activity. For, remarkably, ekphrasis here consists of a description that refers to the art of craftsmanship, of painting (evoked by the passage's color symbolism), and of interpretation (through a script specifying the destination of each object). Thus the *Queste*'s author uses ekphrasis in a way that amplifies the function of the rhetorical device as a representation of art objects that "speak out" to the public.[14] The pommel, hilt, blade, and scabbard of the sword are the "exterior signs" that visibly and verbally translate Galahad's "internal dispositions,"[15] enabling his two companions to acknowledge the analogical resemblance between those objects and the preordained hero of the quest.

Although the chromatic translation of Galahad's virtue seeks to confirm the universal value of the *Queste*'s hero, the resulting colorscape nonetheless generates confusion rather than enlightenment. What, for example, is the significance of the red, gold, and blue tints evoked in the episode of the Miraculous Ship? And how does this colorscape cohere with the one introduced earlier in the narration during the episode of the Tree of Life (210–26)? In the latter case, the colors are mentioned not simultaneously but in succession: white when it grew from the seed that Eve planted after the Fall, the Tree of Life became green after the birth of Abel the fair, and then red ("vermeux") after Abel's murder by Cain. The chromatic transformation of the Tree of Life[16] retraces the history of postlapsarian humanity in a manner that evokes its redemptive significance. Both the moral death provoked by the primordial couple's transgression in the Garden of Eden and the physical one provoked by the first murder will be overcome by the saving birth of God's Son. However, the episode alludes to but does not specify the type

[13] Thus they urge Galahad: "Sire, essaiez a ceste epee. Car nos savons bien que vos acheverez ceste aventure, a ce que nos i avons failli" ("Lord, do test this sword. For we know well that you will complete successfully this adventure, in which we ourselves have failed": *Queste*, trans. Matarasso, 203).

[14] According to Hellenistic rhetoricians, like Hermogenes, ekphrasis "must through hearing operate to bring about seeing" (cited by Krieger, *Ekphrasis*, 7). Whereas Hellenistic rhetoric gives an unrestricted meaning to ekphrasis as "a verbal description of something, almost anything, in life or art" (Krieger, *Ekphrasis*, 7), Jean Hagstrum distinguishes between ekphrastic objects and "iconic" ones, the latter term designating those art objects whose representation does not imply any verbal message: *The Sister Arts: The Tradition of Literary Pictorialism and English Poetry from Dryden to Gray* (Chicago: University of Chicago Press, 1958), 18–29.

[15] Linda M. Clemente, *Literary "Objets d'Art": "Ekphrasis" in Medieval French Romance, 1150–1210* (New York: Peter Lang, 1992), 3.

[16] According to Paul Vincent Rockwell, the Tree of Life and its "transcoloration" serve as a positive counterpoint to "the mortal tree of the Fall" in Genesis: *Rewriting Resemblance in Medieval French Romance*, 113, 115.

of connection that supposedly links Christ to Galahad, nor does it clarify the meaning of the original color (white) of the Tree. Indeed, part of the confusing character of the *Queste*'s message results from its author's tendency to expound, without solving, such ambiguous elements as the colorful art objects found in the Miraculous Ship. A comparable ambiguity marks Galahad's armor: to the circular form of his shield in reflecting the rotundity of God's Creation corresponds the pointed shape of his sword as an instrument of lethal empowerment. Are we presented with the spiritual figure of a "miles Christi," or with the martial figure of a crusader? With the latter, it appears, given the function of shield and sword in empowering Galahad, as it does Achilles, to act as the "representative and defender of his culture [Christianity] against all outsiders, and representative of the gods [God] who protect that culture through him" (Krieger, *Ekphrasis*, xv).

The various objects that the three friends discover during the episode of the Miraculous Ship bear inscriptions that emphasize in that regard the hyperbolic value of the *Queste*'s predestined hero ("cil passera de son mestier toz"; "mielz fere que autre et plus hardiement": 203). What is noteworthy is the relative rather than absolute significance of these superlatives, indicating that Galahad's valor is so measured in comparison with that of the other questers. As Kaeuper notes, to be "the best" in the world means to display the greatest prowess, whence a spirit of competition among knights who are each determined to emerge as winner "by fighting everyone else who wants the same honour" (*Chivalry and Violence*, 132, cf. 149). The battle that takes place at the castle of Carcelois challenges even further the attempt of the *Queste*'s author to introduce with Galahad a non-violent mode of chivalry ("celestiel chevalerie," 116). Because no one at Carcelois is more hated than King Arthur (229), one wonders why Galahad, Perceval, and Bohors identify themselves as being of Arthur's household, especially in view of the anti-Arthurian tenor of the *Queste*. At once, the sound of a trumpet reverberates throughout the castle and a group of armed knights proceeds to ride towards the three friends. In the ensuing battle, the trio kill many of their attackers and pursue the fugitives inside the castle, cutting them down like so many dumb beasts ("come bestes mues," 230). The best fighter is clearly Galahad himself, whose martial skill is such that, from his opponents' standpoint, no human being but the Devil himself has endeavored to destroy them.[17] When in time the trio observe the amount of corpses they have accumulated, they do begin to question

[17] The devilish identification of Galahad by his opponents stands in contrast with the Devil's habitually feminized appearances in the *Queste:* see Jeannine Horowitz, "La diabolisation de la sexualité dans la littérature du Graal au XIIIe siècle, le cas de la *Queste del Graal*," in *Arthurian Romance and Gender*, ed. Friedrich Wolfzettel (Amsterdam and Atlanta: Rodopi, 1995), 238–50, and E. Jane Burns, "Devilish Ways: Sexing the Subject in the *Queste del Saint Graal*," *Arthuriana* 8 (1998): 11–32. It implies here an opposition between male vice (violence) and female vice (lust).

the rightness of their deeds. Only with a monk's (convenient) arrival on stage do they receive confirmation that they acted properly, when the latter reassures them that it was the Lord himself who sent them to destroy people who happened to be worse than Saracens ("poior que Sarrazin," 231). The monk's glorification of Galahad as a crusader, combined with the fact that the hero used his sword as would any one of the Devil's deputies, suggests that, at least at this moment in his story, the *Queste*'s hero is still very much a knight according to the standard of traditional chivalry. The result is to obfuscate the non-violent significance of the "miles Christi," who ends by resembling Roland with respect to the number of dead through which either hero demonstrates his military superiority.

Consider in this connection the crimson tint of both the letters written on the blade of Galahad's sword and its scabbard, as well as the latter's name: "Memoire de sanc" ("Memory of blood," 227). Despite the pious exegesis provided by Perceval's sister,[18] according to whom the scabbard's name is in memory of the blood of Abel, Galahad's weapon appears to have a lethal rather than commemorative function, as confirmed during the Carcelois episode, which happens to take place immediately after the companions' discovery of the sacred sword. Just as problematic is the hero's sporadic appearance as a Red Knight,[19] for it conjures up the very violence that Christ's spiritual "soldier" was supposed to eradicate. The resulting narration fails to approximate the transparency of God's Word inasmuch as it relies on the techniques and themes characteristic of a form of vernacularity, chivalric romance, which it seeks to condemn. Red is so perva-

[18] As Peggy McCracken demonstrates (in chap. 1, "Only Women Bleed" of her forthcoming book *The Curse of Eve, the Wound of the Hero*), the story of Perceval's sister is a story of sacrifice "firmly situated within Christian blood symbolism," although her death "accomplishes no enduring good." Most analyses of Perceval's sister thus point to the ineffectiveness of her sacrifice: e.g. Susan Aronstein, "Rewriting Perceval's Sister: Eucharistic Vision and Typological Destiny in the *Queste del San Graal*," *Women's Studies* 21 (1992): 211–30, here 218; and Jennifer Looper, "Gender, Genealogy, and the 'Story of the Three Spindles' in the *Queste del Saint Graal*," *Arthuriana* 8 (1998): 49–66, here 60. An exception is Philippa Beckerling, "Perceval's Sister: Aspects of the Virgin in the *Quest of the Holy Grail* and Malory's *Sankgreal*," in *Constructing Gender: Feminism in Literary Studies*, ed. Hilary Fraser and R. S. White (Nedlands, Western Australia: University of Western Australia Press, 1994), 39–54, here 50, who considers the way her death ends the evil custom of taking innocent lives.

[19] "Li Chevaliers en armes vermeilles, qui sont de color a feu semblables," 78. The martial rather than spiritual significance of Galahad's armor indicates that the *Queste*'s author develops a view of divine authority that conjures up God's commanding image in the Old Testament. For example, as R. W. D. Nickle remarked (*Light and Colour* [London: Hodder & Stoughton, 1889], 72), the shield of God's soldiers is frequently characterized by its red coloration: "The shield of his mighty men is made red, the valiant men are in scarlet: the chariots shall be with flaming torches in the day of his preparation, and the fir trees shall be terribly shaken" (Nahum 2:3). It is not incidental that French crusaders were recognized by the red cross they wore as their emblem (Faber Birren, *The Story of Color* [Westport, CT: Crimson Press, 1941], 90).

sively associated with Galahad's equipment and behavior that it seems on its way to becoming his dominant coloration, consistent with the working of memory (Abel's murder or Christ's death on the Cross) in spelling out his mission as the agent of God's vengeance.[20]

3. Whiteness as Non-Signification

Not only does the *Queste*'s author resort to motifs (like the quest) and objects (the sword) which evoke the violent "modus operandi" of traditional chivalry, he also relies on a legend the Celtic origins of which betoken a story of revenge. Such appears to be the core of a Welsh tale (*Peredur ab Evrawc*)[21] with respect to a hero whose adventures parallel those of Chrétien's Perceval in many respects. At the castle of one of his maternal uncles, Peredur witnesses a strange procession, beginning with two lads who enter the hall carrying a spear with streams of blood running to the floor. This sight causes all the people in the hall to cry out in unison, and so does the arrival of two maidens bearing a large platter which holds a man's head covered with blood. The fact that a maternal uncle has previously initiated Peredur into the art of knightly weaponry, combined with the hero's lineal connection with his host at the castle, discloses the nature of Peredur's mission in ensuring the restoration of lineage. Indeed, he learns in time that the bleeding head in the platter belonged to his first cousin, who was killed by evil hags; that the hags had also lamed his avuncular host at the castle; and that he is supposed to avenge both relatives. This Peredur proceeds to do by killing the chief hag, while Arthur and his men pursue and destroy the other hags. Red is here the unequivocal coloration of prowess in both its negative (the hags' evil deeds) and positive (Peredur's exploits) effect. We are presented with a successful founding myth, one in which the lance and the platter tell a story of rivalry, and with a successful founding hero as well, considering Peredur's triumph in eliminating the cause of discord and, hence, in restoring order and prosperity.

Read in the light of the Welsh tale, the ambiguities constitutive of the *Queste del Saint Graal* lose much of their mystical appeal, if not their confusing character. Is Galahad a Red Knight, or a White Knight as emblematized by both the ground of his shield and the color of his armor ("armes blanches," 29)? Is the hero supposed to have a Christological significance, as evoked in the White Stag he encounters in the forest (which transforms itself into Christ during the service

[20] As Kaeuper shows convincingly in *Chivalry and Violence*, the problem with knighthood in both history and literature is that it purports to restrain violence at the same time that it glorifies violence.

[21] *Peredur* is part of a collection of Welsh tales (*Mabinogion*) which are preserved in thirteenth- and fourteenth-century manuscripts, the redaction of which (between 1000 and 1250) is based on an oral tradition that may date back to the sixth or seventh century.

of the mass, 235), or does the color red, "spotting" the whiteness of the *Queste*'s hero, associate him with the realm of strife and competition?[22] It is only in the concluding episode of Galahad's adventures in Britain (262–73) that the hero's bicoloration receives a scriptural interpretation, suggesting that the author, aware of the Roland-like character of his hero, attempts ultimately to dispel it. This occurs at the castle of Corbenic ("Blessed Body"), when Mordrain sees the arrival of his predestined savior and praises Galahad for being the lily of purity ("lys en virginité") or, like the perfect rose, a flower of strength and healing with the tint of fire ("droite flors de bone vertu et en color de feu," 263). Mordrain then rejoices at the fact that the fire of the Holy Ghost ("li feus dou Saint Esperit") burns so brightly in Galahad that his own flesh, which was withered and dead, is about to be made young and strong again. White is here associated with red as the two virtues that guarantee Galahad's regenerative power.

Yet, although the *Queste*'s narrative resolution confirms Galahad's role as the ultimate hero of the quest, it does not elucidate the reason that this task can be assumed only by the ninth descendant of Mordrain's line. Why does the *Queste* assign to Galahad a mission which, in both Chrétien's Grail romance and Robert de Boron's trilogy, was to be Perceval's? That Galahad is the predestined hero does not demonstrate the holiness of either quester or quest, so much as it demonstrates, I would suggest, the gratuitous priority here assigned to this "new" model of heroic behavior (Galahad) as opposed to conventional ones (Perceval). The superiority of Galahad over Perceval is in that sense a strategic device used by the *Queste*'s author to assert the superiority of his text over the texts of his predecessors. Evidence of the author's competitive stance is his obsessional praise of virginity (whence his criticism of Bohors for having begotten a son) as a means thus to condemn the principle of genealogical transmission on which aristocratic society, as well as its fictional replica in traditional romance, is grounded. The anti-dynastic tenor of the *Queste* also contributes to the effect of its narration in terms of a failed founding myth, as illustrated by the fact that Mordrain recovers his health and youth only to die a moment later. As himself a failed founding hero,[23] Galahad avoids, by dying, a mission that was bound to make of him an

---

[22] To the ambiguity of Galahad's bicoloration corresponds the ambiguity of each of these two hues. Red may be—among other things—the ancient sign of Aries, the Christian color of martyrdom, the hue of hell, and the tincture of courage; white is marked by a similar multivalence, as the color of purity, innocence, and faith, but also of death (Birren, *The Story of Color*, 323). In John's Revelation, the fourth Horseman rides a "pale horse: and his name that sat on him was Death, and Hell followed with him. And power was given unto [the four Horsemen] to kill with sword, and with hunger, and with death, and with the beasts of the earth" (6:8). See James, *Light and Colour in Byzantine Art*, 105–7. On Apocalypse illustration see Elizabeth S. Bolman, "*De Coloribus*: The Meanings of Color in Beatus Manuscripts," *Gesta* 38 (1999): 22–34.

[23] According to Birren (*The Story of Color*, 66), the traditional color of the Holy Grail is emerald: "its green hue, signifying the Great Mother Nature, may also have related to Venus." There is no such mention in the *Queste*, wherein the narration disconnects its colorless Grail from the vital forces of nature.

avenger or a warmonger of the likes of Roland. Thus the whiteness emblematic of the *Queste*'s hero separates him from the heroes of the epic and chivalric tradition only to the extent that the ending of his story has the effect of a blank page. Consider anew the momentous scene during which Galahad is allowed to contemplate the content of the holy vessel: while the hero reiterates three times ("voi ge") the revelatory value of his vision, the characters who witness the scene are merely able to look "at" Galahad as he is looking "into" the Grail. Neither Galahad nor the *Queste*'s author ever undertakes to translate the figurative meaning of the vessel, which retains till the end its hidden and enigmatic character.[24] Hidden behind Galahad's remark that no word could ever describe the mysteries of the vessel ("langue ne porroit descrire") lurks the author's criticism of those forms of vernacularity, like traditional romance writing, the language of which lacks the power to express such non-perceptual truths as the ones metaphorically contained in the vessel. Yet the *Queste*'s own language proves itself to be just as inadequate inasmuch as the brightness characterizing both the Grail and its hero does not enlighten their witnesses so much as it blinds them.[25]

It is perhaps symbolic that, in the course of their journey together, Perceval and Galahad reach the edge of a forest called *Aube* ("dawn"; from Latin *alba*). The analogy between the whiteness of both Galahad and the forest suggests that

[24] Medieval theologians believed in the power of visuality inasmuch as practices like gazing at relics, icons, or the Eucharist served to "translate" the divine presence and render it perceptible (Frank, "The Pilgrim's Gaze in the Age Before Icons," 103, 174, 180). Adhering to Donald Maddox's view (*Fictions of Identity in Medieval France* [Cambridge: Cambridge University Press, 2000], 204) that Galahad's gaze into the depths of the sacred vessel "constitutes a closed vision," I argue that the type of visuality described in the *Queste* fails to produce meaning. The only "translation" is therefore a literal one, as Galahad carries the ciborium away from the realm of knightly society towards the Holy Land whence Christological history originated (279). In the narrative conclusion, the Grail retains its mysteries and withdraws into Heaven, as does the Good Knight himself (278–79), in an ascending movement the effect of which is to distance, rather than join, this world and the next.

The inability of the *Queste*'s author to reveal the Grail's ethical values, which is linked to the fictional character of a quest that ends at Sarraz rather than Rome or Jerusalem, as Antoinette Saly astutely observes ("Les dénouements du *Didot-Perceval* et de la *Queste del Saint Graal*," *PRIS-MA* [=Pour une Recherche sur l'Imaginaire et le Symbolique au Moyen Âge] 28 [1998]: 193–203, here 203), finds an echo in manuscript illustrations. As Alison Stones remarks, "although the Christianization of the Grail plays such an important part in the development of its iconography," representations of the Grail itself tend to amplify "the healing and curing properties of the Holy Vessel" in ways "that have no parallel in the theology of the Eucharist": "Seeing the Grail. Prolegomena to a Study of Grail Imagery in Arthurian Manuscripts," in *The Grail: A Casebook*, ed. Dhira B. Mahoney (New York and London: Garland, 2000), 301–66, here 338.

[25] Experiments in optics demonstrate that illumination lessens the perception of a given object: "the illumination difference is an obstacle; the greater it is, the more [the observer] will react against it, and his reaction may well be more than proportional to the obstruction": Yun Hsia, "Whiteness Constancy as a Function of Difference in Illumination," *Archives of Psychology* 40 (1943): 5–63, here 6.

the hero's emblematic color is of a dull (*alba*) rather than brilliant (*candida*) shade. Because Galahad's coloration is not reflective,[26] it does not provide any clue as to why he escapes the temptation of the flesh, or why virginity is a precondition for achieving the quest. The forest of Dawn brings to mind the site (Alba) which, in the myth of the foundation of Rome, is a locus of indistinction until Romulus decides, by killing his brother, to affirm his autonomy as the future leader of the city. Unlike Romulus, however, Galahad's distinction ceases to exist when both he and the Grail disappear into Heaven, leaving behind no other trace than the memory of an ultimately undecipherable whiteness.

4. Whiteness as Communication

If Galahad's bicoloration does not signify, this is because in his case red and white do not combine as much as they clash in such a way that each tint contradicts and finally nullifies the other. By contrast, Bohors' bicoloration produces meaning inasmuch as the black traces that "spot" the whiteness of the third bull in Gauvain's dream will serve to inscribe the *Queste*'s story into memory.[27] Thus Bohors leaves the Holy Land after the death of Galahad and Perceval and returns to Arthur's court, where he endeavors to relate the adventures of the Holy Grail as he witnessed them. His relation was in time couched in writing and preserved in the library at Salisbury; Walter Map, a learned man, eventually used this manuscript to write a Latin rendition of the Holy Grail, which was in its turn translated into French (*Queste*, 279–80). In contrast to the intransitive character of Galahad's whiteness, Bohors' coloration emblematizes the function of storytelling in transmitting the truth about the Grail. From his relation resulted the account inscribed on the "white pages" of the manuscript, henceforth ensuring the preservation of the Holy Grail as a scripture whose authenticity did, via Latin, in time impregnate the vernacular rendition of the story. The *Queste*'s author thus reaffirms the supremacy of his romance as a vehicle of truth by virtue of a language which, in

[26] Unlike the dull coloration of *alba*, whiteness as *candida* shines, which is the basis of the difference between blackness as absorption and whiteness as reflection. If you "take a pure white material and direct the rays upon it, it will not take fire, because that which is white receives and reflects the rays of light" (Nickle, *Light and Colour*, 14).

[27] As Bruce Holsinger points out, black is not always the mark of evil, considering the Bride's self-description ("nigra sum sed formosa") in the Song of Songs: "The Color of Salvation. Desire, Death, and the Second Crusade in Bernard of Clairvaux's Sermons on the *Song of Songs*," in *The Tongue of the Fathers: Gender and Ideology in Twelfth-Century Latin*, ed. David Townsend and Andrew Taylor (Philadelphia: University of Pennsylvania Press, 1998), 156–86. An example is the color's function in bringing out "the essential beauty of whiteness" (166); another is the way Christian thinkers conceived of redemption as a metamorphosis from black to white (168, 179).

his case, strives to approximate the transparency of God's Word. His romance is presented as the end term of a transmission that was born out of Bohors' oral recounting, which begot the *Queste* as a sort of scriptural progeny. In this light, Bohors as the father of Elyan "the White" warrants the authenticity of the *Queste* in terms of an unaltered rendition of the Grail's mysteries.

But if Bohors plays an indispensable part in the transmission of the truth about the Grail, then this indicates that the transmission of that truth is, like Bohors himself, of necessity imperfect and that, like the third bull in Gauvain's dream, the resulting text bears "traces of spots." An illustration of the mendacious character of the *Queste*'s language is provided in a colorscape that amplifies its "textile" rather than textual component, in reference to the cloth of red samite that covers the Grail or to the one that adorns the sword of the Mysterious Ship. There results an opacity that works against the principle of "sermo humilis" in terms of a naked language which—to quote Eric Jager (*The Tempter's Voice*, 215)—must shun the "verbal coverings" of eloquence in order to avoid falling, as did Eve, into the traps of the Serpent's seduction. Such is the core of the criticism, by the early Christian moralist Tertullian (ca. 155–ca. 220), of all those strategies of material or linguistic beautification which run counter to the virtue of chastity (*De cultu feminarum*, trans. Turgan, 134). In this line of argument, vanity induces women to cultivate ornamentation at the risk of imitating Eve as "the devil's gateway" (*diaboli ianua*). For women to avoid eternal damnation requires, therefore, that they imitate instead the Virgin Mary as *ianua celi* (Heaven's gateway) by renouncing all artifices of seduction.[28] Tertullian's equation between woman's nature and postlapsarian language focuses on euphemism as an obstacle to truth and transparency, which are the two characteristics of a redemptive mode of expression. Yet the problem with "redemptive language" is that it resorts to the conventional techniques of narration in order to express its condemnation of those techniques.[29]

Like the *Queste*, verse hagiography tends to use a textile rather than textual form of eloquence inasmuch as it portrays its protagonist in a manner that amplifies the saint's aesthetic quality at the expense of his or her ethical

[28] *Ianua celi* is the qualification that the Virgin Mary often receives in biblical and religious literature. See for example the twenty-fourth miracle in the second part of the *Miracles de Notre-Dame de Rocamadour au XIIe siècle*, trans. Edmond Albe (Toulouse: Le Pérégrinateur, 1996), 216.

[29] On the one hand, language is redemptive to the extent that it shuns (*sermo humilis*) the ornaments of euphemistic eloquence. On the other hand, its moral lesson can be conveyed only by means of amplifications and descriptions that will teach the public how to avoid sin and practice virtue. As Jager observes (*The Tempter's Voice*, 213–20), the resulting language is just as fallen as the one that the *Queste*'s author intends to redress, because it oscillates inevitably between the unadorned style of *sermo humilis* and the elevated style of *sermo sublimis*.

significance.[30] The vernacular glorification of the saint (like Christina in the hands of Gautier de Coinci) fails in that sense to achieve transcendence, just as the glorification of "Saint" Galahad by the *Queste*'s author fails to transform the tradition of knightly "malitia" into a spiritualized form of chivalry. To be convincing, the portrayal of perfection needs to blossom outside the conventional features of chivalric heroism, indicating that the protagonist will be "good" only inasmuch as he renounces being a "knight."

Such a renunciation is integral to the perfection of the hero extolled in Guillaume de Berneville's verse *Vie de Saint Gilles* (between 1168 and 1173). In addition to being a non-military and non-violent narration, the uniqueness of this Life also lies, I suggest, in Guillaume's ability to avoid the black-and-white perspective that is often the mark of Old French redemptive discourse. Responding by anticipation to Teresa of Avila's wish that "God save us from dour-faced saints," Gilles displays a constant serenity while contending with the various vicissitudes of his journey, and Guillaume de Berneville de-dramatizes in this way the frequently doleful rendition of life on earth in verse hagiography. Moreover, the individuals that Gilles encounters along his way are themselves the embodiment of a compromise between a cunning use of intelligence and a brute form of stupidity. Guillaume's characters are, in other words, a lifelike representation of human nature in combining greatness and weakness. At first, however, both Gilles' lineage (one of the noblest families of Athens) and appearance (good manners and a blond-haired, white-skinned kind of beauty) assign to the hero a prominent social position, suggesting that his renunciation will have—as is the case with Saint Alexis—an equally exceptional character. Although Gilles does indeed share Alexis' desire to forsake his preeminence in knightly society, his motivation differs in that, unlike Alexis, he does not flee the realm of the flesh so much as the danger of fostering the envy of others.[31] Thus Gilles sails away from Greece and lands in Marseille, where his activities as miracle-worker soon make him so famous that he decides to leave the city and take refuge in the midst of a dense thicket.

Gilles' ensuing life in the wilderness, a happy experience, evokes as such the blissful sojourn in the forest that Tristan and Yseut enjoy in the "courtly" renditions

[30] A typical example is provided in Gautier de Coinci's verse *Passion de Sainte Christine*. When he discovers that his daughter has destroyed the temple's idols, Urban orders that Christina be divested of her clothes ("les dras k'elle a viestus," l. 1486). Divestment has here a voyeuristic rather than revelatory effect. (Stripping the female confessor naked is a topos in late antique hagiography: cf. Susan Ashbrook Harvey's work on female saints.)

[31] "I.a oil u volt; / Ke oil ne veit al quor ne dolt" ("what one sees, one desires; what the eye does not see, the heart does not grieve over," ll. 547–548). Guillaume de Berneville's proverb brings to mind the warning, by a Coptic preacher to his flock (in the fifth century), that "what the eye sees it appropriates" (cited by Frank, "The Pilgrim's Gaze in the Age Before Icons," 107). For the connection between envy and the "evil eye" cf. MacCoull, "Philoponus' Theory of Vision."

of the legend, that is, in those poems, like Thomas' (between 1173 and 1176),[32] wherein love ("amors") is inevitably a cause of pain ("dolors"). In light of the tragic tenor characterizing these courtly renditions, their optimistic take on the forest episode is surprising, as is equally surprising its tragic assessment in those "vulgar" renditions, like Béroul's (ca. 1165), which consistently exalt reciprocal love as a source of joy. On the one hand, Béroul and similarly "vulgar" versions of the legend depict the lovers' experience in the wilderness in terms of severe hardship, such that, when the effect of the love potion disappears, Tristan and Yseut are "delighted to terminate their love affair and go back to their places in society" (Lewes, *The Life in the Forest*, 25). It is on the other hand just as remarkable that the "courtly" versions of the legend (including Thomas') glorify a mode of life in the wilderness that is so openly antithetical to the values cherished by courtly society. For Lewes (*The Life in the Forest*, 2, 53), this incongruity is linked to the fact that Thomas and Guillaume de Berneville were working at the court of Henry II of England during the same period (between 1173 and 1176), indicating that Thomas borrowed his idyllic take on life in the wilderness from Guillaume's *Vie de Saint Gilles*. The secular poet's borrowing of a motif that is integral to the Gilles legend is noteworthy, not only because the resulting narrative resemblance between hagiography and romance places both squarely in the realm of imaginative literature, but also (and more importantly in the context of my analysis) because this resemblance discloses the fact that, regardless of the author's specific intention, the language of narration is inevitably ornamental. Guillaume de Berneville's text owes its lifelike quality to the acknowledgment that everything in this world is of necessity a compromise, such that language stands mid-way between the unadorned language of truth and the decorative language of eloquence.

For three years, Guillaume's saintly hero enjoys the freedom of mind and lightness of spirit which life in the wilderness obtains. His serene existence is, however, about to end when a hunting party organized by King Flovent resumes Gilles' contact with courtly society. As is his task, the master of the royal hunt has identified an animal worthy of pursuit, which—unbeknownst to him—happens

[32] Although this episode has not survived in Thomas' fragmentary text, this lacuna is compensated for by the three extant courtly Tristan poems which are known to be redactions of Thomas' original and whose striking agreement is evidence that "the material existed in the original as well": Ulle Erika Lewes, *The Life in the Forest: The Influence of the Saint Giles Legend on the Courtly Tristan Story* (Chattanooga, TN: Tristania Monograph Series, 1978), 3. Those three poems are: Gottfried von Straßburg's *Tristan*, ca. 1200–1210; Brother Robert's Old Norse *Tristrams Saga ok Isondar*, ca. 1226; and the Middle English *Sir Tristrem* (1294–1330). On the basis of this textual testimony, we can assume the presence of a similar investment of the episode in Thomas' version, wherein Tristan and Isolt achieve their purest fulfillment in the forest and "lapse to a lower level of existence after their return to the court" (Lewes, *The Life in the Forest*, 1).

to be the God-sent hind whose milk ensures Gilles' daily sustenance.[33] The ensuing track is punctuated by the sounds of many horns and hunting shouts ("la criée") which cause the doe to flee and take refuge in the hermit's abode.[34] Given that the deer is traditionally the emblem of Christ in his capacity to triumph over the Serpent, the upcoming encounter between hunters and prey is bound to conclude with God's avenging protection of the holy victim against his persecutors.[35] If this had been the case, however, Guillaume's narrative, like the *Queste*, would glorify its saintly protagonist as an active and aggressive representative of divine justice. Guillaume rejects this alternative by focusing on Gilles' merit as God's servant rather than as Christ's soldier. At the moment that a bowman shoots his bolt, the saint protects the deer by placing himself in such a position that the arrow pierces him in his midsection. Because the bowman's action was unintentional, and because the prey of Flovent's hunting party was animal and not human, the conclusion of the episode eradicates the presentation of Gilles as a victim and of the hunters as his persecutors. The noisy encounter between saint and king turns into a friendly relationship, thereby reiterating the value of Guillaume's protagonist as peacemaker and producer of order. Although Gilles would rather pursue his solitary existence in the company of the forest's "silent animals" ("beste mues," l. 5), he complies with Flovent's request that he become the abbot of the newly-built monastery, as he will in time comply with Charlemagne's request to come to his royal court at Orléans and help him obtain forgiveness for a sin he committed.[36]

Gilles embodies a model of perfection that is far more convincing than Galahad's to the extent that, in Guillaume's text, goodness blossoms away from the

[33] As the master tells King Flovent, the doe may well be a fairy-like animal ("ne sai si c'est chose fae," l. 1780), considering that it has disappeared without a trace. Realizing that this creature has a supernatural character and that they are about to enter a dangerous part of the forest, Flovent invites the Bishop of Nîmes to join the hunting party, which begins the following morning.

[34] Noise plays a similar part in the Tristan courtly poems, alerting the lovers to the presence of a hunting party, whose prey—also a deer—ends in taking refuge in their cave. Considering that "there is no reason for the deer to run to Tristan and Isolt's dwelling," the animal's intrusion into the lovers' story confirms that the authors of the courtly renditions of the legend modeled the episode "on the story of a friendly deer running 'home' to his protector" in Guillaume's *Vie de Saint Gilles* (Lewes, *The Life in the Forest*, 43).

[35] The cult of the Precious Blood associates the image of the stricken deer with the blood that Joseph of Arimathea gathered in a vessel after Christ's death on the cross: thus it is a deer that leads to the discovery of the blood relic and to its veneration at the Benedictine abbey of Fécamp in Normandy. See Jean-Guy Gouttebroze, *Le Précieux Sang de Fécamp: Origine et développement d'un mythe chrétien* (Paris: Champion, 2000), 34.

[36] Whereas Guillaume de Berneville does not reveal the nature of Charles' sin, a number of texts link it to the emperor's incestuous relationship with his sister and to the ensuing birth of Roland (Lewes, *The Life in the Forest*, 12).

realm of aggressive pursuits. Forsaking the convention of both courtly romance and hagiographic romance, wherein the quest frequently entails the pursuit of a white prey of an animal or human kind,[37] Guillaume does not assign this traditional coloration to Gilles' deer. Seen against Galahad's bicoloration, the blood of Gilles' wound has no symbolic function, nor does red ally with white to justify the vengeful mission of Christ's soldier.[38] Additionally, although the location of Gilles' wound ("par mi le cors," l. 1883) connects him with both the Fisher King introduced in Chrétien's *Perceval* and the Wounded King of the *Queste* (considering that those two characters are also said to have been struck in mid-body),[39] the saint's injury does not have any sexual and lineal connotations. Gilles' silence about his wound, combined with the latter's invisibility,[40] contribute to an internalization of the hero's holiness, which here results from humility and self-abnegation. At the opposite of Guillaume's hero stands Galahad in his capacity to "make a noise" in this world, that is, in Attali's definition, to break a transmission, to unhook, and to kill (*Bruits*, 53). Evoking in that sense the hissing sound produced by the equally represented frequencies of background noise as they beat against each other, the whiteness of the *Queste*'s hero is not a signal but a "sound" as meaningless and random as the static heard between the stations of an FM radio. This suggests that, much like the closed system considered in thermodynamics, Galahad's energy ends in turning unto itself, indicating that death is the fate awaiting the *Queste*'s hero as the inevitable result of the incommunicable and uncommunicated character of his perfection.

[37] In Chrétien's *Erec and Enide*, for example, the object of Arthur's pursuit (a stag) and that of Erec's quest (Enide) have in common their whiteness. The romance thus begins with the king's renewal of a custom, the hunt of the White Stag, which finds its parallel in the Custom of the Sparrow Hawk, wherein Erec obtains possession of Enide, "the maiden with the white garment" ("la pucele au cheinse blanc," l. 1071). For other examples of white prey, see Marcelle Thiébaux, *The Stag of Love* (Ithaca: Cornell University Press, 1974).

[38] While in Marseille, Gilles finds shelter in the house of a certain Theotrita, whose mother has been ill for quite some time. Asked by Theotrita to help her mother, Gilles realizes that the latter fell ill as a punishment for her pride. The saint then proceeds to entreat God to forgive Theotrita's mother for, regardless of the gravity of one's transgression, God in His infinite compassion never attempts to avenge Himself on the sinner ("Sire, ne vus busuigne mie / Ke vus sulum nostre fesance, / Pernez de nus vostre vengeance; / Vus estes pius e merciables," ll. 1130–1134). Gilles thus stands for mercy, not requital.

[39] The nature of the wound of Chrétien's Fisher King varies according to the manuscript tradition: alternately, the king is said to have been struck between the thighs, between the hips, or between the legs.

[40] From the moment he is struck by the bowman's arrow until the day of his death, Gilles will never show or speak about his injury. When Gilles narrates his story to King Charles, for example, he tells him everything, except for what concerns his injury ("Fors de la plaie ke il out," l. 2681), which will never heal ("Unc de la plaie ne guari," l. 2153).

By contrast, what differentiates the hero of Guillaume's *Vie* is his role as mediator and protector. Whereas Galahad interacts minimally with his fellow human beings (and when he does, it is with occasionally lethal results), Gilles confirms repeatedly his readiness to cure and save those who come and seek his assistance.[41] That Gilles facilitates the coming together of heaven and earth is demonstrated by the effect of his death in enabling two of his monks to hear and retain the angelic melody emanating from Paradise, as well as by his function in guaranteeing that Guillaume's listeners will never enter the realm where one hears only weeping and crying (l. 3790). The "white noise" of Gilles' perfection thus refers to the harmonious effect of his sanctity as it finds itself expressed in a narration that praises the value of its hero as a positive trigger generating concord and peace among God's creatures. As the quotation that opens this chapter illustrates, Gilles' whiteness is a matter of internal purity expressed through a semantic field that roots the hero's goodness of heart ("cors," l. 2979) in his silent veneration of the Body of Christ ("cors," l. 2977). Further proof of the difference that separates "Saint" Galahad and Saint Gilles is the allusion to the mute animals ("bestes mues") which characterize the hero's human enemies in Galahad's story, whereas in Gilles' story they are integral to the peace and serenity of the saint's sylvan existence. In his slaughtering of the Carcelois knights, it is in reality Galahad himself who acts like a wild creature, evidence of his incapacity to communicate with his fellow human beings other than through aggression.

That the animal realm may serve as a metaphor of man's worst impulses calls attention to the potentially voracious character of human interaction, as illustrated in those other meanings of the word "cors" which—as we examine in the following chapter—amplify its significance in terms of an alimentary and sexual type of absorption. The synesthesic character of vernacularity does not, in that case, represent the authors' attempt to reflect and express God's truth. To the contrary, they use the cross-sensory connotations of the Old French language deliberately to destabilize, by ignoring or undercutting, the orderly world view articulated in the discourse of orthodoxy. We are, in other words, dealing with works of imaginative literature that exploit synesthesia in ways which cultivate language in its deliciously transgressive capability.

[41] Gilles demonstrates his healing power early on when he cures the misshapen and makes the dumb speak ("parler muz," l. 494). While living in a site near the Rhône river, Gilles witnesses the arrival of four men, who carry a sick man; complying with the four men's request, Gilles restores their friend's health (ll. 1319–1417). The sick man mentioned in this episode is not without reminiscence of the numerous Wounded Kings of the Grail tradition. Yet Guillaume de Berneville does not endow the man's illness with moral significance, nor is it the result of combat. In addition, Gilles is in no way connected with the character. The saint's action is thus one of pure generosity, with no resemblance to Galahad's preordained mission as the descendant of the Grail lineage and curer of its king.

IV

PARASITIC HOMOPHONES

> "Au quart jour [prendrons] le vassal
> Tout le daerrain membre aval
> Dont li delis lor soloit plaire,
> Si en fache on un mangier faire;
> Li cuer avoec nous meterons."
> ("Four days hence, we will remove from this vassal the fifth member that stands in front, as the source of the delight [our wives] used to enjoy, and we will order that it be prepared as a course, along with his heart.")
> (*Lai d'Ignaure*, ll. 541–545)

Integral to the entertaining value of imaginative literature is the malleability of its language in reflecting and at times relishing the slippery character of the human realm. Nowhere is such a malleability better expressed than in those works of the culture of literate orality which play on the ambiguity often produced by the concomitance of words that are similar in sound but different in meaning.[1] In the elevated style, the resulting homophony has for its goal to glorify the harmony of God's creation in terms of measure and proportion.[2] By contrast, in works that display a resolutely secular inspiration homophony has a frequently subversive effect inasmuch as it records a cosmology marked by fluctuation rather than immutability.[3] Keeping in mind the significance of noise in information theory

[1] The presence of homophony in vernacular literature is a natural outcome of a number of processes (such as the fall of unstressed vowels and the weakening of consonants between vowels) which led to the transformation of post-classical Latin and the emergence of the Old French language. See R. Howard Bloch's exploration of the word *lai* in disclosing "the polysemic plasticity of the Old French Language": "The Lay and the Law," *Stanford French Review* 14 (1990): 181–210, here 181.

[2] On the moral value of homophony, see Paul Vincent Rockwell, *Rewriting Resemblance in Medieval French Romance*, 105–85, and Brigitte Cazelles, *La faiblesse chez Gautier de Coincy* (Saratoga, CA: Anma Libri, 1978), 98–160.

[3] In her analysis of Shakespeare's language, Patricia Parker notes the interest of puns and wordplays in providing "glimpses into the relation between the plays and their contemporary culture, in a period when English was not yet standardized into a fixed orthography, obscuring on the printed page the homophonic networks possible before such boundaries were solidified." Exploring these homophonic networks discloses the way they "shaped politics, institutions, and laws, as well as discourses of the body and all that we have subsequently come

as an interference whence emerges a meaning at variance with the *logos* of narration, I designate as "parasitic homophones" the puns and wordplays by means of which secular authors undermine, often deliberately so, the hierarchical and stable world view articulated in the discourse of orthodoxy. In this perspective, parasitic homophony produces a type of synesthesia which is bereft of transcendental value to the extent that combining several of our five sensory perceptions here violates and disrupts the ordered structure of language and knowledge.

My analysis focuses on the homophonic network created by the concomitance of words such as "cors" (body, from Latin *corpus*; or horn, from *cornu*), "cort" (court, from post-classical Latin *cortis*), "cuers" (heart, *cor*, *cordis*), "cous" (cook, *coquus*), and "cos" (cuckold, *cuculus*).[4] Examining successively the equivalence thus established among abundance and the body politic (*cors/cort*; section 1), lubricity and the body poetic (*cors/cuers*; section 2), nutrition and predacity (*cors/cous*; section 3), I suggest that the resulting soundscape ends by eliminating any distinction among courtliness, emotion, lubricity, and nutrition.[5] Listeners are here offered a polyphonic register of the workings of society which discloses, paradoxically, the monochromatic character of human interaction when it takes the form of a reciprocal devourment. The fourth section ("Storytelling as *Entremés*") defines imaginative literature in terms of a deliciously transgressive concoction, one in which cognition (knowing, from *noscere*) is primarily a matter of appetite (gnawing, from *gnoscere*). Moralists and grammarians would undoubtedly reject as unworthy exemplars most if not all of the characters and stories examined in this chapter, considering the specificity of these texts in glorifying the "lower" part of human nature. In their perspective, understanding God's Word can be achieved only through the medium of vision and audition as two distance senses best suited for the development of the spiritual propensity

---

to think of as literature": *Shakespeare from the Margins* (Chicago and London: University of Chicago Press, 1996), 1, 272). On the subversive effect of puns and wordplays in underpinning the ideologies of Shakespeare's society (even if his plays appear to celebrate those ideals), see de Grazia, "Homonyms."

[4] The list could also include "cor" (corner, extremity), "cors" ("course" as race), "cos" (rooster), and "coe" ("queue" as tail). Considering the orthographic fluctuation generated by grammatical inflexion, and also by dialectal pronunciation and scribal errors, the spelling of these monosyllabic words is marked by variety. The decision here to choose a specific spelling (for example, "cuer"[s] instead of the possible "coer"[s]) is meant to simplify the exploration of their significance. In my quotations from the original texts, however, I reproduce the manuscript spelling of those words.

[5] The leveling effect of secular literature resembles the effect of a "trickster" as that which is "inimical to boundaries": Kathryn Gravdal, *Vilain and Courtois: Transgressive Parody in French Literature of the Twelfth and Thirteenth Centuries* (Lincoln, NE, and London: University of Nebraska Press, 1989), 117.

which also characterizes human nature.[6] Although neither vision nor audition is necessarily conducive to transcendence, as I examine in the chapter's last section ("*Veoir* and *Oïr*: Delusion or Accuracy?"), moralists nonetheless maintain that putting the more "animalistic" modes of sensory perception in a privileged position is a sinful choice the consequence of which will be one's downfall into the racket of eternal damnation.

1. Abundance and the Body Politic (cors/cort)

In traditional romance, horns of plenty ("cors") are images of the beneficent value of Arthur's court ("cort") in sustaining the knightly forces throughout the land. Communal food-sharing at Camelot punctuates in that sense the metamorphosis of the warrior class into a joyous and prosperous community. The banquet becomes the figure, in both the literal and allegorical meaning of the word, of the nurturing quality of life at court, where competition takes in principle the form of a strictly sportive display of prowess. Indeed, the revelries, like tourneys and jousts, that take place at Camelot in Chrétien de Troyes' Arthurian romances betoken a use of chivalric armor that obliterates its warlike function in favor of its festive and aesthetic value. This is corroborated by Chrétien's reliance on rhetorical figures, such as allegory, enigma, and ekphrasis, that are characteristic of the elevated style, in an attempt thus to subvert what Vance designates as the "*proprietas* of chivalric war" by making it "figurative" (*Mervelous Signals*, 121). The goal is to translate warlike impulses into the impulse of friendship and love, thus accelerating the transformation of feudal aristocracy from "a form of direct political coercion"—in Vance's terms—to a collectivity marked by harmonious exchange, as emblematized by the circularity of Arthur's Round Table. In this perspective, the sonorous similarity of "cors" (as cornucopia) and "cort" (Arthur's court) seeks to glorify the king's role as the orchestrator and guarantor of the "joie de la cort." In Chrétien's first four romances, royal revelries thus take on a civilizing quality that evokes the effect of Ceres' gift to humankind in classical mythology when the goddess endeavored to distribute "grain to the fields of all

[6] See Joan Ferrante: "*Scribe quae vides et audis*: Hildegard, Her Language and Her Secretaries," in *The Tongue of the Fathers*, ed. Townsend and Taylor, 102–35. Evidence of this hier- archical view of the sensorium is the contrast between Hell and Heaven in affecting our senses in an either abhorrent or blissful manner. As Thomas H. Seiler notes, apocalyptic writers described the place of eternal punishment through images of filth and stench that evoked "the antithesis of all that [is] civilized, desirable, and good," whereas Paradise is a garden of light, colors, and sweet smells: "Filth and Stench as Aspects of the Iconography of Hell," in *The Iconography of Hell*, ed. Clifford Davidson and idem (Kalamazoo, MI: Medieval Institute Publications, 1992), 132–40, here 132.

nations, so that they and their posterity might more easily be distinguished from the wild beasts by their diet."[7]

Far from entailing a vegetarian diet, however, the banquets offered at Camelot or any great courts of contemporary aristocracy centered on meat as the trademark of social status.[8] The famous feasts organized by noble households served primarily as a demonstration of power,[9] and "there is little evidence that the quality of cooking played much part in the success of these occasions," for, "quantity was all."[10] Food distribution at Arthur's court serves in that sense as the king's means to assert his preeminence through displays of his generosity. In the opening section of Chrétien's *Yvain*, for example, Arthur organizes a festival at such a great cost ("coust") that it is properly called Pentecost ("Penthecouste", in rhyming position; see *Yvain* [Ms. BN fr. 1433], ed. Hult, ll. 5–6). The primarily secular celebration of Pentecost in traditional courtly romance is, expectedly, much criticized by Grail authors. In their perspective, Arthurian munificence is evidence of the materialistic component of life at court, the result of which is that "cors" and "cort" become similar emblems of the appetite for power and glory that governs both the king and his companions. Thus the *Queste del Saint Graal* opens with a gathering of Arthur's Round Table as is customary during the Pentecost season. A banquet soon takes place (15–16), during which Arthur and his guests hear a clap of thunder so loud that it seems as if the palace is about to fall, while the hall is lit by a light that sheds an indescribable radiance. Struck dumb and gazing at one another like dumb animals ("bestes mues," 15), the diners now witness the appearance of the Holy Grail, which circles the hall and furnishes each plate with food. Despite the seasonal setting, the scene does not have the illuminating effect of a renewed Pentecost. Instead of providing the witnesses with understanding and eloquence, in a Pentecostal manner, the Grail strikes them dumb such that they appear now to regress to the speechless nature of the animal realm. Because they are clueless and blind in the face of the luminous apparition of the Grail, they can absorb it only in the form of a literal ingestion. This banquet scene illustrates the manner in which Grail authors disparage Arthur's court as a mode of life that satisfies the lower part of human nature through a superabundance which ignores the effect of waste, whence the role that Grail literature traditionally imparts to the leitmotif of the waste land.

[7] According to Hyginus, a librarian of Augustus, in his compendium of star myths entitled *De Astronomia*: trans. Condos, 142.

[8] Martin Aurell, Olivier Dumoulin, and Françoise Thelamon, eds., *La Sociabilité à table: Commensalité et convivialité à travers les âges* (Rouen: Université de Rouen, 1992), 122.

[9] Alice Planche, "La Table comme signe de la classe: le témoignage du *Roman du Comte d'Anjou* (1316)," in *Manger et boire au Moyen Âge*, ed. Denis Menjot (Paris: Les Belles Lettres, 1984), 239–60, here 258.

[10] Stephen Mennell, *All Manners of Food: Eating and Taste in England and France from the Middle Ages to the Present* (Urbana and Chicago: University of Illinois Press, 1996), 59.

Whereas Chrétien de Troyes' first four romances corroborate the essentially secular character of the values that regulate life at court, his last extant romance, *Perceval ou le Conte du Graal*, appears to introduce a model of chivalry that emphasizes its spiritual function. This is at least what transpires from the episode that narrates Perceval's encounter with his eremitic uncle (ed. Roach, 183–91). There, Perceval learns that the sacred dish he saw at the Grail castle is destined for another uncle of his, to whom it daily brings a consecrated wafer ("D'une sole oiste le sert on," l. 6422). Seen against the profusion of aliments which externalizes the power of either Camelot or any one of the great courts of contemporary aristocracy, the single wafer brought to Perceval's uncle betokens a mode of life grounded in asceticism and contemplation. Perceval's mission in Chrétien's romance and Galahad's in the *Queste* thus seem to entail a service focusing on Christ's Body ("cors") as the ultimate source of moral sustenance.[11] In contrast with secular food habits that are grounded in ostentation and waste, Grail literature elaborates a scriptural approach to nourishment emphasizing apportionment and parity.[12] Whereas food distribution empowers both factual and fictional lords in the political sense, fasting provides a spiritual form of power to both the Grail questers and the saints commemorated in verse hagiography, as it will in time empower women mystics of the late Middle Ages.[13] An example, in the *Vie de Sainte Marie l'Egyptienne* (by the secular poet Rutebeuf; between 1248 and 1277), is the saint's diet during her thirty years in the desert, which consists of two small loaves of bread and the meager grass of the ground (ll. 468–486). In her cell, the heroine of the *Vie de Sainte Thaïs* (after 1250) survives on plants, bread, and clear water (l. 304); and in his abode in the wilderness, the protagonist of the *Vie de Saint Jehan Paulus* (between 1222 and 1254) feeds himself by grazing like the animals (l. 1556). In the latter's case, this vegetarian diet results in his body being "wasted" (l. 1585), which distances Jehan Paulus from the wasting realm of courtly revelries and from carnivorous practices that give priority to venison as a symbol of the knights' favorite occupation: the hunt.[14] Eating sparsely and fasting contribute to a lightness of being thanks to which the saints succeed in

[11] See the *Conte*'s reference to Christ's "cors sains" and to the Grail as a "sainte chose" (ed. Roach, ll. 579 and 6425); and the *Queste*'s presentation of the Vessel as the receptacle that contains "Corpus Christi," described as "la haute viande": ed. Cerquiglini (86, 255, 270).

[12] Christ nurtures the multitude that has gathered "in the wilderness" by multiplying seven loaves and "a few little fishes" such that four (or five) thousand are filled (Matthew 15:32–36; Mark 6: 35–44; Luke 9: 12–17; John 6: 3–14).

[13] See Caroline Walker Bynum, *Holy Feast and Holy Fast: The Religious Significance of Food for Medieval Women* (Berkeley and Los Angeles: University of California Press, 1991).

[14] J. O. Benoist, "Le Gibier dans l'alimentation seigneuriale," in *Manger et boire au Moyen Âge*, ed. Menjot, 75–87, here 77; Anita Guerreau-Jalabert, "Les Nourritures comme figures symboliques dans les romans arthuriens," in *La Sociabilité à table*, ed. Aurell et al., 35–40, here 39.

transcending the senses and elevating themselves toward God's realm. This process of progressive "disincarnation" entails the control of one's mouth as an opening that bespeaks insatiability, and it is not fortuitous that recluses and hermits cultivate silence as a form of restraint that will protect them from the both nauseous and noisy consequences of human appetite.[15]

2. Lubricity and the Body Poetic ("cors"/"cuers")

In the *Queste*'s moralistic reinscription of traditional romance, progress entails the rejection of all the objects of desire that arouse knightly voracity, beginning with the ladies and maidens whom the questers must leave behind as they depart from Arthur's court.[16] This primarily masculine setting contrasts vividly with the social environment characterizing courtly romance. There, knights and ladies are supposed to form a harmonious relationship at both the physical ("cors") and affective ("cuers") level. In Chrétien's *Yvain*, for example, the opening episode that takes place at Arthur's court gathers together knights and ladies united by a similar interest in the affairs of both the heart and the mind. Thus Yvain's cousin, Calogrenant, begins his recounting of an adventure he had seven years earlier in the Brocéliande forest with the admonition to his listeners that they lend him their hearts and their ears, for things that one hears are lost unless they are understood by the heart ("de cuer entendue," l. 152). The language of Arthur's court and that of vernacular romance are shown to emulate the enlightening quality of exegetical discourse. It is in this connection noteworthy that Calogrenant's adventure was a chivalric defeat, suggesting that prowess now equates with verbal rather than military talent. Further evidence of the importance of the heart over the body is demonstrated through Yvain's own adventure at Brocéliande, in the course of which the hero falls in love with and eventually marries the lady of the fountain, Laudine. Yet, the fact that Yvain obtains both the hand of Laudine and the control of her domain as a result of his having fought and killed her first husband suggests that the triumph of love over chivalry is only apparent. Just as significant is the way Yvain loses Laudine once he resumes his existence as knight-errant in quest of adventures. Chrétien's talent lies, in my view, in his capacity to undermine the very mode of life—chivalry—that he

[15] In this light, the fact that the Eucharistic feast entails (in the West) a form of eating which prohibits gnawing the holy Host may be seen as an attempt to counteract the frequently voracious and at times even cannibalistic character of interaction in postlapsarian history.

[16] Peggy McCracken's analysis of the role of gender in Grail fictions sees the marginal status of women as evidence of the authors' desire to promote chastity: "Mothers in the Grail Quest: Desire, Pleasure, and Conception," *Arthuriana* 8 (1998): 35–48, here 46.

appears to celebrate, as is illustrated in a narrative the central topic of which, love, is in reality incidental and peripheral. If love at either Camelot or Brocéliande belongs to fiction, the reason is that love has no place in a society whose primary values are glory and renown.

A metaphor of the knightly thirst for preeminence is the gigantic characters against whom the hero—for example, Chrétien's Erec—typically tests himself.[17] His victory over two such giants (ll. 4395–4468) has so weakened the hero that his wife Enide believes him dead. The sounds of her grief ("a haute voiz crïer," l. 4673) attract the attention of an evil knight, Count Oringle de Limors, who rides to the site and decides to marry Enide on the spot, regardless of her feelings. The wedding ritual takes place, followed by a banquet in the course of which Oringle orders Enide to rejoice and eat ("Maingiez, que je vos en semon," l. 4807). Because Enide persists in lamenting, Oringle endeavors to beat her repeatedly, the result of which is that Erec awakens from his faint, runs toward the count, and kills him with a sharp blow to the head. And thus the unwarranted aggression of Oringle "of Limors" (from the kingdom of death) finds itself punished on the very site—the dinner table—that epitomizes knightly appetite. Banqueting here represents the voracity of those knights whose prestige is acquired through the despoiling and, hence, disempowerment or death of rival knights.[18] Also noteworthy is the sexual connotation of Oringle's appetite inasmuch as it discloses the "dark underside" of communal food-sharing in exposing "the fragility of the social bonds" that ritualistic feasts are supposedly to strengthen.[19] As illustrated by Oringle's command ("maingiez"), banqueting is the locus of an interaction between the participants that is both unequal and one-sided. What governs such gatherings is conflict and competition as the two "driving force[s] of social and cultural development," fostering a balance of power that fluctuates and changes over time (Mennell, *All Manners of Food*, 16).

This type of fluctuation is at the core of the Arthurian revelry recounted in Robert Biket's verse *Lai du Cor* (mid-twelfth century). The title of Robert's novella refers to an ivory horn that functions as drinking vessel, sonorous instrument,

---

[17] As Jeffrey Jerome Cohen points out, "the giant is enmeshed in the romance process of embodiment as a haunting, originary point as well as a constant, intimately strange limit to its selfhood, troubling the chivalric subject as a reminder of his contingency, his fragility, his gigantism": *Of Giants: Sex, Monsters, and the Middle Ages* (Minneapolis and London: University of Minnesota Press, 1999), 81. References to *Erec* are based on ms. BN fr. 1376, ed. Jean-Marie Fritz.

[18] It is not fortuitous that Michel Serres' analysis of parasitism (*Le parasite*) begins and with a banquet scene (9–24, 331–43), corroborating the significance of Oringle de Limors in terms of a parasitic figure who lives and prospers at the expense of others.

[19] Stephen G. Nichols, "Seeing Food: An Anthropology of Ekphrasis and Still Life in Classical and Medieval Examples," *Modern Language Notes* 106 (1991): 818–51, here 820.

and test of conjugal faithfulness.[20] Because the entire court (with the exception of one knight) fails the test, the horn reveals that adultery ("cors") lies at the heart ("cuers") of the ideology of courtly love. At the same time that it reflects the refinement of Arthur's court and the civilizing value of love, the horn also discloses the mendacious character of both. In traditional courtly romance, it appears that the love quest focuses on the body of the beloved, which is either idealized to the extent that the lady belongs to someone else or devoured once the rival to whom she belonged has been eliminated. The function of Robert Biket's horn in publicly exposing the unfaithfulness of the court's ladies indicates that women are not immune from voracious impulses and that they too intend to savor the body of the beloved. An example is the verse tale of *Ignaure* (early thirteenth century; sometimes attributed to Renaut de Beaujeu), whose eponymous hero is the epitome of amorous ardor. Relying on music to captivate and hence capture the hearts of women,[21] Ignaure soon becomes the lover of twelve noble ladies (each married to one of those valiant and rich knights who live at the castle of Riol) and the happy beneficiary of their welcome. However, unlike the poor knights in contemporary society, whose association with noble ladies constituted an important means of self-empowerment,[22] Ignaure accumulates women strictly to satisfy his amorous impulses. It is clear that Ps.-Renaut's hero does not subscribe to a monogamous way of life, whence the interest of this novella in reinscribing ironically such love songs as Bernart de Ventadorn's, wherein the poet claims to be the faithful servant of a single beloved.[23]

Yet Ignaure's plenitude is about to end when, one fine day, the twelve ladies assemble in an orchard and decide to play a "confession" game wherein one among them will act as a priestly confessor, to whom each of the remaining eleven will successively reveal the name of her secret lover (ll. 87–223). Now aware

[20] The symbolic meaning of Robert's magic horn addresses the entire courtly community, given that the object is "male by its external shape but female as recipient" (Nichols, "Seeing Food," 820). For other textual illustrations of the motif of the magic horn, see Magnúsdóttir, *La Voix du cor*, 278–303.

[21] Each morning, Ignaure goes into the woods with five "jougleres," flute players, and pipers, and brings back the tree of May as a token of his amorous energy (which Ps.-Renaut, using the formula dear to courtly poets, parodically describes in terms of "fine amors," ed. Lejeune, l. 36). Women give him the surname of "Nightingale" ("Lousignol," l. 37) in recognition of his talent as musician, love poet, and lover.

[22] Georges Duby, "Les 'jeunes' dans la société aristocratique dans la France du Nord-Ouest au XIIe siècle," *Annales ESC* 19 (1964): 835–46.

[23] When the beloved fails to respond, Bernart takes away from her the distinction ("domna" as lady) that separated her from the mass ("femna" as woman), suggesting that the poet is now disposed to select another "femna" and make of her his new "domna" (canso 26, ll. 32–34). On the ironic play on the pairing "cors"/"cuers" in the lyrical tradition, see Brigitte Cazelles, "Mots à vendre, corps à prendre, et les troubadours d'Aquitaine," *Stanford French Review* 7 (1983): 27–36.

that they had shared Ignaure, the twelve ladies confront and threaten him. Ignaure saves his skin by claiming that he loves each one of them in equal measure and finds equal pleasure in their own sexual bliss and delight ("Et lor solas, et lors delis," l. 315). They nonetheless pressure him to select one among them to become his sole lover and, despite Ignaure's sadness at losing the others' bodies if not their affection, monogamy thus triumphs over polygamy. However, this happy compromise does not endure: in time, the ladies' husbands learn their secret and decide to take their revenge for, if they do not, they will lose their status as lords and be viewed as cowards ("recreant," l. 451). Seen against the affectionate character of the relationship that Ignaure continues to entertain with the twelve ladies, the reaction of the latter's husbands qualifies as proprietary, disclosing the centrality of the "cors" in defining and at the same time disrupting order at the castle of Riol. Thanks to a judicial proof obtained "in flagrante delicto," they catch Ignaure in the act[24] and in time kill him. Removing from the hero that organ which their wives used to enjoy ("Dont li delis lor soloit plaire," l. 543), they order that it be mixed with Ignaure's heart ("cuer") and prepared as a dinner course. The ladies finally agree to eat what looks like a most delicious and tasty food, but when they discover that they have absorbed the very object of their desire, they vow never to eat again and die soon after. And thus ends the tale, composed in memory of this ardent man "Ki por amours fu desmembrés" ("who was castrated on account of love," l. 664).

In the pseudo-Eucharistic structure of *Ignaure*, twelve ladies lust for a single body, whose absorption takes the form of a meal wherein "cuers" and "cors" are finally united. At the core of Ps.-Renaut's story is not only the beloved's "cuers," but his "cors" as well; and not only his body, but its "fifth member" as a metonymy illustrating the erotic component of desire. Deconstructing the mystique of courtly love and deactivating the tragic connection between love and death as articulated in the Tristan legend, Ps.-Renaut commemorates the both cerebral and sensual pleasures of love. For Milad Doueihi, the author's ritualized parody of the Last Supper bespeaks his effort to rehabilitate the body against its disparagement by the Christian tradition and against its loss "in the domination of an ethical discourse privileging soul over body."[25] At the same time, the rehabilitation of the body does not signify a corresponding depreciation of the soul so much as an indictment of the joyless and proprietary mode of consumption

[24] Ignaure is now thrown into a cell (l. 511) and his disappearance causes much distress among the twelve ladies, who unanimously declare that they will refrain from eating until they know of his whereabouts. Their decision creates an additional challenge to each husband's authority over his wife's body, and the twelve knights respond to that challenge by transforming Ignaure's body into food.

[25] Milad Doueihi, "The Lure of the Heart," *Stanford French Review* 14 (1990): 51–68, here 65–66.

which inspires the twelve husbands to force-feed their wives as their (failed) attempt to recover some measure of marital control.[26] The poet's claim, enunciated in his prologue, that he is about to tell the whole truth about love because the meaning is lost when it remains covered generates a highly fleshly text which in that sense stands at the opposite of the textile character of the *Queste*'s narration, wherein the mysteries of the Grail remain hidden under the red samite that covers the receptacle. The "truth" that Ps.-Renaut intends to reveal is that eating *is* knowing, in reference to a love experience that enables Ignaure and his twelve "disciples" to enjoy and cultivate the delights of human nature. In presenting love as a pleasure shared rather than as a predatory pursuit, his novella differs in that respect from Chrétien's courtly romances as well as from Robert Biket's *Lai du Cor.* Following Ignaure as their model exemplar, the twelve heroines do not give priority to physical attraction over affect, indicating the presence of what I term a Pan-like capacity to respond to the needs of the both upper and lower parts of human nature.[27]

In both Platonic and Christian thought, however, Pan is the emblem of inebriation, disorder, and predation. The sound of his pipes, which causes fear (panic) and confusion (pandemonium), bewitches its listeners in such a way that they lose their capacity to reason and regress to a bestial stage. For Socrates (in Plato, *Cratylus* 408), Pan's music represents human language in its mendacious propensity, as confirmed by the name of the deity's father (Hermes) in connecting speech (*eirein*) and fabrication (*emesato*). Truth is "the smooth and sacred form which dwells above among the gods, whereas falsehood dwells among men below, and is rough like the goat of tragedy" (ed./trans. Hamilton and Cairns,

---

[26] In deciding to dismember their rival, the twelve husbands focus on Ignaure's organ ("le daerrain membre *aval*," l. 542) in a manner that enunciates a form of devouring (*avaler*, to swallow) for the purpose of destruction.

[27] The two names for the tale's protagonist—"Ignaure" and "Lousignol"—may be interpreted as an implicit indictment of rational *logos* in its simultaneously reductive and dominating effect. Seen against the twelve husbands' proprietary stance and legalistic behavior, the protagonist's surname of "Nightingale" portrays him as a free spirit who sings aloud the pleasures of love experienced in both the "cors" and the "cuers," much to the delight of his beloved ladies. In his analysis of the motif of the eaten heart, Allen J. Grieco connects the motif to hunting practices wherein the prey is dismembered and its parts distributed in a way that maintains a safe distance between hunters and prey: "Le thème du coeur mangé: l'ordre, le sauvage et la sauvagerie," in *La Sociabilité à table*, ed. Aurell et al., 20–28. But if the successful hunter is entitled to take for himself the prey's lower parts (24), then this indicates that he absorbs the "wild" aspect of the animal realm along with its uncontrollable sexuality. I also disagree with Grieco's conclusion (27) that the *Ignaure* poet indicts his hero's amorous rapport with the twelve beloved ladies in terms of an adulterous transgression that deserves to be punished by a culinary transgression (in reference to the motif of the eaten heart).

408c).[28] And if falsehoods are linked to a tragic or goatish mode of life, "then surely Pan, who is the declarer of all things (*pan*) and the perpetual mover (*aei polon*) of all things, is rightly called *aipolos* (goatherd), he being the two-formed son of Hermes, smooth in his upper part, and rough and goatlike in his lower regions" (408d). That Pan's body combines reason and instinct proves that his lying and his telling the truth are concomitant and, hence, that the truth about pandemic language is that it cannot ever tell the truth. Socrates denigrates the confusing effect of Pan's tune and instead praises Apollonian music as a truthful and rational form of elocution.

In Ovid's *Metamorphoses* (11.116–193), the contrast between Pan and Apollo takes the form of an "unequal" musical contest wherein Tmolus is to act as judge and Midas as witness. The sweetness of Apollo's sounds is such that Tmolus declares Apollo's lyre superior to Pan's pipes. But Midas challenges this verdict and calls it unjust, which prompts the god of Delos to punish "such stupid ears" by transforming them into the ears of an ass. The opposition between Pan and Apollo in Ovid's story develops a dualistic perspective on man's nature, wherein the rational side should and will triumph over the irrational. All those who, like Midas, let themselves be governed by impulse and instinct are bound to incur loss of humanity and be marked by the brand of animalism. It is therefore both logical and predictable that Midas "of the *golden* touch" be transformed into Midas "with the ears of a lumbering ass."[29] This is why the music of Pan, the half-goat god, is in Christian thought the sonorous symbol of evil.[30] Yet the result is to increase the distance between humans and nature or, more specifically, the result is to effect the triumph of argumentative *logos* at the expense of intuition. It is in that context noteworthy that, in the "unequal" contest opposing the two deities, Apollo's victory is pre-ordained, indicating that his superiority over Pan is not a matter of superior musical talent and that his capacity to reason is eristic

[28] Augustine develops a similar opposition between the divine voice, which comes "from above," and the diabolical voice, "from beneath" (*De libero arbitrio* 3.25.74). As Eric Jager notes (*The Tempter's Voice*, 109), the Fall as false or abusive eloquence was a paradigm for theater as the medium was relentlessly denigrated by patristic authors and medieval moralists.

[29] Ovid's description of Apollo's "golden head" is noteworthy, for it associates the coloration of the god's hair with rational lucidity, which is precisely what thick-minded Midas lacks. For this story see David Brumble, *Classical Myths and Legends in the Middle Ages and Renaissance* (Westport, CT: Greenwood Press, 1998), 216–18 (s. v. "Midas").

[30] Accordingly, goats will be charged with the sins of the world, whence the fate awaiting any and all scapegoats that endanger Apollonian reason and order. Thus it is said that Aaron laid the sins of his people on the head of a goat, which was then led away into the wilderness (Leviticus 16:10). The chasing away of the scapegoat ("caper emissarius") symbolizes the collectivity's desire to distance itself from its irrational and instinctual tendencies.

in nature.[31] Just as noteworthy are the circumstances which, according to Ovid, lead to the revelation of Midas' secret, considering that it is the swaying of reeds that tells the truth about the "vile shame" hidden behind Midas' turban.[32] Although Apollo's victory in the musical contest is supposed to mark the triumph of reason (the lyre) over instinct (Pan's pipes), man's irrational side is not eradicated so much as transformed into an underground force. Revelation emerges by means of the melodious sounds produced by the reeds, disclosing that, in the last analysis, Pan's music survives alongside Apollo's as an index of man's ambivalent nature. In this perspective, the interest of Ps.-Renaut's *Ignaure* consists, I suggest, of an acknowledgment that human nature combines an upper and a lower part and that promoting one aspect at the expense of the other can only lead to unbalance and excess.

The motif of the eaten heart, which appears in a multiplicity of texts including Ps.-Renaut's novella,[33] is given a particularly remarkable function in the verse *Roman du Castelain de Couci* (by "Jakemes," late thirteenth century).[34] Like Ps.-Renaut, Jakemes places the corporeal register in a privileged position over the symbolic through a narration that focuses on the love experience between the Châtelain and his lady, the Dame de Fayel, in a manner which amplifies

[31] Wes Folkerth analyzes the contest between Apollo and Pan in similar terms, noting that Apollo considers Midas' preference for the music of Pan to be "a serious threat to his cultural hegemony": *The Sound of Shakespeare*, 90.

[32] Having discovered Midas's secret, his barber digs a hole in the ground, murmurs that his master has ass's ears, and fills up the hole again. A cluster of reeds begins to grow on the spot and proceeds to broadcast the words of Midas' barber.

[33] Ranging from Ovid's *Philomela* to the *Roman de la Poire* (mid-thirteenth century) and Boccaccio's *Decameron*, the motif is already present in the Dionysus myth according to which the Titans kidnapped Dionysus, cut him up, tossed his limbs into a cauldron, and ate them all except the heart. As Doueihi notes ("The Lure of the Heart," 56–57; see also idem, *A Perverse History of the Human Heart* [Cambridge, MA: Harvard University Press, 1997]), the heart that is not eaten and survives the savage murder of the Titans "becomes the object of [a specific] prohibition": cannibalism. For other analyses of the motif, see Sylvia Huot, "Troubadour Lyric and Old French Narrative," in *The Troubadours: An Introduction*, ed. Simon Gaunt and Sarah Kay (Cambridge: Cambridge University Press, 1999), 263–78; Gregory B. Stone, *The Death of the Troubadour* (Philadelphia: University of Pennsylvania Press, 1994); Roberta L. Krueger, *Women Readers and the Ideology of Gender in Old French Verse Romance* (Cambridge: Cambridge University Press, 1993), 183–216; Jean-Jacques Vincensini, *Pensée mythique et narrations médiévales* (Paris: Champion, 1996), 335–58; Helen Solterer, "Dismembering, Remembering the Châtelain de Coucy," *Romance Philology* 46 (1992): 103–24; Grieco, "Le thème du coeur mangé"; and Bloch, "The Lay and the Law."

[34] Guy de Thourotte, surnamed the Châtelain de Couci, was known for the love poems he composed between 1170 and 1202, the date of his death, which he met during his voyage as a participant in the fourth crusade. The author known as Jakemes is the first French romance writer to base the protagonist of his narrative on a historically authentic figure; also unique is the way Jakemes incorporates several of the Châtelain's poems within his tale.

the protagonists' "mutual fascination with the body of the beloved" (Solterer, "Dismembering, Remembering," 105). Yet Jakemes pays equal attention to the sentimental quality of love, as is illustrated by the pairing of "cors" ("coers") and "cuers," which reoccurs with significant frequency as an index of the plenitude of the lovers' experience in uniting body and soul.[35] Thus, like Ps.-Renaut, Jakemes glorifies love in terms of a Pan-like capacity to savor the at once cerebral and sensual type of pleasure dispensed by the beloved. At the same time, Jakemes' narration differs from Ps.-Renaut's by focusing on a single duo of lovers, the result of which is a para-Eucharistic assessment of the eaten heart motif grounded on interiority and self-sacrifice. Indeed, it is the Châtelain himself who offers his heart as a token of his eternal devotion to the Dame de Fayel, proof that the "cuers" is here the emblem of "an intimate communion between the lovers that involves a sacrificial meal" (Solterer, "Dismembering, Remembering," 116).[36] Although Jakemes' narration concludes with a repast scene that resembles the ending of Ps.-Renaut's tale,[37] the eaten heart motif serves primarily to confirm the Châtelain's merit as an exemplary lover. The physical act of offering his heart shows the Châtelain (as lover) to be true to his lyric word (as poet) inasmuch as this gesture "confirms what has already been projected poetically" (Solterer, "Dismembering, Remembering," 112). Far from a gruesome episode (as the motif is usually interpreted), the eating of the Châtelain's "cuers" enables the Dame de Fayel to incorporate her lover's body in a virtually sacramental manner. Not only does she thus recover, by absorbing, the Châtelain's love; he is himself immortalized "as a type of textual reliquary," suggesting that the eaten heart motif in Jakemes' romance associates "the figure of eating with the process of reading" (Solterer, "Dismembering, Remembering," 118, 120).

---

[35] An example, early on in the text, is the effect of love in inducing the Châtelain to devote his entire being to its service: Love strikes him through his eyes such that "coer et corps assentir / Li fist a loiaument amer" (ed. Delbouille, ll. 78–79). See also ll. 353, 836, 1072, 3136, 3497, and 3536.

[36] The Dame de Fayel's husband is not without fault in precipitating the events that lead to the lovers' separation and, ultimately, to the Châtelain's death. When he discovers his wife's infidelity, her husband takes his revenge by announcing—without intending to do so—that both he and his wife will go to the Holy Land. The Châtelain decides to join in the crusade in order thus to remain close to his beloved and only belatedly discovers the husband's ruse. In fighting the infidels in the Holy Land, the Châtelain is fatally wounded and before dying makes the following request of his servant, Gobert: Gobert is to open his body, take his heart, and carry it back to the Dame de Fayel. But the latter's husband succeeds in taking hold of the Châtelain's heart, which he offers to his wife as a course especially prepared for her.

[37] After the Dame de Fayel is served with the Châtelain's heart, she is delighted by the taste of the course, wondering aloud that it must be quite costly, considering that they have never been offered such a delicacy before. When her husband tells her the truth of the matter, she decides never to eat again and dies soon after.

Compared to its role in *Ignaure*, the heart does not serve here as an ironic deconstruction of courtly love. Rather, nutrition functions as the metaphor of a Body Poetic wherein the "cors" of the sacrificed lover is the founding stone of Jakemes' poetic corpus. In this way the author detaches the motif from the socio-political role of feasting at Arthur's court, while also distancing himself from a negative form of orality wherein knowing comes from gnawing. This negative form of orality refers to the mouth as "the place where lips, teeth, tongue, palate, and throat engage in their specific labor of biting, savoring, triturating, masticating, and swallowing."[38] By contrast, a positive form of orality focuses on the speaking voice articulated through the mouth as a sonorous producer of meaning.[39] Both *Ignaure* and the *Roman du Castelain de Couci* combine these two forms of orality understood as eating and speaking by investing the pairing "cors"/"cuers" with both sensual and sentimental significance, as does Marie de France in a tale, *The Laustic* ("Nightingale"), which evokes Ps.-Renaut's hero in his capacity to cultivate the combined pleasures of body and heart.

3. Nutrition and Predacity ("cors"/"cous")

The animalistic aspects of nutrition and sexuality account for their rejection by many poets and most moralists as two topics that belong to the lowly style,[40] over against which is Jakemes' lyrical amplification of the eaten heart motif in ways that seek to transcend the lover's body and demonstrate the sublime value of both the Châtelain's and his own language. Nonetheless, it remains that his *Roman* is embedded in transgression inasmuch as the resulting Body Poetic superimposes itself over Christ's Body. Surely the *Queste*'s author would have disapproved of Jakemes' lyrical appropriation of eucharistic imagery and argued that we are dealing here with a typical case of secular literature as a fallen medium.

---

[38] Louis Marin, *Food for Thought*, trans. Mette Hjort (Baltimore and London: Johns Hopkins University Press, 1989), 35–36.

[39] As Madeleine Jeay points out, most medieval reinscriptions of the eaten heart myth normalize its violent component by emphasizing its courtly significance; the tale's cannibalistic aspect is thus replaced by a presentation of the violence of desire as being both "acceptable" and "unavoidable": "Consuming Passions: Variations on the Eaten Heart Theme," in *Violence Against Women in Medieval Texts*, ed. Anna Roberts (Gainesville: University Press of Florida, 1998), 75–96, here 91. On the animalistic character of nutrition, see Gutton's remark that the noise of gluttony reveals "the animal in us" (*Bruits et sons*, 49).

[40] Medieval rhetoricians maintain that images and figures of a trivial nature may occasionally serve to evoke the sublime, whereas those of an elevated kind can never signify lowly reality. See Nancy Freeman-Regalado, "*Des Contraires Choses*. La fonction poétique de la citation et des exempla dans le *Roman de la Rose* de Jean de Meun," *Littérature* 41 (1981): 62–81, here 74–75.

In this perspective, Ps.-Renaut's and Jakemes' narratives are mirror images of each other, following a process of metonymic reduction that focuses on Ignaure's "fifth member" and on the Châtelain's heart with equal ambiguity.

As a rhetorical figure entailing substitution and transformation, metonymy is integral to the pleasure of imaginative literature in its undecidable character. An example of the function of language as a source of metamorphosis is the pervasive use of nutritive imagery by means of which both Ps.-Renaut and Jakemes register the changing dynamics between consumers and consumed. It is not coincidental that the art of cooking is itself the site of constant shifting and mutation, as corroborated by the type of culinary logic that characterizes the language of cookbooks and food preparation.[41] Much like those founding myths which Bruce Lincoln (*Myth, Cosmos, and Society*, 65–73) classifies under the rubric "sitiogony" (creation through food; from *sitos*, grain), *Ignaure* and the *Roman du Castelain de Coucy* seem to connect the survival of the beloved as consumer to the lover's death and being consumed. Unlike the process of transformation evoked in sitiogony, however, the sacrifice of the lover does not effect the survival of the beloved since the consumer dies soon after the act of absorption. In reality, consumer and consumed are similarly victims at the hands of a series of actors and agents, which includes the treacherous spy who divulges their secret love, the vengeful husband(s) who orchestrates the lover's demise,[42] and, not incidentally, the cook ("cous") who transforms the lover's body into a meal.

The *coquus* figures prominently in historical documents and literary texts as a character whose function is not only culinary, in reference to the "Coquus Franciae" or "Magister coquorum" at the French king's court (the ancestor of the "maître queux"), but also diplomatic.[43] Indeed, the master cook of Saint Louis served occasionally as royal representative, as does the cook Rainouart in the epic *Chanson de Guillaume*.[44] This dual expertise in nutritive transformation and verbal transmission, which points to the similarity of both activities, explains the frequent prominence of the "cous" at the courts of both factual and fictional

[41] Culinary logic works along two principal axes: the paradigmatic axis (which pertains to the lists and items found in the book) organizes and classifies the realm of edibles as units the function of which imitates that of lexicology; the syntagmatic axis (which pertains to the description of the activities that take place in the kitchen) combines those elements and prescribes "the ways in which [they] can be arranged and connected to each other" (Marin, *Food for Thought*, 117–18). On the history of medieval cookbooks, see Bruno Laurioux, *Les livres de cuisine médiévaux* (Turnhout: Brepols, 1997).

[42] For Krueger (*Women Readers and the Ideology of Gender*, 206–16), revenge is indeed central to the plot of Jakemes' romance.

[43] Jacques Merceron, *Le Message et sa fiction: communication par messager dans la littérature française des XIIe et XIIIe siècles* (Berkeley: University of California Press, 1998), 23, 28–29.

[44] Jacques Merceron, "Cooks and Messengers: Food and Language in Twelfth- through Thirteenth-Century French History and Literature," *Chronica* (1992): 39–40.

kings. In the Arthurian tradition, for example, it is the king's seneschal, Keu, who assumes the organization of royal feasts and banquets. The occasional spelling of his name ("Ques," at line 2180 of Chrétien's *Yvain* [ed. Roques]) confirms Keu's status as Arthur's "maître-queue," while his relentlessly sarcastic attitude confirms his mastery in the art of innuendo. Keu's aspersion is often expressed through culinary metaphors: witness his reaction when Yvain vows that he will go to Brocéliande and avenge the shame incurred there by his cousin Calogrenant. Opening his comment with the remark that food and wine make a knight talkative, Keu then focuses on Yvain and notes that the latter has obviously a full stomach. For a meal induces any knight to boast—but without stirring in the least ("sanz remüer," l. 595)—that he will go and slay such pagan kings as Loradin or Forré.[45] Arthur's seneschal enunciates here a caustic assessment of both chivalric behavior, when the knight's only deeds take the form of empty speech acts, and courtly language as an elevated style that hides or embellishes reality. The glorious Round Table is transformed into a collectivity of satiated and inebriated individuals, who proceed either to fall asleep (as does King Arthur; *Yvain*, ll. 42–48) or engage in self-praise (as does Yvain). Purposely resorting to the lowly style of proverbial wisdom, Keu disregards the rules of civility and speaks an uncourteous language in order to expose the reality of chivalry in its most literal and material urgencies.

That Arthur's companions are ordinary human beings with respect to corporeal needs is demonstrated repeatedly in the course of Yvain's adventures. A salient illustration occurs at the moment when the hero learns that he has lost Laudine's love for having failed to comply with his own promise to return to her at the end of a year. At once Yvain takes leave of his companions and enters the forest, where he soon loses his mind and roams about, naked and senseless. Loss of social contact transforms the hero into a wild man ("Hom forsenez et salvage," l. 2830) who spends his days tracking down the game of the woods and eating it raw ("et se manjue / La venison trestote crue," ll. 2827–2828).[46] Then chance takes the wild man to the abode of a hermit, whereupon he is provided daily with such

[45] Keu's allusion to those two pagan kings satirically amplifies the less-than-heroic stature of the Round Table, whose members prefer the prosaic pleasures of life at court over the sublime exploits of soldiers, like Roland, who sacrifice their lives in fighting the infidels.

[46] In his classic analysis of culinary practices in pre-industrial societies, Claude Lévi-Strauss (1964, 1968) adhered to a structuralist approach and saw the "gustemes" as constituent elements of social order. See *The Raw and the Cooked*, trans. John and Doreen Weightman (New York: Harper & Row, 1990), and *The Origin of Table Manners*, trans. eidem (New York: Harper & Row, 1978). Lévi-Strauss' binary oppositions (like the raw and the cooked, or the raw and the rotten) serve here to delineate the conditions necessary for the emergence of a viable social order (the cooked), away from such excesses as loss, waste, or destruction. The function of parasitic homophones in imaginative literature enunciates a much more complex and less benevolent picture of social organization.

essential aliments as bread, along with venison cooked without salt and pepper ("Venison sans sel et sans poivre," l. 2880). That the hermit's bread happens to be coarse and rough as well as moldy and dry is a measure of Yvain's hunger, while his lack of concern for taste indicates that he has regressed on the social scale.[47] At the same time, the substitution of cooked venison for raw meat signals that Yvain is on his way to regaining awareness of his status. Before his eventual reintegration into knightly society, another food provider intervenes in Yvain's story in the form of a lion whose life the hero has just saved. As a token of its gratitude, the lion captures for his new master the wild beasts of the forest, beginning with a roe-deer which Yvain, who is henceforth extremely fond of the animal, proceeds to roast and eat; but not without deploring the lack of wine, salt, cloth, and knife ("ne fu deduiz / Qu'il n'i ot pein ne vin ne sel," ll. 3462–3463). The hero's reaction establishes a distinction between animals and men on the basis of culinary practices (like the cooking of meat) and table manners (like the use of a knife) the absence of which affects taste in the sensory and social meaning of the term. In the context of Yvain's story, "the raw" signifies a type of behavior that is unrefined inasmuch as it is natural, in opposition to "the cooked" as the emblem of one's capacity to contain and repress nature. "The raw" may thus be viewed as a metaphor of excess, either when one overeats and falls asleep, as does Arthur in the opening episode of Chrétien's romance, or when one devours his food without proper decorum and tasty condiments, as does Yvain when he no longer remembers his identity and social allegiance to the extent that he ends up losing both his manners and his mind.

Reasoning entails remembering, which the twelve ladies of Ps.-Renaut's *Ignaure* proceed to do once they decide to avenge themselves ("nous vengerons") through abstinence ("ne mangerons"; in rhyming position at ll. 601–602). Because fasting is a slow death, this gives the ladies an opportunity to commemorate the details of Ignaure's appeal (ll. 588–607): one regrets his beauty, another his limbs; a third evokes his elegant body, and a fourth his eyes and torso; a fifth remembers his loving heart, and a sixth his beautiful feet; and all lament the loss of the sensual delight (*delit*) he used to provide them.[48] In reality, remembering

[47] As "one of the languages of human culture by which cultures are constituted," culinary logic stresses status differences between individuals or classes (Marin, *Food for Thought*, 118). Spices and pepper (imported and expensive) thus played an important part in identifying the nutritive habits of the aristocracy: see Benoist, "Le Gibier," 81. As Lévi-Strauss notes (*The Origin of Table Manners*, 484), boiling, which provides a method of preserving all the meat and its juices, suggests economy and is plebeian, whereas roasting, which involves destruction and loss, suggests waste and is aristocratic.

[48] That their respective plaints articulate the ladies' appetite for a specific part of Ignaure's anatomy contradicts the claim of medieval rhetoricians according to which images and figures of an elevated kind can never signify lowly reality.

equates with dismembering, as confirmed in Ps.-Renaut's epilogue by the poet's reliance on *praeteritio* as his means to describe that which decency requires him not to mention. Alluding to the beloved lady who keeps him affectively prisoner, Ps.-Renaut evokes the beauty of her neck and the whiteness of her complexion and then claims that he will not talk openly about "that part of her which is covered," except to say that, from where he stands, he can see "her breasts raise up her tunic when those go up a little, for they seem to be quite firm" (ll. 635–643). The author now proceeds to praise the pleasure generated by the metaphoric chain that binds him to his beloved, thus dismantling the presentation of the lover as sufferer in the lyrical tradition. Delight is all the sweeter when it feeds one's imagination, enabling Ps.-Renaut to see beyond the lady's tunic and deconstruct her body.[49] By contrast, the Châtelain de Coucy's poetic and affective remembrance of his beloved has a restorative effect inasmuch as "recorder" and "remembrer" resolve the disruption ("desmembrer") of the lovers' story as caused by the jealous husband and, primarily, by those slanderers who seek "to destroy [the hero's] lyrical paradise" (Solterer, "Dismembering, Remembering," 109). That the poet-lover lives forever "in the body of his text kept alive by countless readers" (122) would mark the Châtelain's ultimate victory over the slanderers who caused his downfall. In surviving as a heart now integrated into the body of his beloved, the Châtelain does outwit the jealous husband, who fails in his attempt to regain control over his wife. Yet the lovers' story leads nonetheless to a fatal outcome, indicating that the slanderers, if not the husband himself, have the last word in this matter.

In Ps.-Renaut's tale of *Ignaure*, this role is assumed by a most cruel "losengier" (flatterer and, hence, liar; l. 378), who discovers the secret shared by Ignaure and his lady disciples. Taking advantage of a meal that has gathered the twelve husbands together, the traitor joins them and undertakes to reveal the truth about Ignaure. His action qualifies as parasitic on two counts: first, because his words seek to perturb the husbands' ignorant bliss and interrupt their wives' sentimental felicity; and second, because he behaves here as a "lechiere" (whose root means "to lick"; l. 386), a word that describes someone who is motivated by lust, gluttony, or perfidy. In view of the specific setting of the scene, it appears that the traitor lets himself be governed by each of these three impulses. Thus he endeavors to narrate his story with manifest lubricity, all the while feeding himself at the twelve companions' expense, and leaves after having received from them the reward they promised as payment for his words. Also noteworthy is the fact that the traitor is truthful when he reveals how the twelve ladies betrayed their husbands by sleeping with Ignaure and by remaining loyal to him

[49] That savoring the sight of the beloved is as enjoyable as possessing her corroborates the saying according to which "man eats with his head." Both *Ignaure* and the *Roman du Castelain de Couci* also vividly illustrate the proverb according to which "revenge is a dish best served cold."

afterwards. Their secret could have remained safe, were it not for the interference of the traitor, who thus embodies the author himself in his capacity to spin a tale and disclose the whole truth about this and any other love quest. In the absence of the traitor, there would be no story, no revelation about the object of desire, and no disclosure.

Much like the role of noise in information theory, the parasite becomes in this way a producer of meaning. It is through him that the story unfolds and that the audience realizes the resemblance between eating and speaking as two equally parasitic activities.[50] And the ultimate parasite is of course the storyteller himself, consistent with his capacity to invent songs and tales that narrate the history of human interaction as it finds itself beautified and transformed into a Body Poetic, or rehashed and presented to its public as a meal of a deliciously transgressive quality.[51]

4. Storytelling as "Entremés"

The remark made by one of the angry husbands portrayed in *Ignaure* that the traitor is about to serve them with "malvais entremés" ("evil talk," l. 392) is an apt description of the multivalent function of the parasite.[52] Indeed, "entremés" ("placed between")[53] may designate the interrupting effect of interference, the

[50] To quote Michel Serres (*Le parasite*, 107, 326, 341), the parasite is "a creature of relation" and the site of exchange; it is a mouth that "eats, speaks, shouts, sings, belches, hiccups, and gurgles"; the parasite "never ceases to eat and drink, scream and burp, produce a thousand types of noise, and fill the space with his pullulation and uproar." Of course the original parasite (of this type) was a stock figure in classical New Comedy.

[51] Seen against the ethical criterion used by medieval moralists in their denigration of bawdy entertainment, the pleasure listeners and spectators derived from obscene literature was primarily rhetorical. As Bruno Roy notes in regard to farces, "the richer the metaphor, the more comic the play": "Getting to the Bottom of St. Caquette's Cult," in *Obscenity*, ed. Ziolkowski, 308–18, here 317.

[52] Deriving from the same root (*missus*, from *mittere*, to send), the Old French "més" designates the messenger or his message, as it may designate the meal placed on a table, in reference to one of the eventual meanings of *mittere*—"to place"—in post-Classical Latin (see Merceron, *Le message et sa fiction*, 296 n. 7, 298 n. 26; and Michel Jeanneret, *Des mets et des mots: banquets et propos de table à la Renaissance* [Paris: Corti, 1987], 9). In the context of my analysis, "entre-més" thus describes a culinary and linguistic type of "farcissure."

[53] When an "entremés" was served in between courses, it included a variety of dishes ranging from pheasants (served in between the second and third course) to the head of a wild boar (after the fourth course); sweet "entremés" (or "issues") were served as desserts concluding the meal, according to *Le Ménagier de Paris* (an anonymous treatise on domestic economy composed in 1393), e. g., articles 34 and 36, ed. and trans. Georgina E. Brereton and Janet M. Ferrier: 557, 567. The *Ménagier* describes in great detail the remarkable lavishness of aristocratic banquets: see Planche, "La Table comme signe de la classe," 256.

cross-sensory and synesthesic quality of the vernacular language (see Larry Crist's delicious concoction of a word—"pornonomie"—in order to describe the role of the author as "bricoleur sexuel"),[54] or the mediative function of the go-between. I propose in this section to examine successively each of these three meanings of the Old French *entremés*.

The interfering effect of the traitor as liar finds an emblematic example in Ganelon's reaction when Charles and his army hear the sound of Roland's horn (*Chanson de Roland*, ll. 1755–1757). Charles surmises that his men must be in a fight, but Ganelon refutes the soundness of this interpretation by declaring that if such words had been spoken by any one else, they would surely have been taken for a lie. For everyone knows the extent of Roland's pride ("le grant orgoill Rollant," l. 1773) and how Charles' nephew is prone to blow his horn all day in pursuit of nothing more than a hare. Surely Roland is showing off for the benefit of his peers, as is his wont, and there is therefore no reason for Charles to stop instead of riding on. The traitor speaks here a language that stands midway between truth and lie: thus his assessment of Roland's character is correct; but the allegation that Roland is simply playing is not, for this coheres neither with the sacred function of his olifant (to be blown only in the gravest of dangers) nor with Roland's relentless desire to kill the greatest number of opponents possible. This is the reason that Naimes now corroborates the emperor's interpretation against Ganelon's, whose attempt to prevent Charles from returning to Roncevaux indicates that he has betrayed Roland. Acting upon Naimes' advice, Charlemagne undertakes to punish the traitor by entrusting him to Besgon, his master-cook (ll. 1817–1820). In his turn Besgon gives Ganelon to the hundred servants of the kitchen, who proceed to pluck the traitor's hair from his beard and mustache and beat him with sticks and clubs, before putting an iron collar around his neck and chaining him in a cage as they would a bear (ll. 1821–1827). The substitution of the chief "cous" for the leader of the Christian host connects both characters in a manner that focuses on their parallel contribution to the cause of Christianity. As the representative of God on earth, the emperor is assigned a mediative function, indicating that his language is a faithful rendering of the divine Word. Similarly, the emperor's master-cook is in charge of the physical well-being of the French army, consistent with an expertise in the art of food preparation that knows how to transform raw nutrients into aliments designed to foster the warriors' energy. He, too, is at the head of an "army" of diverse individuals, and his task is to control this army and ensure that they work in harmony at the service of Charles' host. The gravity of Ganelon's action in attempting to break the channel

[54] Larry S. Crist, "Gastronomie et pornographie dans les fabliaux," in *Continuations: Essays in Medieval French Literature and Language in Honor of John L. Grigsby*, ed. Norris J. Lacy and Gloria Torrini-Roblin (Birmingham, AL: Summa Publications, 1989), 251–60, here 253, 260.

of communication between Charles and his nephew deserves a punishment that consists in his being judged by the master-cook's army, and not by his own peers. This social degradation, which effects the traitor's transformation into a wild beast, situates him on the lowest rung of the social ladder.[55] Of equal significance is Ganelon's helplessness at the hands of the kitchen myrmidons, signaling a complete reversal in the balance of power between consumers and consumed. What takes place at the court of Charles' master-cook is the silencing of the traitor, as befits Ganelon's parasitic action against his rival, Roland, which eventually caused the destruction of Charles' rear guard.

Another form of parasitic interference is embodied by those seneschals, like Laudine's in Chrétien's *Yvain*, who resort to innuendos and double-entendres as their means to attain preeminence at court. Because Laudine's knights, including her seneschal, are—in Lunete's assessment—all cowards when it comes to fighting (ed. Hult, ll. 1631–1637), Laudine's sole recourse to ensure the protection of her domain is to marry Yvain. She thus entrusts her seneschal with the task of announcing to her court the news of her upcoming marriage, which the seneschal proceeds to do with great eloquence. However, his speech to Laudine's knights significantly alters Lunete's remark concerning their cowardice by focusing exclusively on Laudine's weakness as the reason that they should advise her to marry Yvain.[56] In addition to being self-serving, the seneschal's silence signals the presence of a conflict between him and Lunete as the Fountain Lady's closest counselors. The balance is about to lean in his favor when Yvain fails to honor his promise and return to Laudine's domain within a year, for this failure provides Laudine's seneschal with an opportunity to charge Lunete with treason and thus obtain preeminence as Laudine's sole counselor. As Lunete eventually recounts to Yvain through the walls of the chapel in which the seneschal has imprisoned her (ll. 3562–3720), the latter, realizing that he could now stir up great enmity between the two women ("Si vit bien quë il pooit faire / *Entre moi et lui* grant

[55] Ganelon's downfall, which takes him from knighthood to kitchenhood, evokes the frequent view according to which the cooks were "the most despised of medieval trades" due to "the countless acts of violence in which [they appeared] to be embroiled" (Merceron, *Le Message et sa fiction*, 180, cf. 171). There ensues "a singular pattern of conjunction-disjunction between cooks and knights" (182) in terms of uncontrolled violence. Also remarkable is the fact that "medieval cookbooks read much like medieval epic warfare or the martyrdoms of saints in hagiographic literature" (172) for, taken together, these remarks corroborate my contention that secular Old French works construct a cosmology grounded in fluidity and fluctuation, in such a way that the lowest of *torchepots* (scullions) may end in resembling both a saint and a knight.

[56] The seneschal reminds his audience that a woman does not know how to bear a shield or strike with a lance: ergo, let us all advise her to take a husband ("Löez li tuit que mari prengne", l. 2102).

courous"), accused her in open court of having betrayed her mistress.[57] Lacking the bravery that is supposed to distinguish the constituents of knightly society, Laudine's seneschal is also a master at parasitic language, an expertise which empowers him to place himself between Lunete and Laudine ("entre moi et lui") by rallying the entire court against his lady's formerly favorite counselor. Not only does the seneschal interrupt, by interfering, the mode of amicable exchange between the two women; he also interrupts, by inferring, the amorous interaction that used to unite Laudine and Yvain.[58] In alleging that Lunete betrayed her lady on Yvain's account ("pour vous," l. 3571), the seneschal alludes to an illicit love affair between Lunete and Laudine's new husband. The parasite is here a producer of disorder who misuses his nutritive function as Laudine's master "cous" as well as his function as spokesman at her "cort" by means of a language that transforms Yvain's "cuers" into a transgressive "cors," the result of which is a portrayal of his betrayed lady as "cos" ("cuckold").[59] His culinary language concocts a tale which "effects the formation of a dialectic between logos, eros, and *sitos*, [that is], between words within a system of language and communication, words within a kinship system, and goods within an economic order" (Marin, *Food for Thought*, 124–25).[60] The resulting connection among those three sys-

[57] The seneschal's charge reads as follows: "Et quant che seut li seneschaus, / Un fel, .i. lerre, .i. desloiaus, / Qui grant envie me portoit / Pour che que ma dame creoit / Moi plus que lui de maint afaire, / Si vit bien quë il pooit faire / *Entre moi et lui* grant courous. / En plaine court, et voiant tous, / Me mist sus pour vous l'oy traÿe" (ed. Hult, ll. 3563–3571; my emphasis). ("And when this became known to the seneschal, a wicked, treacherous, and disloyal man, who was jealous of me because my lady believed me more than him in many matters, he saw clearly that he could now stir up great enmity between me and her. In open court and public view, he charged me with having betrayed her on your account.")

[58] Because his goal is to sever the lovers' amorous relationship, Laudine's seneschal acts contrary to the function of the mediators (most of them aged and bawdy women) analyzed by Leyla Rouhi, *Mediation and Love: A Study of the Medieval Go-Between in Key Romance and Near-Eastern Texts* (Leiden: Brill, 1999). The go-between's primary role—to facilitate nonmarital encounters—completely subverts the "laws of courtly love and violates the sacred codes of discretion, honesty, and loyalty" (93). The Church relentlessly condemned them for thus transgressing Christian morality (66).

[59] On the interconnection between "cos" (cuckold) and "cous" (cook), see Marie-Thérèse Lorcin, "Manger et boire dans les fabliaux: rites sociaux et hiérarchie des plaisirs," in *Manger et boire au Moyen Âge*, ed. Menjot, 227–37, here, 232, 235. As Michel Serres observes (*Le parasite*, 291), cuckoldry functions according to the principle of the "included middle" ("tiers inclus"), considering that the betrayer inserts himself or herself in between the two members of a couple. By contrast, the jealous figure (like Laudine's seneschal) excludes the middle (Lunete) and reasons according to the Aristotelian principle of the "excluded middle" ("tiers exclu"). Thus the jealous figure is both parasitic and paranoid.

[60] The treacherous character of Laudine's seneschal consists in abusing his function as her representative and spokesman. In the medieval metaphor of the body politic, as Claire Richter Sherman notes (*Imagining Aristotle* [Berkeley: University of California Press, 1995], 216), leaders were the head, while seneschals, bailiffs, and provosts were the eyes and ears.

tems of exchange has for its goal to disrupt the previous order, in such a way that the seneschal will henceforth supervise and control all channels of communication at Laudine's court. Lunete's expression "entre moi et lui" encapsulates the role of the seneschal as an "entremés" whose action, in imitation of the bloodsucker in biology, empowers him to appropriate for his own benefit the role previously occupied by Lunete.[61]

A second meaning of *entremés* reflects the cross-sensory quality of the vernacular creation in mixing that which should remain distinct and separate according to the discourse of orthodoxy. In that sense, language as a source of parasitic fabrication describes not only the traitor (like Ganelon) and the rival (Laudine's seneschal), but the art of storytelling as well, when storytellers resort to culinary imagery in order to transform a lowly story "into an exquisite and agreeable poem" (Marin, *Food for Thought*, 132). Listeners are offered a meal that is all the more pleasing as it feeds their imagination by combining the lowly and the sublime so as to blur the distinction between the lower and upper parts of human nature.[62] Socrates would surely banish cooks from his ideal city (as he does those poets whose "appeal is to the inferior part of the soul") in concocting feasts that satisfy "the unreal and incontinent part" of the soul.[63] In his view, cooking and poetry are equally treacherous arts of deception in that the culinary and lyrical signs persuade in favor of falsehood instead of truth. Such confections turn the consumers into voracious and lustful beasts, each one ever hungry for more delights and thus ready to eliminate, by devouring, his or her rivals in matters of appetite. For the less philosophically inclined, however, like our vernacular storytellers and their audiences, part of the pleasure of language lies in the capacity of the Body Poetic to "speak" a desire that belongs to both body and soul.

[61] Not for long, however: assuming Lunete's defense, Yvain as the Knight with the Lion presents himself at Laudine's court to fight and ultimately kill Lunete's accuser.

[62] The art of imaginative literature in its entertaining function consists of a "deliberate pairing of the two faces of the sacred" ("sainteté" and "souillure"), which storytellers achieve "by performing such logical and narrative operations as juxtaposition, equivocation, interpenetration, and inversion": Merceron, "Obscenity and Hagiography," 336. In the moralistic view, these operations also describe the power of the Devil in using a simultaneously invasive and perverted language, which is the reason that the depiction of Satan and his cohort presented an extraordinary opportunity for innovation, individuality, and artistic evolution: "diabolic iconography survives all forms of censorship—Church, state, social, and personal—to remain the means by which is expressed that which all men in all ages have most feared: chaos": Barbara D. Palmer, "The Inhabitants of Hell: Devils," in *The Iconography of Hell*, ed. Davidson and Seiler, 20–40, here 35.

[63] In Socrates' description, the devotees to such feasting have "their eyes ever bent upon the earth and heads bowed down over their tables [. . .] like cattle, grazing and copulating, ever greedy for more of these delights, and in their greed kicking and butting one another with horns and hoofs of iron they slay one another in sateless avidity" (Plato, *Republic* 398a, 605b, 586a–b).

Rhetorical figures like allegory serve here as "entremés" in that they establish a to-and-fro movement between the lowly and the elevated, as is illustrated by the tension between Fasting and Feasting described in the verse *Bataille de Caresme et de Charnage* (thirteenth century).

The parodic tonality of this poem consists in using the figures and themes of the elevated style (epic allegory) to devise a story that proposes to its audience the most appetizing of all meals. Therein follows a detailed enumeration of the dishes that constitute the host of Charnage (Carnival or Feasting), whose victory over the army of Caresme (Lent or Fasting) concludes with a treaty whereby Caresme's presence at court will henceforth be limited to a yearly period of six weeks. Excess, it appears, characterizes austerity rather than abundance, whence derives a type of balance that gives priority to sensory and cerebral pleasure as a means of covering up the dire reality of existence. Also noteworthy is the proposal, made by one of Charnage's allies, to act as the messenger who will gather together the soldiers of his host. That this personage happens to be an "escoufles fameilleus" ("famished kite," ed. Lozinski, l. 140) is a telling acknowledgment of the centrality of parasitism as both a primary component of human interaction and the reason for its constant fluctuation. Among the constituents of Charnage's host, the kite is the only one to receive an attribute, "fameilleus," which has as its remarkable characteristic the suggestion that hunger does exist at Charnage's court, indicating that Charnage owes his abundance to predatory activities. Another exceptional element is the fact that the kite is the only one among Charnage's allies to be a non-edible animal:[64] not only may the "escoufle" thus escape the fate awaiting his companions, his force also resides in his capacity to transform every prey into a meal. Because the kite does not participate in the ensuing combat, his unique function as Charnage's messenger signals that the latter's victory results, not from feats of arms, so much as from a type of devouring that enables the soldiers of his host to feast on their enemies and ensure both the latter's demise and their own preeminence at court. This and similar works of imaginative literature therefore constitute a powerful way to feed the audience's imagination, thereby disclosing the role of culinary language in exorcising such calamities as hunger and famine.

Beyond this literal investment of language, the art of storytelling also qualifies as "entremés" inasmuch as it transmits, translates, and entertains—the latter in reference to the singing and dancing which accompanied the pauses in between the courses of a banquet. Such is the goal of Marie de France when she

[64] The other non-edible animal mentioned in Charnage's host is the "taulle," a word which, according to Lozinski (*Bataille de Caresme et de Charnage* [Paris: Champion, 1933], 52–53) could be read as "touille" (shark). Because sharks were not eaten in medieval Europe, this confirms the unique status of the *escoufle* within the poem.

endeavors to perpetuate the memory of oral Celtic legends by reinscribing them in French verse ("M'entremis des lais assembler, / Par rime faire e reconter," ed. Warnke, ll. 47–48).[65] Significantly, the core of Marie's tales is a narration that focuses on the disassembling effects of parasitic characters who seek to disunite two lovers (e. g., *Yonec*) or, conversely, on the harmonious value of go-betweens when these contribute to the blossoming of affective reciprocity (e. g., *Eliduc*). In Marie's perspective, the lower part of human nature is internal, as emblematized by the bestial treatment that the knight Bisclavret ("werewolf") receives at the hands of his wife. If the tale of *Bisclavret* is of special importance, provoking Marie's decision ("m'entremet," l. 1) to render it into French verse, the reason appears to lie in its significance with regard to the respective value of appearance and reality. Hidden behind the seemingly animalistic figure of the werewolf is not a savage beast who eats men (ll. 9–11) but a loving husband who is devoted to his wife in body and soul. The ogre is in reality Bisclavret's wife, as she forces her husband to retain his animalistic appearance and proceeds to marry a neighboring knight. She eventually endures a punishment that condemns her and her female posterity to be noseless. Her being deprived of the organ for olfactory perception does not mean that she is henceforth unable to smell; rather, the point is to render visibly the animalistic and predatory components of her character.[66] Marie's work as artistic matchmaker ("entremetteuse"), that is, as a mediator whose language praises love in terms of affective reciprocity (in contrast to the bawds' language and function), brings forth the mediative function of language in its capacity to invent tales and stories that are food for thought.

---

[65] Marie's art of "assemblage" (amalgam) is also at the heart of the coherence of her collection of novellas, as masterfully demonstrated by Douglas Kelly, *The Art of Medieval French Romance* (Madison: University of Wisconsin Press, 1992), 99, 110–14 and Rupert T. Pickens, "History and Meaning in the *Lais* of Marie de France," in *Studies in the Seven Sages of Rome and Other Essays in Medieval Literature Dedicated to the Memory of Jean Misrahi*, ed. Hans R. Runte et al. (Honolulu: Educational Research Associates, 1978), 201–11.

[66] The predatory character of Bisclavret's wife connects her to the realm of the wild ("lupa" as wolf, also meaning procuress), of sexual perversion ("lupanda" as "lupanar," bordello), and social transgression ("lepra" as leper, leprosy being a disease that often caused loss of the nose): see Milena Mikhaïlova, *Le présent de Marie* (Paris: Diderot, 1996), 194. Citing what he describes as an "old law," the jurist Philippe de Beaumanoir (second half of the thirteenth century) notes that "if a person caused loss of limb to another, the same was done to him as he had done, hand for hand and foot for foot; but things are no longer done this way according to our custom" (30.841): *The "Coutumes de Beauvaisis,"* trans. F. R. P. Akehurst (Philadelphia: University of Pennsylvania Press, 1992), 305.

5. "Veoir" and "oïr": Delusion or Accuracy?

At the heart of the moralists' denigration of resolutely secular artifacts lies the disconnecting effect of the latter's language in recording "a world of human turmoil" (Vance, *Mervelous Signals*, 278) rather than reflecting the stable laws of the universe. In this perspective, the sonorous resemblance between the horn as bugle, its cornucopian function, and its "horny" appearance should not be perceived as a playful reinscription of cosmology but, rather, as an index of the process of degradation wherein pride leads to gluttony, and gluttony to lust.[67] According to the discourse of orthodoxy, the only worthy use of language is a righteous (*rectus*) one, in both the logical and legal sense of the word. Thus moralists and grammarians value hagiographic and epic narratives inasmuch as these writings depend "on idealism and stark contrast, uncomplicated by nice distinctions, the vagaries of personalities, and grays of all sorts."[68] For them, the danger of imaginative literature consists precisely in its ability to construct an illusory "edifying" tale, similar to the sophistication of talented cooks in constructing "culinary illusions or tricks for the eyes" (Merceron, *Le Message et sa fiction*, 175).[69] In both cases, the resulting "edifice" is of course deprived of edifying value in the moral sense and, in the worst of cases, may even provoke the listeners' downfall.

The parasitic homophones that testify to the realistic quality of Old French literature are, in the moralistic view, evidence of the latter's danger in titillating the worst impulses of their listeners. That the term parasitic is synonymous with such words as vulturous and wolfish, and the term sycophantic with reptilian,

---

[67] In his previously quoted sermon (in Le Goff, *L'imaginaire médiéval*, 258–59), Jacques de Vitry points to the effect of pride in inducing the knight to impress his peers by giving sumptuous banquets (hence Jacques' criticism of the knight as glutton), or to shine in combat so as to attract the attention of ladies and damsels (hence the knight's sin of lust). Old French vocabulary confirms the sonorous equivalence among vainglory, gluttony, and lust through a semantic field in which pride ("bofoi"), blowing ("bofer"), and feasting ("bobance") appear each to derive from noise (Latin "bombus", rumbling sound). On canonists' condemnation of songs, stories, or pleasurable spectacles as a menace to clerical purity, see James A. Brundage, "Obscene and Lascivious: Behavioral Obscenity in Canon Law," in *Obscenity*, ed. Ziolkowski, 246–59.

[68] See Russell, *Chaucer and the Trivium*, 136–37. Unlike the heroes of romance or of the fabliau, "saints and exemplars may have varied stories and even checkered careers, but in the end they are never ambivalent: if it is not sharp and unambiguous, an exemplar is worthless" (137).

[69] The famous nineteenth-century French chef, whose name was amusingly Antonin Carême ("Lent"), was well aware of the cerebral quality of gastronomic pleasure. He would thus erect "extraordinary edible edifices called *pièces montées*, entirely in order to delight dinner guests before they happily demolished them": Margaret Visser, *Much Depends on Dinner* (New York: Collier Books, 1988), 314.

is in that respect integral to the moralists' criticism of imaginative literature in transforming its audience into the "beste mue" mentioned in the *Queste del Saint Graal* (230). Therein ensues an indictment of chivalric appetite that transforms the knight into a ferocious and lethal beast or, in Yvain's case, that causes the hero's regression to animality. It is not by chance, as Serres remarks (*Le parasite*, 11), that carnivory is the realm of Mars, the god of warring and hunting. Nor is it by chance that hunting activities are grounded in noise and that hunting vocabulary is marked by an abundance of onomatopoeias, as is the case of those French words which reproduce sounds relative to hunting ("haro," "taïaut," "vloo," and "hallali").[70] The profusion of echoic words (like bang, crash, splash) that are formed in imitation of natural sounds indicates that reason is unable to control this type of acoustic phenomenon and that, if these sounds can be described through reproduction, they can never be truly defined and contained.[71] Whether the first component of the word "cacophony" is itself of onomatopoeic origin, the fact is that *kakos* refers to that which is physically or intellectually disagreeable, ugly, defective, and lowly. By analogy, also classified as lowly—at least, by moralistic authors—are those vernacular works which cultivate ambiguity through wordplays and double-entendres, consistent with the status of this literary production as a fallen medium.[72]

What interests me in the moralists' warning against the danger of imaginative literature is the way they thus implicitly acknowledge the power of the vernacular language "to convince, seduce, confuse, obfuscate [. . .], whether the author consciously seeks to exploit that power or not" (Russell, *Chaucer and the Trivium*, 202). This in itself is proof of the popularity enjoyed by the reciting of deliciously transgressive concoctions, as well as demonstrating that gifted storytellers and their listening public did not constitute an ignorant mass but were, on the contrary, endowed with remarkable hermeneutic talent for interpreting parasitic homophones.

---

[70] Again compare Clément Jannequin's programmatic chanson "La Chasse": see Brown and Freedman, "Jannequin."

[71] Echoic words in ancient Greek, for example, include *ktupos*, which refers to inarticulate sounds as produced by horses, thunder, and laments; *patagos*, to sounds generated by the wind, by the fall of a stone, by the clanging of weaponry, by wind instruments, and by idle and vain gossiping; and *psofos*, to sounds caused by the encounter between two objects, the chattering of teeth, the lapping of waves, the rumbling of thunder, and the clanging of arms. See Anatole Bailly, *Dictionnaire Grec-Français* (Paris: Hachette, 1950), 1144, 1498, 2175. In the French language, onomatopoeias often serve to record the circumstances of pandemonium (e.g., "chahut," "charivari," "hourvari," and "tintouin").

[72] It is perhaps not incidental that, to describe the slaughtering of Latin grammar at the hands of the less educated members of society, grammarians invented the expression "Kitchen Latin" (Merceron, *Le Message et sa fiction*, 187).

The capacity to decipher the enigma of the world recorded in the soundscape of imaginative literature is not, however, an exercise accessible to everyone. This is particularly the case of those spineless heroes, like Guilliaume in Jean Renart's *L'Escoufle*, whose approach to life is the complete opposite of the typically predatory mode of life at court. Separation from his beloved has in that sense a disastrous effect on Guilliaume, who for a while adopts the parasitic form of chivalry that is embodied in the bird evoked in the title of Jean's romance. In the course of his wanderings, the protagonist joins a hunting party and is thus provided with the opportunity to capture a kite (ll. 6868–6917). In the presence of the master hunter and his companions, Guilliaume now proceeds to plunge his fingers into the bird's body and extract its heart, which he undertakes to eat without any bread or salt. He then prepares a fire, dismembers the bird, and burns the pieces to dust. In Solterer's view ("Dismembering, Remembering," 115), this scene connects the act of dismembering and the faculty of remembering in a manner that focuses on the heart of the bird as an emblem for Aélis, for, "once the lover eats the heart of the bird [. . .], he is remembered in the body of their love." Although this interpretation seems to cohere with Jean Renart's remark in the epilogue of his romance that the bird whose heart Guilliaume ate enabled him to reunite with his beloved ("par celui dont il manja / Le cuer, retrova son amie," ll. 9096–9097), it should be noted that this remark refers to the *escoufle* incident as a prerequisite to the unfolding of the story: without the bird, no misadventure; without separation, no romance. In thus apologizing for a title that gives prominence to one of the most despicable birds of prey, Jean also praises his own talent in having concocted a rose out of a thorn (l. 9081). At the same time, the author clearly condemns the predatory character of chivalric behavior when it consists in dismembering and eating any potential rivals.[73] Rather than announcing the upcoming fusion between the two lovers, then, Guilliaume's consumption of the kite's heart emblematizes chivalry in its most feral and lethal proclivity. In devouring the bird's heart, Jean's habitually spineless protagonist seems to adhere to the aggressive mores and customs of traditional knighthood. However, Guilliaume's reaction at the end of the scene demonstrates that the hero is well aware of, and regrets, the bestial character of his gesture. Having blamed

---

[73] Although Jean Renart's romance provides ample details on the practical aspects of daily life, it also shows a significant restraint regarding nutrition and eating. There are only two scenes of banqueting: the first occurs in the beginning section of the narrative (when the King of Jerusalem honors Richart's arrival by organizing a feast, ll. 676–723), and the second, in its concluding episode (to celebrate the coronation of Guilliaume as the new Emperor of Rome, ll. 8980–8986). The liminal role of those two feasting scenes in Jean's romance, combined with the author's reserve in describing them, suggest his awareness of the socio-political meaning of food distribution and of the metaphorical significance of appetite in its severing and depredatory effects.

the bird as he would a human being, Guilliaume now feels shame for his entire conduct, indicating that he does not or cannot resemble—in deeds, thoughts, or language—the constituents of his social group.

The resulting distance that Jean Renart establishes between his lackluster protagonist and the typical heroes of courtly romance appears also to distinguish Chrétien's Perceval as a "niche" (ignorant and naive) Welsh boy who has so far lived in the forest, away from courtly life. Realizing that Perceval wants to leave the vale of his childhood in order to find King Arthur's court, his mother laments the fact that (to cite the prose *Roman du Graal*) her last surviving son will most probably be eaten by the wild creatures ("li sauvecine de le forest," 198) which inhabit the forest. The problem confronting Chrétien's ignorant protagonist as he enters the realm of chivalric society is that he knows nothing of its traditions. Nor does he know that Logres, as Arthur's kingdom is traditionally designated, may well be a "land of ogres."[74] What distinguishes Perceval is his literal and pragmatic approach to the world that surrounds him, which accounts for his lack of interpretative sophistication. Because of the incomplete state of Chrétien's last extant romance, the illuminating quality of Perceval's quest for the Grail remains undetermined and so does the nature of its completion, although vision seems to be the medium that will help him achieve maturation.[75] Will Perceval survive amidst "li sauvecine de le forest"? The opening of Chrétien's romance suggests a negative response to this question through a presentation of traditional chivalry that points to its aggressive character. One fine day, as the lad is playing with his javelins near the forest, he is suddenly distracted by a noise he hears coming from the woods ("moult grant noise," ed. Méla, l. 101). The din is such that Perceval assumes he is dealing with devils, who, according to his mother, are the most hideous things in the world (ll. 110–112). Although Perceval's ignorance causes him to assign a demonic origin to what is nothing other than the sounds made by the equipment of five armed knights, his acoustic perception is in reality accurate. For, in the twilight stage of Arthurian history developed in this last of Chrétien's romances, chivalry *is* noisy, just as the constituents of Logres *are* devilishly aggressive. While Perceval still ponders the din he has just heard, the five knights emerge into the open. And when the lad sees the glittering hauberks, the bright and gleaming helmets, and the lances and the shields, along with the white and the scarlet ("le blanc et le vermeil") shining in the sunlight,

[74] "Terre as ogres," ll. 6169–6170, ed. Roach (from Ms. BN fr. 12576). On the significance of Logres and of its manuscript variations (Nogres, Norgres, and London), see Brigitte Cazelles, *The Unholy Grail* (Stanford: Stanford University Press, 1996), 42–53.

[75] See Donald Maddox, *Fictions of Identity in Medieval France* (Cambridge: Cambridge University Press, 2000), 87; and Barbara Nelson Sargent-Bauer, "'Avis li fu': Vision and Cognition in the *Conte du Graal*," in *Continuations*, ed. Lacy and Torrini-Roblin, 133–61, here 133–44.

and the gold, the sky-blue, and the silver ("l'or et l'azur et l'argent"), this sight is so magnificent that, he concludes, those wonderful creatures are undoubtedly angels (ed. Roach, ll. 123–132). The deceptive capacity of vision[76] could not be better captured than through this superabundance of light and color imagery, which dupes Perceval into taking these knights for God's deputies. Hearing had enabled him unwittingly to perceive the sonorous reality of knightly aggression. Seeing the brightness of chivalric equipment changes the lad's opinion as he now admires and, hence, desires the objects that materialize one's standing in society. From Perceval's perspective, white, scarlet, gold, and silver fuse into a single coloration, the luminosity of which erases in him any memory of the deafening sounds that accompany the march of these and many other knights-errant of traditional romance.

The scene evokes in that respect the principles of heraldry as a visible mark of nobility. To the white and silver corresponds the metal of "argent" which, in blazoning, signifies faith and purity; and to the gold, the second metal of "or" as the emblem of honor and loyalty. The other colors mentioned in Chrétien's description of chivalric equipment have also an equivalent in blazoning: to the scarlet corresponds the hue of "gules," which signifies courage and zeal; and to the sky-blue, the hue of "azure" as an emblem of piety and sincerity (Birren, *The Story of Color*, 89–93). Among the five hues used in blazoning, "sable" (black, an emblem of grief and penitence) is here conspicuously absent, and so are "vert" (green, signifying youth and hope)[77] and "pourpre" (purple, signifying royalty and rank). As a result, Perceval is presented with an embodiment of chivalry which amplifies such values as faith and purity, courage and zeal, and piety and sincerity. Considering that this presentation does not cohere with the noise generated by chivalric equipment in echoing the clashes and clangs of martial encounters, it appears, then, that vision here decreases the sensitivity of the lad's ears. Lacking the capacity to interpret what he sees, Perceval proceeds to "correct" the assessment he made via audition, which leads him now to utter an incorrect appreciation of the sight. Also interesting is the juxtaposition of "argent" ("blanc") and "gules" ("vermeil"), and of "or" and "argent," for it happens to contradict the laws that regulate the tinctures of heraldry, according to which metal cannot be placed upon metal any more than hue can be placed upon hue. Regardless of

[76] As Maddox observes (*Fictions of Identity*, 139), many of the visual encounters related in the Tristan legend illustrate the potentially delusive effect of vision. On the problematic relations of sight to truth in medieval romances, see A. C. Spearing, *The Medieval Poet as Voyeur: Looking and Listening in Medieval Love-Narratives* (Cambridge: Cambridge University Press, 1993).

[77] Although the version of this episode of Chrétien's romance in Ms. Bern 354 replaces the white mentioned here (ed. Roach) by "vert": see ed. Méla, l. 127.

Chrétien's putative interest or expertise in heraldry,[78] the colorscape of the scene merits attention to the extent that it combines that which cannot combine and mixes its hues in a manner that blinds Perceval to the concrete reality of chivalric equipment. Whereas the lad habitually evolves in the realm of the literal, he is here offered a chance to enter the realm of the figurative without realizing the latter's capacity to deceive. In this perspective, the language of noise speaks the truth, whereas the language of sight is grounded in illusion and mendacity. Were he to possess adequate interpretative acumen, Perceval could later establish a connection between the devilish din he heard coming from the woods and the "gules" ("vermeil") that is so often the color of such predatory knights as the "Vermaus Chevaliers," who is at that very moment in the process of stealing Arthur's royal cup and pouring its content on the queen. That "gules," "golos," and "gloton" may each be associated with the mouth as an organ that processes absorption discloses the occasional significance of "vermeil" as the crimson color of aggression and devouring.[79]

Old French imaginative literature exploits parasitic homophony in ways which, as we saw, disclose the frequently voracious character of social interaction. From this ironic use of wordplays and puns results the construction of a cosmos wherein the sole constant law consists of an alternative between eating or being eaten. The moralists are expectedly not amused by this impish take on the human experience. At issue, in their perspective, is the tendency of secular works to play on the cross-sensory character of the vernacular language in ways which end by erasing the hierarchical organization of the five senses, the five constitutive elements of nature, the classifications of tripartite society, as well as the upper and lower aspects of human nature. In referring simultaneously to that which is harmful ("nocere"), that which provokes seasickness ("nausea"), and that which

[78] Evidence of the systematic use of hereditary devices on the shield begins in the West in the eleventh century, while true heraldry came into being in the first half of the twelfth century: see Anthony Richard Wagner, *Heralds and Heraldry in the Middle Ages* (London: Humphrey Milford for Oxford University Press, 1939), 12, 17 (on heralds and heraldry in twelfth- and thirteenth-century medieval romance, see 25–40). See also Michel Pastoureau, *Traité d'héraldique* (Paris: Picard, 1979), 37–58.

[79] According to the Larousse *Dictionnaire étymologique* (378), the word "gueule" (Old French "gole," "goule," "gule") derives from the Latin *gula*, "gosier" (throat) and by extension "bouche" (mouth). Originally, the heraldic hue of "gueule" was obtained from the skin of a marten's throat; whence the meaning of "gules" as "ermine dyed red" (OED). Expanding on this definition, the OED then states that, although the word ("gules") "coincides in form with the pl. of the Fr. ["gules"] and med. Latin word [*gulas*] for 'throat,' [its] ulterior etymology is disputed." At issue is whether the word refers to "the colour of the open mouth of a heraldic beast" or, "more likely," to "the heraldic use transferred from the sense 'red ermine'." But what about the throat ("gule") of the said heraldic beast, from whose skin the color was supposedly obtained?

smells,[80] the word noise emblematizes the intoxicating effect of this secular production in launching its audience on a downward journey. The fate awaiting Old French producers, their consumers, and any individual guilty of gluttony (like the twelve female characters introduced in the tale of *Ignaure*, whom their husbands describe as "gloutes" [debauchees] and "goulouses" [insatiable]) is Satan's "gula" as a monstrous mouth[81] that engulfs its victims and absorbs them into a realm where teeth are forever gnawing.

[80] To reiterate the remark I made in the Introduction, it may be that nose, *nausea*, nuisance, and noise have nothing in common etymologically. From an acoustic perspective, however, the resulting homophonic network discloses the capacity of secular literature to question and hence dissolve the rigid classifications and boundaries characteristic of scientific thought (de Grazia, "Homophones," 151). For the latter, such a network is in itself a risk of "contamination, sullying, or mixing" (Parker, *Shakespeare from the Margins*, 5); for secular entertainers, it is the soundscape of human relations as a dynamic and fluid organism.

[81] It is not incidental that Hell resembles a kitchen and that "the Harrowing of Hell play at Chester was performed by the Cooks": Richard Rastall, "The Sounds of Hell," in *The Iconography of Hell*, ed. Davidson and Seiler, 102–31, here 112; nor that the stage direction in the *Jeu d'Adam* specifies that the entry of Adam and Eve to Hell is to be accompanied by the banging of "caldaria et lebentes" ("cauldrons and pans"). On the description of Hell as a cauldron, see Clifford Davidson, "The Fate of the Damned in English Art and Drama," in *The Iconography of Hell*, ed. idem and Seiler, 41–66; and Pamela Sheingorn, "'Who can open the doors of his face?': The Iconography of Hell Mouth," in *The Iconography of Hell*, 1–19.

V

SONUS MORTIS

> Si oënt plaintes dolereuses,
> Que font les ames angoisseuses
> Cui on tourmentoit la dedens.
> Si fort estraignoient les dens
> Qu'i[l] les enbatent es genchives.
> Toutes crioient les caitives,
> Communement a un acors.
> (They hear the doleful moaning made by those tormented souls who were tortured within the place. The latter were grinding their teeth so fiercely that they would ram them into their gums. All the condemned souls were crying together in unison.)
>
> (*Vie de Saint Jehan Paulus*, ll. 61–67)

Following my loosely eschatological sequence, I propose in this last chapter to examine a number of accounts wherein transgression takes an acoustic manifestation, with particular attention to those apocalyptic texts which describe the end of time. As with the preceding chapters, my selection of textual examples is based on content (the sonorous consequences of sin) rather than metric form or date. The moral tenor of these examples signals that we are dealing here with what contemporary moralists viewed as a "worthy" form of vernacularity, in reference to the capacity of Old French texts to edify and enlighten. In such texts, noise is invested with negative connotations and functions as a phonic interference that works against the revelatory value of vision.

The potentially disturbing effect of sounds calls attention to the complicated mechanism by means of which movements are transformed into audible phenomena (Gutton, *Bruit et sons*, 150–51). Entering the ear canal, waves of air molecules make the eardrum vibrate, which in turn activates three small bones: the hammer, the anvil, and the stirrup. The stirrup then presses like a piston against a fluid-filled, snail-shaped region of the inner ear called the cochlea, creating waves that agitate tiny hair cells on its walls.[1] Expounding the description of the ear's structure, this chapter's first section ("'Visions' of Hell: A Sonoscopy")

---

[1] In a normally-constituted organ, the motion of the hairs stimulates nerve endings, and the brain recognizes the motion as sound.

examines its metaphoric significance with respect to the thudding, clanging, and crunching manifestations that typically signal the presence of Satan and describe his action as trickster. Although succumbing to temptation is not necessarily fatal for one's soul, it often entails a sonorous type of punishment, either when the protagonist loses his capacity to speak, or when he is possessed by devils whose invasion transforms their victim into a senseless creature (section 2: "Tongue-Tied Sinners"). Should they fail to repent in time, those sinners are ultimately condemned to the realm of pandemonium that characterizes the kingdom of the infernal Hunter (section 3: "Trumpeting The End of Time"). The resulting soundscape constitutes a language which in my terminology qualifies as *diabolos* either because it temporarily blurs the channel of communication between creature and Creator or because it annihilates any possibility of ever hearing the melody that emanates from the kingdom of Heaven.

In this connection, it may be that vision is the optimal if not solely operative modality through which to weave our way to a harmonious network of exchange and communication, thereby justifying the "ocularcentrism" of Western thought. The final section ("Painting a New Beginning") compares the respective value of vision and audition as they are illustrated in texts that enunciate a non-hierarchical assessment of sensory perceptions. The wisdom of those works lies, I suggest, in the acknowledgment that sentience is best achieved through a synesthesic mode of perception as this mode is registered and fostered by the Old French language in its cross-sensory resonance.

1. "Visions" of Hell: A Sonoscopy

Assigning to Pan's pipes the power both to captivate and to alienate their listener, Platonic and Christian thought views the half-goat god as the emblem of the ambivalence of human nature. Because Pan's pipes produce a tune that satisfies our lower impulses at the expense of our spiritual self, they are dangerous and should be avoided. Like the panpipe, the drum appears also to possess the power to delight and bewitch alike, whence the dual assessment inspired by this instrument in manufacturing a type of sound either creative or destructive.

That "each culture seems to invent drums and flutes before anything else"[2] suggests the presence of a universal need to translate the spirit of life into beats and blows, respectively, while confirming the drum's potentially generative quality. A Melanesian myth from the people in the Banks Islands thus recounts how Qat created mankind by carving six figures from the wood of the dracaena tree.

---

[2] Diane Ackerman, *A Natural History of the Senses* (New York: Vintage Books, 1990), 224.

He stood those figures in a row and danced before them, until those images began moving a little, weakly and stiffly:[3]

> When Qat saw that, he began to beat upon his drum. Soon the wonderful rhythmic magic of the drum filled the air. The figures began to move a little more, slowly and carefully at first, in time with each drum beat, then faster and faster, until they too were dancing the life dance of the drum. At last they were able to stand and walk and run by themselves (Leach, *The Beginning*, 178–79).

Another generative quality of the drum is the effect of its beats in ensuring social order. Thus an Orphic myth relates how the goddess Rhea plays on her drum to prevent bees from swarming in the wrong place, the beehive emblematizing here the ideal republic (Graves, *The Greek Myths*, 1: 30–31). Such is also the core of the Dogon's view on drumming to the extent that this particular African ethnic group equates rhythm with "law and order."[4] Drumming is therefore the prerogative of the Dogon's social leader (the Hogon) as well as those individuals—the griots—whose specialty is language. The griots demonstrate their mastery of communication through both the commemorative voice of their songs (in praising the village's ancestors) and the powerful voice of their drums, which has the ability to resolve conflicts or punish transgressors. The alternately interfering and mediative effect of the griot's drumming accounts for the respect and fear he commands in Dogon society, situating him (and the shaman of Asian tradition) among those sacred experts—like the blacksmith—who are empowered to control the natural elements.[5]

---

[3] Compare the myth of Pygmalion as reinscribed in Jean de Meun's verse *Roman de la Rose* (ca. 1275), which reiterates the life-producing power of sounded rhythm. To animate the statue he has just created, Pygmalion dresses her as he would a queen and then plays many "tabor et fleüste et tymbre" for her (l. 21015). Cf. Brumble, *Classical Myths and Legends*, 288–91. On the Pygmalion myth in courtly culture, see "The Medieval Pygmalion (1200–1500)," in E. Joshua, *Pygmalion and Galatea: The History of a Narrative in English Literature* (Aldershot: Ashgate, 2001), 6–20, and J.-D. Mueller, "Pygmalion, höfisch mittelalterliche Erweckungsphantasien," in *Pygmalion: Die Geschichte des Mythos in der abendländischen Kultur*, ed. M. Mayer and G. Neumann (Freiburg: Rombach, 1997), 465–95.

[4] See Geneviève Calame-Griaule, *Ethnologie et langage: La parole chez les Dogon* (Paris: Institut d'Ethnologie, 1987), 103. Regarding the generative function of drumming, Calame-Griaule cites the concomitance in Dogon mythology between the first drum and the first rain (487); and regarding its protective function, the effect of drumming in ensuring that seeds will not be eaten by birds at the moment when they germinate (118). One could also cite the role of drumming during an eclipse: in many cultures, people beat drums to prevent the moon from swallowing the sun.

[5] A Yakut proverb affirms that "blacksmith and shaman are from the same nest" (cited by Mickey Hart and Fredric Lieberman, *Planet Drum* [New York: Harper Collins, 1991], 125). The preeminence of the griot in Dogon society is also linked to the effect of his drumming in

In his *De planctu Naturae*, we recall, Alan of Lille establishes a hierarchy of sounds wherein instruments like the harp and the lyre come first by virtue of their soothing quality (Metre 9, trans. Sheridan, 209–11). At the bottom of Alan's scale stand musical instruments, among which are trumpets, horns, cymbals, and sistra, the ecstatic rhythm and percussive noise of which generate license and ribaldry. Drums present a special case in that their "muted boom" tends to slow the stream of music and the swiftness of its song, but may also produce "honorable" sounds when struck with "a friendly touch of the hand" (*Plaint*, trans. Sheridan, 210). Although Alan's specific treatment of the drum is connected with the musical perspective developed in his treatise, it also reflects the dual view that this instrument inspired during the Middle Ages. On the one hand, drumming became the emblem of Satan as a source of eternal torment, which Hieronymus Bosch's "Garden of Earthly Delights" vividly expresses through the figures of demons that are in the process of beating on a field drum in which a sinner is imprisoned. On the other hand, drums had an important military role in orchestrating and controlling the rhythm of battles, whence came the drummers' privileged position on the battlefield. Before the time when European leaders came to recognize the martial value of the drum, however, "taburs" appear to have been the sonorous device of Saracen armies. It is thus said that, at the battle of Zalaca in 1086, the Moors triumphed over the host of Alfonso VI in part because of the sounds of their drums, which had never before been heard in Spain and generated great fright in the king's soldiers.[6] The Moors' phonic specificity is reflected in the epic tradition, witness the *Chanson de Roland*, which mentions the presence of drums in exclusive reference to the pagan host. Thus Marsile initiates his battle against Charlemagne's rear guard by bidding his drummers to play ("Fait suner ses taburs," l. 852), and so does Baligant as he prepares his attack of Charles' host ("taburs suner," l. 3136). Yet, in contrast with factual history, fictional history grants neither Marsile's drums nor Baligant's the capacity to overpower their opponents. By way of the imagination, the *Chanson* thus enables the Christians to avenge Alfonso's defeat against the Moors. What takes place at Roncevaux is the spectacular silencing of pagan "taburs" as the acoustic mark of the enemies of Christianity, who are presented as both savage and primitive warriors.

That griots and shamans constitute a distinct and fearsome caste in traditional cultures is linked to their uncanny mastery of language as well as their ability to communicate with the spirit world. Drumming induces in them a trance-like state, and it is again to the sounds of the drum that their souls are able to leave

---

dispelling evil charms by means of a rhythm which creates waves that clash with, and destroy, demonic forces.

[6] Noted by Gérard Moignet in his edition of the *Chanson de Roland* (83).

this world and undertake an out-of-body journey to the other world. A similar experience occurs to one of the protagonists introduced in the verse *Vie de Saint Jehan Paulus* (between 1222 and 1254), which begins with an episode recounting the circumstances in which the fictional Pope Basil took leave of his body, went to Satan's abode, and, after his return from the seven loci of Hell, related his experience as a warning against the consequences of sin. Consistent with the antipathy of devotional authors for this and any other magical practices, Basil's out-of-body journey is provoked not by the sound of a drum but by the will of God. Thus the archangel Michael leads Basil's soul to the iron doors of Hell, which are as crimson ("vermel") as burning flames. The coloration characterizing the gate of Satan's abode seems to cohere with the habitual designation of journeys through Hell as "Visions." Indeed, medieval accounts of those journeys have for their main distinction the fact that the other world is described in visual terms,[7] beginning with the *Visio sancti Pauli* in its earliest extant version (eighth century). Here too it is Michael who guides Saint Paul's soul through the places of torments, which vary from the pain endured through extreme cold to that of extreme heat, inspiring the author of a thirteenth-century verse adaptation of the *Visio* to depict one of the loci as a burning oven the seven-colored flame of which symbolizes the seven types of hellish tortures.[8] This colorscape justifies the qualification of Paul's journey in terms of a "vision," and so does, in the verse

[7] The medieval corpus of visionary literature (derived from late antique roots) is much too vast to be accounted for here: see Bernard McGinn, *Visions of the End: Apocalyptic Traditions in the Middle Ages* (New York: Columbia University Press, 1979). Cf. Jane Baun, "The Moral Apocalypse in Byzantium," in *Apocalyptic Time*, ed. Albert L. Baumgarten (Leiden: Brill, 2000), 241–67. Of particular interest regarding Visions of Hell in the Old French tradition is Douglas David Owen, *The Vision of Hell: Infernal Journeys in Medieval French Literature* (Edinburgh: Scottish Academic Press, 1970). Another visionary journey very popular during the Middle Ages—the *Visio Tnudgali* (ed. V. H. Friedel and Kuno Meyer [Paris: Champion, 1907])—inspired the "Last Judgment," a painting attributed to one of Bosch's pupils (Peter Huys) and perhaps a copy of a lost original by Bosch. The culmination of the genre is of course Dante's *Inferno*, a pit the labyrinthine construction of which provides the pilgrim and his guide, Vergil, with a viewpoint whence to measure the depth of the misery of the human soul. Satan's monstrous shape, shaggy body, and vivid coloration visibly render the extent of his perversion. See for example in Canto 34 the pilgrim's reaction when he sees the three faces on Satan's head: "L'una dinanzi, e quella era vermiglia [. . .] / E la destra parea tra bianca e gialla" ("One [was] in front and it was red [. . .] and the right one seemed between white and yellow," trans. Singleton, ll. 39, 43). On Dante's apocalyptic vision, see Richard Kenneth Emmerson and Ronald B. Herzman, *The Apocalyptic Imagination in Medieval Literature* (Philadelphia: University of Pennsylvania Press, 1992), 104–44.

[8] They include tortures by snow, fire, snake, blood, ice, lightning, and fetid smoke: see ll. 26–33 of Henri d'Arci's verse adaptation of the *Visio sancti Pauli* (mid-thirteenth century; ed. L.-E. Kastner, *Revue des Langues Romanes* 48 [1905]: 385–95). The seven-colored flame of Hell is also mentioned in the other verse renditions of Paul's vision, ed. idem, *Revue des Langues Romanes* 49 (1906), 49–62, 321–51, 427–50.

Voyage de Saint Brendan (by the Anglo-Norman Benedeit, early twelfth century), a peregrination in the course of which the saintly protagonist reaches the site of Hell (a hill with dark earth) before being granted to see Paradise (a luminously golden mountain).[9]

In striking contrast with this tradition, Basil's journey through Hell as narrated in the opening episode of the *Vie de Saint Jehan Paulus* is presented as an acoustic rather than visual experience. Regardless of the artistic inferiority of the text when compared with such masterpieces as Dante's *Inferno*, Basil's sonoscopic discovery of Hell warrants further investigation in that it provides a sonorous assessment of Satan's abode. When the Pope and his angelic guide enter the hellish place, the site is first and foremost a confusing racket, as generated by the moaning of tortured souls who grind their teeth so fiercely that they ram them into their gums. The darkness is so intense that audition is the travelers' sole means of orientation, and Michael, who does know about the sevenfold topography of the site, must himself rely on sounds to go from locus to locus. The result is a soniferous cartography that eventually leads the two visitors to a place of torment where devils mint ("batoient") their silver money and use as their anvils ("englumes") the heads, bodies, and faces of the condemned souls of usurers (ll. 354 and 352).[10] The devils' gesture, combined with the specific equipment involved in their activities, contributes to a description of Hell as a sort of gigantic tympanum.[11] Among the successive loci of Hell is an abyss whence emerges a noise of such magnitude that it affects the visitors' visual faculty ("tel noise a c'on n'i voit goute," l. 407), prompting Basil to fear for his sanity. In reality, however, audition is here a source of enlightenment, for it is through this soniferous training that Basil learns the moral lesson he is supposed to transmit to his flock. Once his soul has re-entered his body, the Pope thus proceeds to write down his "vision" and, of all the places he visited, remembers with particular acuity the seventh locus of Hell. The centrality of this site in the *Vie*'s narration results from

---

[9] On journeys to heaven in medieval vision literature, see Jeffrey Burton Russell, *A History of Heaven* (Princeton: Princeton University Press, 1997), 101–13.

[10] In a scene represented in the wall painting (ca. 1200) at Chaldon, Surrey, the condemned soul of "a usurer or miser is made to eat coins as he sits over a pile of money heated to redness by fire": Davidson, "The Fate of the Damned," 55.

[11] As noted by Alan of Lille, drumming produces a variety of sounds depending on the frequency and force of the stroke. The voice of the Dogon drum, for example, is obtained by either "striking" the instrument (with the palm of the hand) or "beating" it (with the side of the hand): Calame-Griaule, *Ethnologie et langage*, 531. In the fifth locus described by the author of *Jehan Paulus*, the manner in which demons beat on their victims' heads signals that, in the poet's perspective as in Bosch's, the maximum of pain is the one which results from torture by noise. As Rastall remarks in regard to the sonorization of Hell in mystery plays ("The Sounds of Hell," 117), "a dramatically clear way of indicating hellish activity is the unordered and incoherent noise of shouting and banging" (as described by Lewis in *The Screwtape Letters*).

the fact that it is occupied by the soul of Jehan Paulus' ancestor, where she awaits her deliverance as it will in time be effected by the text's eponymous hero. When he learns about his ancestor's fate from Pope Basil's writing, Jehan forsakes at once his life of privilege and goes to a deserted area near Toulouse where he lives seven years praying and fasting. Fearing that Jehan's saintly behavior will cause the liberation of his ancestor, Satan concocts a strategy of temptation ("engieng," l. 1061) which entails his taking the princess of Toulouse from her chamber and bringing her to Jehan, whose nature deteriorates to such an extent that he rapes and then kills the princess.[12]

This temptation scene develops a contrast between the empowering effect of noise as "engineered" by the Devil and the confusing result it has upon his victims. Diabolic noise is a death sentence for the innocent princess of Toulouse, while diabolic "batestal" (a racket produced by beating, flailing, and fighting; l. 1093) transforms Jehan into a "beste sauvage" (l. 1016). Echoing the circumstances of Yvain's downfall in Chrétien's romance, the hero henceforth loses all memory of his previously pious existence and roams about the forest like a dancing drunkard ("En sanblanche d'ivre dasant," 1228). Jehan's behavior, which brings to mind the presentation of Diabolus as "hylaris" and "gaudens" in the *Jeu d'Adam*, indicates that he is on his way to become Satan's disciple. One morning, however, the sight of the rising sun brings the hero back to his senses by reminding him of God's brightness. This enlightenment scene initiates a process of redemption which leads to the hermit's discovery by the king of Toulouse and to the hero's eventual return to society,[13] wherein God honors him by having all

[12] The fabric of satanic noise as an infernal tympanum points to the significance of the ear as a metaphor for sexuality, whence the success of the Devil's decision to tempt Jehan in the flesh. As Jacques Derrida notes in an essay significantly entitled "Tympan," one could draw a long inventory of the sexual investments that constrain the discourse of the ear: thus, "the horn that is called *pavillon* [the visible part of the outer ear] is a phallus for the Dogon and Bambara of Mali, and the auditory canal a vagina" (in *Margins of Philosophy*, trans. Alan Bass [Chicago: University of Chicago Press], 1982, xiv, n. 6). For Derrida, the labyrinthal configuration of the ear works against putting hearing in a privileged position as a truly communicative organ, considering the effect of the spiraling canals of the inner ear in producing delay and distancing. Because sounds may inflict pain for the listener, the question is whether one should "philosophize with a hammer," that is, whether philosophy means "to tympanize" in the sense of "to criticize" and "ridicule" (*Margins of Philosophy*, x, xii).

[13] The king of Toulouse decides to go on a hunting party in order to capture some wild boar. All day long, hunters and dogs run through the forest with great noise ("grant noise" and "grant bruit," l. 1615), until the king's master hunters reach Jehan's grove. Because of his ascetic existence, the holy man has by then become as hairy as a bear ("pelu si com un oursel," l. 1622). The king and his men bring this strange creature back to Toulouse and expose it in public. The onlookers' recognition of Jehan's sanctity arises at the moment when an infant reveals that God has forgiven Jehan and that the latter's merit has effected the liberation of his ancestor's soul. For an analysis of the hunting episode, see Brigitte Cazelles, "Bodies on Stage and the Production of Meaning," *Yale French Studies* 86 (1994): 56–74.

the bells of the city ring on their own (ll. 1995–1997).[14] In the *Vie*'s sonoscopic perspective, the voice of the bells signals the metamorphosis of the protagonist from a raging beast to a sounding board of redemptive value. Although the sight of the rising sun plays a pivotal part in Jehan's return to consciousness, nonetheless the poem gives priority to phonic phenomena in a manner that discloses their significance with respect to the story's moral lesson. Good and evil manifest themselves through opposite sonorous fields that seek to develop the listeners' capacity to distinguish between evil sounds and benevolent ones. The power to resist temptation resides in the acuteness of one's auditory perception, which enables God's creatures to recognize, and exorcise, the presence of Satan and his disciples.

Sonoscopy here refers to audition as a "distance sense" that helps humans to orient themselves in the right direction ("le droite voie": *Jehan Paulus*, l. 2061) and avoid the fate that could have been Jehan's in roaming away from Christian rectitude ("desvoie," l. 2062). Being attentive to the sounds of the world provides the perspective necessary to stay on the path toward Heaven, while transgressors will ineluctably end in the abyss, belly, or mouth of Hell (as Satan's abode is usually described: see Sheingorn, "The Iconography of Hell Mouth") or, to amplify the metaphor employed in this analysis, in the infernal Tympanum, where the condemned souls will forever endure the sundering noise of damnation.

2. Tongue-Tied Sinners

Once he recovers his mental and moral sanity, Jehan resumes his life in the wilderness and vows never to utter a word unless or until God should grant him forgiveness. The hero's sense of guilt is so deep, or the hagiographic poet so enamored of symbolic numerology, that the divine announcement—via an infant's

[14] Ringing bells produce a variety of "voices," ranging from the joyous sounds of the carillon, to the doleful sounds of the knell, down to the fearsome sounds of the tocsin. Many examples illustrate bells' exorcising or protective function during the Middle Ages. Thus it is said that Pope Sylvester II ordered in 1000 that all the bells of Christendom be rung to ensure the safe arrival of the new millennium. During the plagues, the charitable society of the "Charitons" used to bury the dead in the course of funeral processions led by a bell ringer. One of the bells of the church of Saint-Porchaire at Poitiers was tolled in order to protect the city from the danger of storms. In contrast with the harmony of divine sounds, Satan is a producer of discord, as is illustrated by a miracle that Jehan Paulus performs when he liberates a man possessed by the devil. At the moment when the saint makes the sign of the cross, Satan comes out of the man's body with a noise as great as that of a tornado ("Ausi bruians com fust uns tors," l. 2018). On the contrasting sounds of heaven and hell, see Kathi Meyer-Baer, *The Music of the Spheres and the Dance of Death* (Princeton: Princeton University Press, 1970).

voice—that Jehan is redeemed must be heard three times before the hero dares respond to this miracle. Experience has taught Jehan that the best means to ward off the temptation of the flesh (*license*) is *silence:*[15] an anagram which breaks, by inverting, the noisy power of Satan's seduction.

Silence is also the core of the verse *Roman de Robert le Diable* (late twelfth century), the very title of which predicates a negative association between the protagonist and the Devil. The story begins with the marriage of two pious and good individuals (the Duke of Normandy and the daughter of a count), whose happiness is hampered by the fact that they are childless, until the Duchess undertakes to call upon Satan's help and thus succeeds in conceiving a child.[16] Although Robert is the product of a legitimate and human union, the circumstances of his conception point to Satan as his true father. Expectedly, the child turns out to be a monster, who spends nights and days screaming ("crie et brait et pleure," l. 98) and kicks and bites his wet-nurses so ferociously that they end up using a horn to feed him his milk. Robert grows in size and beauty, and in meanness as well, considering the number of people he has killed by his fifteenth birthday at his putative father's instigation ("Si com li fist faire diables," l. 350). In time, Robert discovers that his evil behavior was caused by his mother's pact with Satan, whereupon he abandons his former mode of existence, cuts his hair, dons pilgrim clothes, and departs for Rome. There, Robert is told of the fourfold condition that will grant him God's pardon.[17] He must, first, act like a madman; second, endure the people's ensuing mockery and mistreatment; third, nourish himself with food that he will take out of a dog's mouth; and fourth, never utter a single word, whether foolish or wise, for this would at once place him anew under Satan's control (ll. 865–868). By a sort of homeopathic process, Robert's best protection against devilish impulses is to act like a possessed being, which provokes great hilarity at the court of Rome, until the emperor takes pity on this poor creature and provides him with shelter. Robert henceforth lives in the emperor's dog-kennel and for ten years behaves in compliance with the terms of the contract.

---

[15] The view of pastoral writers was that "words about sexuality could kill", that is, provoke "the eternal death of the soul": Ruth Mazo Karras, "*Leccherous Songys*: Medieval Sexuality in Word and Deed," in *Obscenity*, ed. Ziolkowski, 233–45, here 235.

[16] One day, while her husband is hunting in the woods, the Duchess laments their fate and blames God for granting to poor women that which she cannot obtain. She then calls upon Satan ("Diable," ed. Löseth, l. 45) and promises to become his disciple if he grants her to bear an heir. When the Duke returns from his hunting party, desire overwhelms him so irresistibly that he takes his wife on the spot and thus Robert is conceived. Scholarly works on the Old French *Robert le Diable* are cited by Kaeuper, *Chivalry and Violence*, 265–72, and by Cohen, *Of Giants*, 119–41, who also analyze other (English) renditions of the legend.

[17] On the Pope's advice, Robert consults a saintly hermit who soon receives from Heaven a letter specifying the terms that will ensure the hero's remission.

True to the formula typical of romance, a series of adventures is about to perturb the emperor's realm. Disorder begins when the emperor's seneschal requests of the emperor the hand of his daughter but finds himself rejected on the argument that the princess is too young to marry (ll. 993–1001), a rejection which prompts the seneschal to become the emperor's declared enemy. Weakened by his seneschal's repeated attacks, the emperor is also threatened by the Turks and owes his victory to a mysterious White Knight. The sole individual to know about the White Knight's identity is the emperor's daughter: from her chamber window, which opens on the garden where Robert comes to drink and pray, the princess has seen an angel bring to Robert a white armor with which to participate in the emperor's fight against the Turks. But the princess suffers from aphasia[18] (which may be the true reason that the emperor is opposed to her marriage) and must rely on sign language in her attempt to tell her father what she knows about the White Knight.[19] Instead of trusting his daughter's message, however, the emperor curses her for having foolishly fallen in love with his poor fool. Although his

[18] Many female characters in imaginative literature suffer from accidental (and temporary) muteness, indicating—in the view of Claude Thomasset, "Des jeunes filles accidentellement muettes," in *L'Hostellerie de Pensée*, ed. Zink and Bohler, 459–66—the emergence of their identity as sexual beings. An example is the princess introduced in the fabliau "Do mire de Brai," whose muteness would externalize what Thomasset characterizes as "the temptation of incest." Whether caused by the fish bone that strikes the fabliau's heroine momentarily dumb or by a fleshly obstruction (in the case of Dona Marinha, the mute heroine evoked in the fourteenth-century Portuguese text of the *Livro de Linhagens do Conde D. Pedro*), silence often refers to a type of sexual temptation or transgression that endangers the perpetuation of lineage. See Danielle Bohler, "La Discrète," in *L'Hostellerie de Pensée*, ed. Zink and eadem, 75–84. But this line of interpretation does not entirely apply to the story of the mute princess in the *Roman de Robert le Diable*. Not only does she appear to fear her father, but the latter also displays a deep-seated animosity toward his daughter. Unable or unwilling to provide a sexually-grounded reason for her infirmity, the author resorts instead to a moral argument (that she has committed some kind of sin: "ne sai quel desloiauté," l. 980), while at times relying on psycho-physiological explanations (the "escap," "folie," "gas," and "malencolie" evoked at ll. 4095–4606). In premodern society, melancholy was said to inflict all types of physical and mental aberrations, including one's nocturnal transformation into a werewolf. In contemporary society, extreme timidity, combined with lack of control over one's immediate environment, may lead to a psychological reaction (mostly in young girls) known as "selective muteness."

Despite the author's attempts thus to indict his character, the princess' muteness is clearly not the result of transgression. Her story contrasts in that respect with the adventure related in a miracle assigned to Our Lady of Rocamadour. It recounts how a blind woman recovers her sight thanks to the Virgin's intercession and vows to go to Rocamadour. Because the woman fails to fulfill her promise, the Virgin punishes her such that a bone obstructs her throat and she loses her capacity to speak. Eventually, the Virgin does heal the woman, who at once takes the road to Rocamadour (see ed. Albe, 106–9).

[19] "En baubiant comme muële / Gargone a son pere la bele, / Qui ne set qu'ele li vaut dire" ("Mumbling as mutes do, the fair maiden 'jargonizes' something to her father, who does not understand what she means to tell him," ll. 2315–2317).

choice of words has a derogatory intent, there are many indications that, indeed, the princess is under the spell ("asoté," l. 2886) of her amorous feelings toward Robert ("cest fol"). Thus she weeps at the sight of Robert's bleeding thigh when the hero is wounded in the course of an ambush motivated by the emperor's desire to discover the identity of the White Knight. The motif of Robert's wound, combined with the silent love of the emperor's daughter, suggest that the narration will lead to a romance-like, happy outcome. It may be that love will complete Robert's transformation from a cruel and savage character into a domesticated and civilized human being.

This possible outcome is temporarily delayed by the emperor's decree (ll. 4429–4430) that he will offer both his kingdom and his daughter's hand to the White Knight, provided that the latter prove his identity by displaying both his wound and the piece of lance that caused it. Because his desire to become the leader of the kingdom is as strong as ever, the seneschal undertakes to wound himself in the thigh, don white armor, and present himself at the emperor's court with the required evidence at hand. Recognizing his own seneschal in the White Knight who stands before him, the emperor welcomes him as befits a champion, a future son-in-law, and the emperor-to-be. But when the emperor orders the princess to take him as her husband, she reacts by declaring aloud that this man is lying about his identity (ll. 4490–4494). The princess' miraculous recovery of speech, which appears to have been provoked by both her anguish at marrying the seneschal and her sorrow at not marrying Robert, indicates that her aphasia was a form of escape from the unspeakable cruelty of life. Thanks to her newfound eloquence, the identity of the White Knight is revealed and Robert is summoned from his kennel and brought before the Roman emperor. Yet the resolution of the story is once more delayed by the arrival at court of messengers who tell Robert that his parents have both died, that his land in Normandy is under attack, and that he must at once leave Rome and return to his homeland in order to protect his heritage and become the new Duke. Robert's response to both the Norman messengers and the Roman emperor is that he will neither claim his inheritance nor take possession of the emperor's daughter and land,[20] at the risk of succumbing to vainglory and finding himself under the hold of the "anemis."

Therein ends, before it ever began, the possible love story between our aphasic princess and tongue-tied repentant sinner. The narrative unfolds along a series of spectacular transformations wherein Robert the Devil becomes Robert the Fool, Robert the White Knight, Robert the Hermit, and, ultimately, Robert the Saint. The miracle of the talking princess is replaced—and erased—by the

[20] Never, Robert affirms, will this maiden be by him "violée / Ne baissie ne acolée" ("raped or forced [kissed] or seized [embraced]," ll. 4959–4960)—a remarkable description of "love" in feudal conjugality.

miracle of the silent saint, who opts henceforth to live speechlessly as his means to achieve presence and repletion. No more is said about the princess, who may well have resumed her aphasic reaction to the tyranny of fate, indicating the author's intention to turn his romance into an edifying story. Like Galahad in the *Queste del Saint Graal*, Robert abandons the white noise of chivalry for the white silence of perfection, leading to a form of redemption that appears similarly to blossom in total disregard for the well-being of others. In Robert's case, however, silence is the ultimate trick by means of which Satan's son succeeds in silencing the Trickster.

3. Trumpeting the End of Time

In the story of *Robert le Diable*, Satan's cunning genius ("engieng") manifests itself as a life force that leads to deadly results. The Devil's power resides here in his capacity to present evil (the birth of a murderer destined to damnation) as if it were good (the continuation of lineage), consistent with the blinding luminosity of "Lucifer" as a source of false enlightenment. Visual imagery thus corroborates the status of Satan as God's rival, indicating that he dupes his victims through a pseudo-revelatory language (what I designate as *diabolos*) which relies on reason in order to negate and annihilate God's *Logos*.

Consider, in the *Jeu d'Adam*, Diabolus' warning to Eva that she is the victim of her Maker's duplicity ("grant engin"). According to Diabolus, the fruit that God (Figura) gave her has no value, whereas the fruit He forbade her to take is a source of life, power, and dominance, as well as the fount of an all-encompassing knowledge in matters of both good and evil (ll. 243–251). The force of Diabolus' eloquence lies in his use of the "colors" of rhetoric in order to abuse and confuse his interlocutor.[21] In a series of rhyming pairs, the garden of Paradise ("gardin") is shown to be the locus of an elaborate ruse ("engin," ll. 243–244); God's gift ("doné"), to stand at the opposite of generosity ("bonté," ll. 245–246); and God's interdiction ("defendu"), to prevent His creatures from attaining mental

[21] In Seneca's threefold classification ("sententiae," "divisio," and "colores"), "colors" refer to those figures that set the tone of the style, either through descriptive amplification or dramatic characterization. See Charles Sears Baldwin, *Ancient Rhetoric and Poetic* (New York: Macmillan, 1924), 98. Geoffrey of Vinsauf (early thirteenth century) composed a treatise on the colors of rhetoric (*Summa de coloribus rhetoricis*) the function of which is similarly to reinforce the persuasive power of the argument: see Edmond Faral, *Les Arts Poétiques du XIIe et du XIIIe siècle* (Paris: Champion, 1962), 92, 321–27. Along with his abuse of rhetoric, Diabolus also shows himself an expert at semantic manipulation. His evocation—at line 250—of the power ("poëste") and dominance ("seignorie") contained in the forbidden fruit echoes and inverts the might and authority of God mentioned in John's Revelation (12:10).

and moral excellence ("vertu," ll. 247–248). On the basis of these inversions, Diabolus concludes his argument by praising the forbidden apple as a container of "grace" (l. 249) endowed with creative and scientific merit. His power of persuasion consists in resorting to a religiously-marked lexicon ("grace") as the most convincing evidence that his is a selfless and generous attempt to empower God's creatures to such an extent that they will escape from His tyranny.[22] Seen against the straightforward nature of Figura's speech, *diabolos* is a twisted language that produces meaning through innuendo and circumlocution. An example is Diabolus' reliance on "similiter desinens" (homophony) to invert the meaning of God's words and disjoint signifiers from their proper signified (Vance, *Mervelous Signals*, 818). He thus affirms, contrary to Figura's claim, that the apple (*malum*) is not the fruit of evil (*malum*) and that biting into it (*morsus*) will not lead to death (*mors*). Also noteworthy is the fact that Diabolus addresses his speech to Eva rather than to Adam, whom he describes as most stupid ("soz"). By contrast, Eva shares with Diabolus a propensity to think and reflect, which leads to a paradoxical portrayal of the First Woman in terms of a highly mental being, one concerned with the realm of ideas (albeit evil ones) rather than with the flesh—*pace* many representatives of the theological tradition.[23] Yet Eva's sentient status is also hampered by her dependence on orality as a mode of communication that is unreliable because of the ephemeral character of spoken utterances.[24] The nature of Eva as a babbling ignoramus is evidenced by the consequences of her transgression. Duped by Diabolus into believing that she has "seen the light," Eva inaugurates postlapsarian language as a production of half-truths, falsehoods, or downright lies, thus causing the downfall of the human species into a soundscape of

---

[22] Exactly the argument used by the tempter figure in C. S. Lewis's *Perelandra* (1943).

[23] Eve inspires a contradictory indictment of woman's nature in its association with both sexuality and heresy. Regarding the latter, Augustine affirms that Eve's error was to take God's command ("you shall die") figuratively instead of literally (*De Gen. ad Litt.* 8.17.36, 11.35.50 [PL 34.387, 450]). Imitating the Serpent as teacher, she became the teacher of Adam and, in Jager's words (*The Tempter's Voice*, 46), a false "Divine Doctor."

[24] In the moralistic perspective, Eve is in that sense the emblematic ancestor of the female species. Although women's connection with orality was a logical consequence of their being in the main excluded from the culture of written textuality, medieval theology used this connection as proof that they evolve in a realm of ignorance and mendacity, thus justifying their peripheral place in medieval society. The primarily oral character of female communication accounts, therefore, for the invisibility of women in the visual perspective of medieval thought, while the equation between male power and the production of sounds accounts for women's inaudibility in imaginative literature. Indeed, structures of power in a given society result from a differential allocation of sensory powers, an example of which is the role of pungency as the reason for the ostracization of women in Suya society (Classen, *Word of Sense*, 86). A counterpoise to this picture, a collection of medieval women's letters, is being published by Joan Ferrante and Roger Bagnall of Columbia University.

confusion and discordance. Will the ensuing history lead humankind to Satan's eternal Pandemonium or to the brightness of Paradise?

Those issues are at the heart of John the Divine's Revelation, the prophetic tonality of which warrants exploration here to the extent that God's truth takes an alternately visual and aural manifestation. Although the text opens with a word, Apocalypse ("unveiling"), which amplifies the revelatory value of vision, audition plays an equally important part in providing John with access to the divine reality. Thus he hears behind him "a great voice, as of a trumpet" (1:10), which prompts him to turn in order "to see the voice that spake with me" (1:12). In addition to sounding "as of a trumpet" (4:1), God's voice evokes the noise of thunder (4:5, 16:18), and so does the voice of the four beasts (6:1) and the seven angels (8:5, 11:19). Hearing God is hearing his power, which forecasts the destructive effects of Judgment Day: "for the great day of his wrath is come: and who shall be able to stand?" (6:17). In John's prophetic experience, the end of the world has arrived, for he hears a great voice saying to the seven angels, "Go your ways, and pour out the vials of the wrath of God upon the earth" (16:1). Thunders and earthquakes now devastate the universe, plunging the sinners into darkness and the Serpent into the infernal abyss.

With the exception of the harps and songs of God's angels (5:8, 15:3), it thus appears that the aural manifestations of God's power are in the main punitive. Yet the fate of humankind will only be known on the day when the "voice of the seventh angel [. . .] shall begin to sound." Because John is not allowed to reveal what message will resonate through the seventh trumpet on Judgment Day, human history may end in a song or it may finish with a bang.[25] Old French accounts of the end of time tend to dramatize the outcome of Judgment Day by giving priority to its discordant effect. An example is the third part of the *Jeu d'Adam*, which consists of an apocalyptic poem (the "Ordo Prophetarum," also known as the *Quinze signes du jugement*)[26] forecasting the destruction of the hu-

[25] See Gilbert Dahan, "Le Jugement dernier vu par les commentateurs des *Sentences*," in *De l'art comme mystagonie: iconographie du Jugement dernier et des fins dernières à l'époque gothique*, ed. Yves Christe (Poitiers: Centre d'Etudes Supérieures de Civilisation Médiévale, 1996), 19–35, here 30–31. A painting by Geertgen tot Sint Jans in the late fifteenth century provides an optimistic illustration of the end of time by showing the infant Jesus with a pellet bell in each of his hands. The sound of Jesus' bells is meant to overpower the sound of the trumpets of damnation. By contrast, Revelation leaves open the eventual ending of human history, although the violence that permeates the text of John the Divine predicates a similarly violent outcome. As Arthur P. Mendel observes, virtually the whole of Revelation "is an account of the violence, devastation, suffering, and death necessary to purge the world and clear the way for the pure and perfect Kingdom": *Vision and Violence* (Ann Arbor: University of Michigan Press, 1992), 39.

[26] As Bullington remarks (*The Alexis in the Saint Albans Psalter*, 230, n. 19), this part of the *Jeu d'Adam* is inspired by a sermon falsely attributed to St. Augustine: the *Contra Judeos, Paganos et Arianos, Sermo de Symbolo*, wherein the prophets announce the coming of the Messiah (PL 42.1117–1130, esp. 1120–1125).

man realm. Stars will fall all over the earth, the sea will invade the land, and the wind will blow viciously, confounding (by destroying and mixing) both lands and trees ("Terres, arbres confundant," l. 1272). Men and animals will be reduced to silence, and so will Saint Peter, so great will be his fear when he sees the sky take its leave and hears the earth howl ("braire," l. 1177) after being burst open. In the final moments of postlapsarian history, the human species is reduced to a state equivalent to prelingual deafness (a condition in which "thinking itself can become incoherent and stunted"),[27] and it is now nature itself that speaks aloud and calls upon God's compassion.[28] The poem concludes with the prophetic sounds of God's "bosines" (horns, l. 1295), which precipitate the eradication of humankind[29] as a consequence of the fact that humans used to prefer hearing songs about Roland to songs about Christ.[30] In citing songs celebrating Roland's prowess, the text of the play establishes an implicit contrast between divine sounds (the "bosines" of Judgment Day) and evil ones (Roland's horn). The message here is that contemporary audiences would be better served in listening to divinely-inspired texts (like the *Jeu d'Adam*) rather than to the noisy accounts of human vainglory (*orguillus*, l. 973).[31]

In the moralistic perspective of the *Jeu d'Adam*, the sound of Roland's horn encapsulates the seduction of imaginative literature, the authors of which deserve the fate awaiting all those who adhere to the values of Babylon (Revelation

---

[27] Oliver Sacks, *Seeing Voices: A Journey into the World of the Deaf* (Berkeley: University of California Press, 1989), 19.

[28] Rivers will express themselves with man's voice ("les fluves parlerunt / E voiz d'ome parler averont," ll. 1151–1152).

[29] The direction in the Chester Harrowing of Hell mentions that Christ's coming is to be accompanied by shouting or a great "material" noise ("fiat clamor, vel sonitus magnus materialis"). Taking the Latin "materialis" as a noun, Rastall suggests ("The Sounds of Hell," 112) that this "great sound of material" refers to an unstructured noise such as one obtained by banging on pots and pans. God's noise on Judgment Day will thus overcome, through drumming, the racket produced by Satan and his disciples.

[30] The original is as follows (ll. 964–973): "Home, que fet, que tote rien veit? / Mult par est plain de coveitié, / Que de Deu n'a nule pitié. / Plus volontiers orreit chanter / Come Rollant ala juster / E Oliver son compainnon, / Qu'il ne ferrait la passion / Que suffri Crist a grant hahan / Por le pecchié que fist Adam. / Por quei sumes nos orguillus?" ("Why does man act in such a way as to render himself blind? He is so filled with ill intentions that he has no care for God. He shows himself more inclined to hear songs about Roland's martial deeds and about Olivier his companion, than to hear about the Passion that Christ suffered, at the price of great moaning, because of the sin committed by Adam. Why are we thus governed by pride?"). According to Paul Aebischer in his edition of the *Jeu d'Adam*, the play refers, not to the *Chanson* itself, but to an episode of the epic song *Girart de Vienne* that narrates a fight between Roland and Olivier (ll. 5100–5967). This does not affect the playwright's diatribe against the secular literary tradition.

[31] In its Babel-like cataclysmic conclusion, the play evokes the oncoming eradication of the human realm by claiming that every tower, regardless of height, will be thrown down at the end of time ("N'a soz ciel si haute tor / Que jus ne chie ai icel jor," ll. 1110–1111).

18:22). As is predicted by John the Divine, a mighty angel will take up a stone and cast it into the sea in order to effect the fall of the city. At that moment, "the voice of harpists, and musicians, and of pipers, and trumpeters, shall be heard no more at all in thee; and no craftsman, of whatsoever craft he be, shall be found any more in thee" (18:22).[32] A verse adaptation of John's text (second half of the thirteenth century) evokes the disappearance of Babylon by means of a word (*trové*) which often describes the inventive talent of secular poets (*trouvères*).[33] In this and other vernacular renditions of Revelation 18:22, the voice of musicians ("vox musicorum") refers to the voice of secular poets and identifies the latter as the Trickster's direct heirs because, like Satan in his power to deceive, jongleurs and minstrels excel in an art that is grounded in illusion. God will spew out of his mouth (Revelation 3:16) all those who used their tongues in order to deceive and abuse. And they will in turn be engulfed by the Dragon's mouth, whose action in devouring newborn children (12:4) vividly evokes the effect of court entertainment in nurturing the voracious proclivity of human nature.[34]

---

[32] The King James version here echoes both the Greek (. . . φωνὴ κιθαρῳδῶν καὶ μουσικῶν καὶ σαλπιστῶν. . .) and the Latin (. . . vox citharoedorum et musicorum et tibia canentium et tuba. . .) versions , and such is also the case in a thirteenth-century verse rendition of John's Apocalypse: "Adont cesserunt ses citholes / Et ses chansons et ses musiques / Et se[s] trumpes et ses violes" ("All the harps, songs, music, trumpets, and viols [of Babylon] will henceforth cease"): H. A. Todd, "The Old French Versified Apocalypse of the Kerr Manuscript," *PMLA* 18 (1903): 535–77, here 568 (ll. 1000–1003).

[33] The text reads as follows: "Jammès ultre *trové* ne serra, / Ne harpe ne musike la ne chantera; / Tibies ne busines erent desornavant; / Voiz de tubes n'erent sonant" ("It [Babylon] will not ever be found, and harps and music will no longer be heard there; nor will there be pipes or trumpets; and the voices of tubas will sound never more"): Paul Meyer, "Version Anglo-Normande en vers de l'Apocalypse," *Romania* 25 (1896): 174–257, here 241 (ll. 1101–1104). In this connection, it is noteworthy that the *Bible de Jérusalem* provides a translation according to which the fall of Babylon will forever hush the song of harpists and minstrels, and of pipers and trumpets ("Le chant des harpistes et des *trouvères* et des joueurs de flûtes ou de trompettes chez toi ne s'entendra jamais plus" [1815]).

[34] Among the many tricksters of secular literature, the protagonist of the *Roman de Renart* embodies to diabolical perfection the link between mendacity and appetite. Renart thus confesses his sins to a priest (who happens to be himself a kite of dubious value) by acknowledging that he often acted contrary to nature ("Mainte chose ai fete a envers," l. 13230) and slept with mothers, daughters, and fathers alike. He then concludes his recitation by eating up his confessor. Claude Reichler examines the significance of Renart's language as deviant discourse and rhetorical debauchery: *La Diabolie: La séduction, la renardie, l'écriture* (Paris: Minuit, 1979), 79–149; and Micheline de Combarieu the carnivorous aspect of his appetite: "Manger (et boire) dans le *Roman de Renart*," in *Manger et boire au Moyen Âge*, ed. Menjot, 415–28, here 422–23. Food is often a metaphor for transgression, as evoked in the *Jeu d'Adam* when Adam and Eve are chased from Paradise by an army of devils as cooks, or in a depiction of sin as cannibalism in Dante's *Inferno:* see Rachel Jacoff, "The Hermeneutics of Hunger," in *Speaking Images: Essays in Honor of V. A. Kolve*, ed. R. F. Yeager and C. C. Morse (Asheville, NC: University of North Carolina Press, 2001), 95–110.

4. Painting a New Beginning

John's apocalyptic experience articulates a gradually less mediated vision of God,[35] as illustrated by the fact that no temple will exist in the heavenly Jerusalem (21:22). Contemplation of the divine presence will henceforth be achieved directly, no longer requiring the help of intermediaries.

The unmediated character of John's vision of God was to inspire an approach to Revelation that sought to internalize this apocalyptic experience. Evidence is provided by the iconographic programs of Apocalypses produced in thirteenth-century England for the benefit of the aristocracy, the cycles of images in which endow the spoken word with conspicuous visibility (Lewis, "The English Gothic Illuminated Apocalypse," 3). To imprint John's vision on the soul's interior eye, the designers of those manuscripts relied on the three principles—order, association, and visualization—on which the medieval rules of artificial memory were founded.[36] Owners of those illuminated Apocalypses are for example invited to admire the beauty of Heaven in terms of measure and proportion, as when an angel gives John a reed with which to measure the temple of God (11:1) and the perfectly-squared shape of the heavenly Jerusalem.[37] Along with order, association constitutes another powerful mnemonic device, an evidence of which is the contrast between the splendor of the future Jerusalem and the horrors of Hell as a double-headed dragon mouth (depicted in an illuminated Apocalypse preserved at Lisbon: see Lewis, "The English Gothic Illuminated Apocalypse," 29). As for the third principle of artificial memory, visualization, a striking

[35] In his commentary on the Apocalypse, Richard of St.-Victor (a prior of the Benedictine abbey of St.-Victor in Paris, twelfth century) thus identifies four levels of perception, ranging from the phenomena of the visible world, to the outward appearances of the invisible, to its internal apprehension, and, finally, to the seer's vision of God face to face (*In Apoc.* 1.1 [PL 196.686B–689A]). See Suzanne Lewis, "The English Gothic Illuminated Apocalypse, *lectio divina*, and the Art of Memory," *Word and Image* 7 (1991): 1–32, here 4–5.

[36] See Jesse M. Gellrich's remark that "the idea of the Book in the middle ages consists [. . .] of specific ways of signifying, organizing, and remembering": *The Idea of the Book in the Middle Ages* (Ithaca and London: Cornell University Press, 1985), 248. Noting how the locus as visual field defines the place of writing, Michael Camille cites the Latin grammarian Varro according to whom "to talk (*loqui*) is said to come from place (*locus*); and he who speaks (*loquitur*) with understanding puts each word in its proper place": "Philological Iconoclasm," 394.

[37] Revelation 21:15–16. On the typological interpretation of the city's shape, see J. T. Rhodes and Clifford Davidson, "The Garden of Paradise," in *The Iconography of Heaven*, ed. Clifford Davidson (Kalamazoo, MI: Medieval Institute Publications, 1994), 69–109, here 78; and Robert D. Russell, "A Similitude of Paradise: The City as Image of the City," in *The Iconography of Heaven*, ed. Davidson, 146–61, here 156. The square-shaped Heavenly Jerusalem is represented on fol. 25 of a thirteenth-century Anglo-Norman Apocalypse preserved at Trinity College, Cambridge, ms. R.16.2. (This all goes back to the cubic universe patterned on the Ark of the Covenant in Cosmas Indicopleustes' sixth-century *Topographia Christiana*.)

component of John's Revelation is its spatialized conception of the end of time.[38] What John contemplates in his ultimate vision is Paradise (from Persian "pari-deiza", the Lord's enclosure) as a site where blessed souls will contemplate the divine presence away from the turbulence of postlapsarian history. That "noisy" and "nauseous" may derive from the same root would explain John's observation that, in the world according to the second Creation, there will be a new heaven and a new earth, but "no more sea" (21:1). Whereas in postlapsarian history the sea emblematized the Serpent as the realm of bitterness and fluctuation,[39] at the end of time the Serpent will be assigned a specific location: the underworld.[40] Another visualized distinction is the darkness of Hades as opposed to the brightness of Paradise, which is detailed in John's evocation of the colors of God (1:13), His throne (4:3), and the New Jerusalem (21:19–21). Painting a new beginning is integral to the lesson of John's prophecy regarding the necessity to absorb and retain God's light, consistent with Aristotle's definition of memory wherein remembering is "the having of an image, related as a likeness to that of which it is an image" (*On Memory*, ed. Barnes, 716). In the vivid picture of eschatology as forecast by the seer, time will end at the moment when space will prevail.

The preeminence of space over time in Platonic and Christian thought[41] is at the basis of the "ocularcentric" tradition of Western philosophy, the history of which Martin Jay has delineated with concise eloquence:

> From the shadows playing on the wall of Plato's cave and Augustine's praise of the divine light to Descartes's ideas available to a "steadfast mental gaze" and the Enlightenment's faith in the data of our senses, the ocularcentric underpinnings of our philosophical tradition have been undeniably perva-

[38] As Jeffrey Burton Russell observes, "traditionally, heaven is a place, a sacred space. The sacredness of this space is expressed in metaphors of kingdom, garden, city, or celestial spheres" (*A History of Heaven*, 13). This place is sometimes described in terms of luminosity: see Russell's list of Old English terms for heaven (104), which includes *wlite* (brightness, beauty) and *wuldor* (glory).

[39] Until the moment when spatialization will generate eternal stability, humans must rely on a sonorous mode of communication with the Lord, who will grant his assistance to all those who "obey" his commands, that is, who "listen" to him "from below" ("obaudire"). See for instance Psalm 130:1's appeal to God: "De profundis clamavi ad te, Domine" ("Out of the depths have I cried unto thee, O Lord"). The element of instability ("chaos" to use Bonting's term), which the Bible often symbolizes as the sea, "will be abolished with the coming of a new heaven and earth" (*Chaos Theology*, 36-37). On the nautical significance of noise and the acoustic environment, see Serres, *Genesis*, trans. James and Nielson, 13, and Folkerth, *The Sound of Shakespeare*, 108–12.

[40] A powerful way to contain disorder and chaos is to confine the producer of disturbance to the underworld (Gellrich, *Idea of the Book*, 88).

[41] In the Old Testament knowledge comes from hearing God's voice and truth emerges from auditory interaction, which may account for the Hebraic taboo on visual representation.

> sive. Whether in terms of speculation, observation, or revelatory illumination, Western philosophy has tended to accept without question the traditional sensual hierarchy [and has therefore built its theory of knowledge] resolutely on a visual foundation (*Downcast Eyes*, 87).

Yet the past hundred years or so have witnessed the emergence of a growing discontent with respect to the "unwise" and, for some, even "dangerous" tendency to give priority to vision at the expense of the other senses. This denigration of visualism entails three principal changes, which Martin Jay identifies as a detranscentralization of perspective, the recorporalization of the cognitive subject, and the revalorization of time over space. Examples of the first form of philosophical change begin with Nietzsche, who mocks the visionary tradition of the medieval period and its neo-Platonic search for the "white ecstasy" of divine illumination as a type of mental aberration that acts contrary to wisdom.[42] Contemporary thought tends to condemn the historical preference for sight on the argument that it is not the ultimate mode of access to knowledge but, rather, a primary mode of domination. In contrast with medieval theories wherein vision (which emits visual rays) is a more active mode of cognition than audition (which just receives), current philosophy inverts this hierarchical schema in favor of audition as more passive and hence less harmful.[43] To quote Levin, "in the body politic

---

With the Hellenization of the Bible, however, seeing came to supplant hearing when thinkers like Philo Judaeus attempted to "make the meaning of the Old Testament intelligible within the Greek cultural horizon," the result of which was to emphasize the non-verbal essence of God's *logos* as light and the importance of human eyes as the primary organ "that will receive its revelation": Blumenberg, "Light as Metaphor for Truth," 46–47.

[42] See Nietzsche's *Daybreak* (examined by Jay, *Downcast Eyes*, 40). As David M. Levin remarks, Nietzsche does not reject ocular thinking, so much as he "turns the very logic of ocularcentrism against itself, altering forever the visionary ambitions of philosophy": introduction to *Modernity and the Hegemony of Vision*, 1–29, here 4–5. What Nietzsche calls forth is the emergence of a new race, one constituted of free individuals who will become active creators of their own fate rather than passively observed creatures. His superman will thus obtain access to knowledge as a *Gay Science*, in contradistinction to the sorrowful existence imposed on the human race by an all-seeing Creator.

From Lacan to Althusser down to Foucault, vision and visual imagery become the very emblem of man's aggression (as elicited by envy—*invidia*—a word which derives from the Latin verb *videre*, to see), of man's subjection by ideology, or of his alienation in the current "empire of the gaze" that Foucault describes in terms of scopic regimes of "malveillance": "L'oeil du pouvoir," in *Michel Foucault: Dits et Ecrits, 1954–1988*, 2: *1976–1988*, ed. Daniel Defert, François Ewald, and Jacques Lagrange (Paris: Gallimard, 2001), 190–207, here 195, 201.

[43] Meditating on Meister Eckhart's remark that "in hearing I am passive and in seeing I am active," Levin notes that, as a lesser control-driven organ, hearing has the "capacity to unify, integrate, reconcile, and harmonize without imposing totality": *The Listening Self* (London and New York: Routledge, 1989), 34. Levin here elaborates a contrast between the visual paradigm associated with "*knowledge* to designate the totalizing, metaphysical functioning of Reason," and the auditory paradigm as a means to achieve thinking and understanding.

of the senses, vision, as we know, is sovereign, and the totalitarian empire of the panoramic gaze, the most reifying and totalizing of our sensory powers, continues to extend the hegemony of its metaphysics" (*The Listening Self*, 30). Jay's second form of philosophical change, the recorporalization of the cognitive subject, calls for an alternative mode of interaction giving a privileged position this time to the voice and the ear. True reciprocity will occur when we abandon the reductive and ultimately alienating gaze by means of which we traditionally contain and reify the other. At the opposite of this violent "avidity of the gaze," Emmanuel Levinas stresses the value of sound as "a ringing, clanging scandal. Whereas, in vision, form is wedded to content in such a way as to appease it, in sound the perceptible quality overflows so that form no longer contains its content."[44] The "scandal" of sound consists in compelling the interlocutor to recognize the essence of the other as a subject, instead of treating the other, as does the ocularcentric tradition, as an object of specularity and manipulative speculation.[45] In short, contemporary thought denigrates the alienating effect of "ocularcentrism" in placing the individual under the control of a tyrannical, because overseeing, source of authority—whether this authority is understood in religious or in political terms.

Illustrating the third form of change mentioned by Jay, postmodern philosophers call for a revalorization of time over space as a means to protect individual freedom.[46] Much like Rousseau's praise of an emotive form of interaction, Levin

---

Whereas vision is distancing, detached, spatially separating, "hearing is intimate, participatory, communicative; we are always *affected* by what we are given to hear" (32). Levin here echoes Hannah Arendt's remark: "If one considers how easy it is for sight, unlike the other senses, to shut out the outside world, and if one examines the early notion of the blind bard, whose stories are being listened to, one may wonder why hearing did not develop into the guiding metaphor for thinking": *The Life of the Mind* (New York and London: Harcourt Brace Jovanovich, 1977–1978), 1: 110–11.

[44] Emmanuel Levinas, "The Transcendence of the Words," in *Totality and Infinity* (analyzed by Jay, *Downcast Eyes*, 556). That knowledge is not necessarily acquired through seeing alone is evidenced by the salutary effect of Freud's "talking cure" in requiring no direct visual contact between patient and analyst.

[45] The celebration of auditory communication by Levinas—along with other representatives of what Jay (*Downcast Eyes*, 547) describes in terms of "philo-Semitism"—may signal the influence of an Hebraic rather than Hellenistic view on knowledge and truth, as emblematized in the distinction between God's creative act in Genesis (a Word calling out of the void) and in John (God as "the light of men," 1:1–5) (notwithstanding the fact that the prologue of John's Gospel is deliberately patterned after Genesis 1). Since this approach of recent decades seeks to reach back behind the late antique rise of silent reading, it would be interesting to investigate the function of silent reading of the Hebrew Scriptures.

[46] Instead of the visual paradigm, which has led to an ontology that qualifies as frontal or optical projection, what should now be cultivated is an ontology that would grant preeminence to temporality as the very foundation and creation of being: "Listening, more sensitive to the passage of time, the great destroyer of this [traditional] ontology, may alone provide the channels for a different historical life": Levin, *The Listening Self*, 31, 275.

for example recommends a form of attention to the world which he designates as "hearkening" in reference to a type of hearing moved by ontological understanding. In a comparable manner, von Franz (*Patterns of Creativity*, 232, 235) proposes an interpretation of the New Beginning that stands at the opposite of the seer's architectural and colorful depiction of Jerusalem. Far from duplicating the First Creation according to the outer and extroverted principles developed by Christian cosmological theories, the Second Creation is to be understood as an inward process and an inner mystical event.

Although there is no question here of contesting the value of hearkening, what appears problematic in the renewed interest in audition is the fact that it entails the rejection of vision as being necessarily the realm of tyranny and totalitarianism. A more adequate way to achieve a certain degree of stability is perhaps to recognize that human nature stands midway between Apollo (ocularcentrism) and Pan (auricularcentrism). More generally, the wisdom of the Pan myth may be to warn us against the danger of giving reason too much pride of place over intuition or vice versa, at the risk of throwing human nature off balance. And such may also be the lesson to be drawn from those artifacts of mythical and imaginative literature which develop a cross-sensory experience of the world and wherein understanding calls upon the combined agency of all of our senses.

My first textual exhibit is the tale of the Pied Piper which, in Robert Browning's rendition, serves to alert children that they should not imitate their elders' too serious and authoritarian mode of life. Consider the adults' treatment of the Pied Piper after he has liberated the town from those subterranean creatures that creep, swim, fly, or run. When the Piper asks for the thousand guilders he was promised as a reward, the mayor and his Council declare that it was never their intention to pay this "wandering fellow / With a gypsy coat of red and yellow." And thus the reader begins to recognize in the Piper an avatar of Pan as both the master of communication and a wandering foreigner who, as such, is a ready-made scapegoat. In reaction to the elders' treachery, the Piper blows his pipe and out come the "merry crowds" of children running, who henceforth vanish from Hamelin, never to return. The children's specificity lies, first, in their being like the Piper rather than a replica of their elders and, second, in the place wherein they reappear, Transylvania.[47] Evoking a rite of passage from childhood to adulthood, this sylvan traversal suggests that they have thus acquired a Pan-like capacity to pay heed to the voices of nature, such that their mode of hearing and speaking now resonates the reality of life itself.

The second example comes from Hindu mythology, in reference to two deities, Krishna and Kali, who emblematize respectively the powers of life and death.

---

[47] My suggestion here is that Browning's version of the legend opposes a sorrowful mode of existence (Hamelin) to a joyful one (Transylvania). In this light, the Piper does not sacrifice the children, but to the contrary saves them from a society whose adults behaved like "rats" and "moles."

Krishna is a young cowherd of unsurpassed beauty whose flute summons every one to lose all inhibitions, adhere to a carefree and playful mode of life, and "indulge in amorous and erotic dalliance."[48] Represented as an ugly woman clothed in dark garments and wearing a necklace of snakes and skulls, Kali embodies the realm of destruction and death, as echoed in her weird and uncanny laughter. Despite their patent differences, Krishna and Kali also share a "jungly" component in that they live on the periphery of civilization, in the realm of that which is "untamed, uncultured, uncaring, and uncompromising" (138), thus disclosing their significance in equally representing that which is completely unbound and primordially free. Registering the sum total of human existence, the vital sounds of Krishna's flute and the deadly sonority of Kali's sword are phonic reminders that life and death are inseparable. Taken together, therefore, these two Hindu deities hold the promise of renewal and continuity, like Pan in his dual appearance, and like Janus as the god of recurrent beginnings (January). In this connection, the value of hermetic language over hermeneutics lies in the former's connecting quality,[49] which brings to mind Janus' association with crossing places and bridges. Similarly regulating any motions of going in and coming out, Hermes is a master of all transitions and, from a linguistic viewpoint, a master translator. It would appear, then, that both Janus and Hermes and by familial association Pan himself facilitate such transactions as those which connect words and ideas, signifier and signified, earth and heaven. In the mythological perspective, the monstrosity of two-faced Janus or goat-like Pan emblematizes human nature in combining reason and instinct. Human existence here finds its equilibrium in the middle space that protects one from both eristic reasoning (the upper part of human nature) and anarchic intoxication (the lower part of transgressive delight).

That vision and audition can either lead to enlightenment or generate confusion, regardless of one's station in life and intellectual acumen, is amply demonstrated by Gautier de Coinci in his collection of verse miracles devoted to the Virgin Mary (first decades of the thirteenth century), which constitutes my third textual exhibit. One of Gautier's tales ("De l'ymage Nostre Dame") narrates the story of a Saracen whose devotion to a painting of the Virgin Mary is such that it inspires him in time to convert to Christianity. Gazing at the icon as is his wont, the Saracen comes one day to wonder about the mystery of the Incarnation,

[48] David R. Kingsley, *The Sword and the Flute* (Berkeley, Los Angeles, and London: University of California Press, 1975), 41.

[49] As illustrations of the status of human nature in combining an upper and a lower part, the Pan myth and its folk renditions are positive counterpoints to the power of Satan in his capacity both to beguile through good music and to alienate through unstructured noise. Rastall ("The Sounds of Hell," 113) proposes to designate the first type of seduction as the "deceit position," and the second the "force of arms position."

which in his perspective defies reason. As he reflects on the pro and con of believing that a deity could be born of a virgin, he sees two breasts coming out of the image's bosom and, thereafter, a clear oil oozing out of the breasts. It is this sight which prompts him to relinquish paganism.[50] Gautier concludes his narration with a warning addressed to all those religious clerics who prefer singing about Ogier[51] rather than venerating the sacred objects of the cult. Instead of cultivating meditation, as nurtured by the contemplation of holy icons, they accumulate material possessions such as covers and rugs without realizing that the Devil hides himself in those rugs, where he sits night and day and defecates. Beyond Gautier's marvelously realistic depiction of the result of heedlessness in the "face" of the Trickster's ubiquitous presence,[52] what is noteworthy in this particular tale is the positive connection it establishes between vision and reflection. The Saracen's persistence in venerating the Virgin Mary is rewarded by a miracle that compels him to convert because, if God can bring life to a painting, then this goes to prove that God has also the power to take flesh through a virginal body.

Just as vision (when it occurs away from any manipulative speculation) may lead to enlightenment, so can audition (when sounding and hearing are neither disassembling nor alienating) become a path toward revelation, as another of Gautier's tales illustrates ("Dou cirge qui descendi au jougleour"). The story

[50] This is a hagiographical topos: see Kathleen Kulp-Hill, trans., *Songs of Holy Mary of Alfonso X, the Wise*, MRTS 173 (Tempe, AZ: MRTS, 2000), 62 (no. 46).

[51] Ogier, we recall, achieves an exploit both spectacular and specular in striking down the standard-bearer of Charlemagne's pagan opponent in the *Chanson de Roland*. Ogier is also the protagonist of a late epic (thirteenth century), whose main characteristic is that he is violent and vengeful. As such, Ogier is mentioned in a hagiography—the Anglo-Norman *Vie de Sainte Osith* (ca. 1200; l. 331)—as the epitome of chivalric aggression. This polyvalent treatment of Ogier illustrates the way vernacular works invest a given motif with various and, at times, divergent meanings and functions. In this connection, I enthusiastically endorse Keith Busby's reminder (echoing my own suggestion: *Le corps de sainteté d'après Jehan Bouche d'Or, Jehan Paulus et quelques vies des XIIe et XIIIe siècles* [Geneva: Droz, 1982], 32–41) that we should "examine the local dynamics" of medieval codices as evidence that miscellaneous manuscripts are in reality "structured according to principles of similitude and contrast": "*Fabliaux* and the New Codicology," in *The World and Its Rival: Essays on Literary Imagination in Honor of Per Nykrog*, ed. Kathryn Karczewska and Tom Conley (Amsterdam and Atlanta: Rodopi, 1999), 137–60, here 159–60.

[52] The depiction of the Devil as defecating or as a stinking "petomane" is a constant in medieval literature (as seen in the famous film "The Seventh Seal"). Breaking wind was "a not unimportant feature of the devils' stage business" in mystery plays (Rastall, "The Sounds of Hell," 11). Sounds and smells here combine in a way that amplifies Tertullian's assessment that Eve is *diaboli ianua* (the Devil's gateway, *De Cultu Feminarum* 1.1) in terms of evil speech and dirty opening. In analyzing what she labels the "talking cunt" motif, Madeline Caviness links the expression "diaboli ianua" to the fact that "one is born between feces and urine": thus "when a woman opens her legs she is a gate of hell": "Obscenity and Alterity: Images that Shock and Offend Us/Them, Now/Then?" in *Obscenity*, ed. Ziolkowski, 155–75, here 163–64.

focuses on Pierre, a lay minstrel ("un jougleour" and "home lai") who uses his craft to pay homage to a painting of the Virgin Mary which is venerated at Rocamadour. One day, the tale's hero begins playing and singing so melodiously that it seems as if his viol wants to speak, and the Lady rewards her musician by having a beautiful candle fly down atop Pierre's viol. Everyone in the crowd rejoices at this miracle, except for one melancholy monk, by the name of Gerard, who takes this for folly and denounces Pierre for being a sorcerer ("enchanteres"), sleight of hand artist ("boutencoroye"), and legerdemain expert ("tregeteres").[53] Despite the monk's repeated attempt to put the candle back into its stick, the miracle reoccurs three times, eliciting great joy among the witnesses and as great a dismay in Gerard, who is henceforth silenced by the sound of collective prayers ("de la noise / Est esbaudis et estonés," ed. Koenig, ll. 158–159). What is noteworthy in Pierre's story or in the Saracen's is that, as in the case of most of Gautier's miracles, the focus is a protagonist who qualifies as an outsider, either because he does not adhere to the true faith or because he practices a profession of dubious value. In medieval society, such individuals stood at the lowest rank and deserved at best to be ignored and at worst to be rejected by the dignitaries of both the secular and the religious orders. That the Saracen, an unrefined and uneducated peasant ("Uns vilains bobelins champestre," l. 214), is rewarded on account of the acuteness of his vision is all the more admirable as he thus demarcates himself from the heedless behavior of those clerics and priests who are so enamored of ornaments and so filled with vainglory that they only turn an inattentive ear to God's Word. As for the story of Pierre the "jougleour," it illustrates

[53] Gerard's qualification of the minstrel as a "boutencoroye" and "tregeteres" equates Pierre's comportment with evil aerobics, in reference to a form of *gesticulatio* to which clerical culture assigns a demonic origin: see Jean-Claude Schmitt, *La raison des gestes dans l'Occident médiéval* (Paris: Gallimard, 1990), 261–73. Considering that a "trick" (from the Old French verb "trichier," to cheat) refers to those feats that are achieved by experts in legerdemain and jugglery, the monk's criticism of the minstrel focuses on a form of entertainment that deceives and delights instead of instructing its public.

Gerard's condemnation of Pierre's expertise reflects the ambivalent attitude to music shown by the Church Fathers and many medieval moralists, as in the examples collected by McKinnon, *Music in Early Christian Literature*. Based on the Boethian triad, the view here is that "musica mundana" (the Music of the Spheres) and "musica humana" (the smaller-scale order of the universe) are not accessible to humankind, which can only produce "musica instrumentalis" (that, is, sounded music). And although "musica instrumentalis" is supposed to reflect "musica caelestis" (the music of Heaven), as the latter's mortal equivalent it is also "the only kind of music open to perversion." Gerard's reaction to Pierre's performance echoes Robert Mannyng's warnings against minstrelsy as a production of good music that is "harmful to the soul [because it] gives way to an appreciation of its beauties at a purely sensual level [and becomes] the path to carnal vice" (Rastall, "The Sounds of Hell," 114–15; see also idem, "The Musical Repertory," in *The Iconography of Heaven*, ed. Davidson, 162–96, here 169–70).

the positive effect of audition when it fosters a harmonious mode of communication between humans and deities.

Gautier de Coinci amplifies the moral lesson of Pierre's story in an epilogue wherein euphonious homophony serves to register the harmony of God's creation and, conversely, wherein parasitic homophony records Satan's disassembling effect (ll. 209–210, 354–358). In the latter case, homophony brings together words that are identical in sound but different in meaning and describes any individual whose words are not in harmony with his thoughts ("ne se concorde"), the result of which is discordance and severance from God ("descorde"). By contrast, all those who flee Satan's bondage ("cordes") will develop a musical type of language ("cordes") allowing them to interact peacefully with one another ("se concorderont") and bring themselves into accord with God ("acorderont"). In Gautier's non-hierarchical cosmology, matter ("cordes") may have an alienating effect or a liberating one; hearing may be intoxicating or uplifting; singing may lead to mental deafness or, if pure and sincere, may enable the singer to taste the fount of eternal life. Also remarkable is Gautier's assessment of transgression as being caused, not by Satan experienced as an external force, but by the unbalanced effect of unduly exalting one specific sensory perception. Whenever seeing and hearing combine rather than compete, there results a perspective which in a Pan-like fashion ensures contact and communication between inner self and outer reality.[54]

In the minimalist approach to the human experience developed throughout Gautier de Coinci's *Miracles*, the true miracle lies in an assessment of human nature that grants to a Saracen the capacity to think rationally and to a "trouvère" that of singing harmoniously. At a time when Saracens and minstrels constitute the scum of humanity and are as such destined to the noisy prison of Hell, Gautier's openness of mind is comforting.[55] It suggests the elaboration of an ontology

[54] The same sensory combination—"synesthesia" in the proper sense of the term—occurs at Pentecost, considering that hearing and seeing enable Jesus' followers to be "all with one accord in one place" and each achieve full revelation of God's mystery. Thus a sound from heaven is heard as of a rushing mighty wind, and "there appeared unto them cloven tongues like as of fire, and it sat upon each of them. And they were filled with the Holy Ghost, and began to speak with other tongues, as the Spirit gave them utterance" (Acts 2:1–4). The linguistic lapsus initiated at both Eden and Babel is symbolically corrected at Pentecost, with the advent of God's spirit as manifested through both acoustic and visual imagery. The multiplicity of languages inspired by the Spirit gives rise to not dissonance but, to the contrary, an expertise conducive to communication and understanding.

[55] According to the prose *Estoire del saint Graal* (1225–1230; ed. Ponceau, 1.282–332 [172–74]), Evalach (also known as Mordrain), the Saracen king of Sarras, is sexually obsessed by the wooden representation of a woman. See Colette-Anne Van Coolput, "La poupée d'Evalac ou la conversion tardive du Roi Mordrain," in *Continuations*, ed. Lacy and Torrini-Roblin, 163–72. Seen against Evalach's Pygmalion-like obsession, which distinguishes him

that is linked to neither a visual nor an auditory paradigm, that is neither a frontal nor a lateral projection, that entails neither an ocularcentric modality nor an auricularcentric one, but which will blossom as an all-encompassing concordance that can be obtained regardless of one's philosophical acumen, religious belief, or station in life. Beyond its devotional character, the vernacular voice of our Benedictine poet—as well as the voice heard in myths and folk tales from Pan to the Pied Piper—echoes the wisdom and vibrancy of the "vox populi," speaks the universal language of compassion, and sings both the visible and the aural beauties of the world. In between the vision of paradise and the noise of death stands a human solution wherein sentience is both a sensitive and a sensible experience.

---

as an enemy of the faith, Gautier de Coinci portrays his Saracen's love for the icon as evidence of the character's internal depth. On the verbal and physical violence committed against Muslims, see David Nirenberg, *Communities of Violence* (Princeton: Princeton University Press, 1996), 93–124.

With regard to Gautier's minstrel: in contrast with the often anonymous character of the protagonists of vernacular literature when they belong to the lower strata of society, Gautier de Coinci gives a name to his hero, Pierre, whose unwavering devotion turns him into a sort of "St. Peter of the poor." In acting here as the spokesman and defender of the lowly, Gautier the author of narrative Miracles demarcates himself from Gautier the hagiographer, as exemplified by the vivid contrast between his innovative portrayal of an admirable Saracen and, in the *Passion de Sainte Christine*, his conventional castigation of pagan figures as being necessarily deaf and blind to the true faith and incapable of reflection. Just as noteworthy is the contrast between the treatment of "vox populi" in the *Vie de Saint Alexis*, silenced as it ultimately is by the Pope's all-seeing authority, and its joyous triumph in Gautier's miracle of the flying candle, wherein the folk's collective prayer reduces to silence Gerard the sad (and probably bad) monk.

CONCLUSION

THE AMBIVALENCE OF NOISE

Par petiz ruisiaus, que Deduiz
I ot fet fere par conduiz
Si en aloit l'eve fesant
Une noise douce et plessant.
(In small brooks, which Delight
Had made there as furrows,
The water ran along, making
A sweet and pleasant sound.)
(Guillaume de Lorris, *Rose*,
ll. 1385–1388)

En sa main une coie espee
Ausinc con de langue copee.
Si la brandist san fere noise,
Qu'en ne l'oïst pas d'une toise.
(In his hand, a sword as quiet
As one whose tongue is cut out:
He brandished it so noiselessly
That it could not be heard a fathom
away.)
(Jean de Meun, *Rose*,
ll. 15459–15462)

From Genesis to Revelation, this acoustemological journey through the soundscape of early French literature has been a journey not through time in the historical sense of the word, but through perturbation. We have encountered a non-evolutional type of teleology, one which leaves undecided the fate of humankind at the "end of time," and also one in which the story of humankind is a succession of ups and downs as haphazardly determined by a blind Wheel of Fortune. This unpredictability and these fluctuations are reflected in a concept—noise—which defies conceptualization to the extent that the word is in reality "rootless." Does noise express the harmful (*noceo*), nauseous (*nausea*), or malodorous (nose) effects of stridence? Is it destructive, or can it also be generative?

My analysis of literary soundscapes submits that noise is all of the above and that it functions as both trigger and trickster. Consider the repercussion of Roland's horn: it is, at the same time, music to Charlemagne's ears and the very song of Christian rightness; an aggressive clamor to the Saracens; the noise of vernacular poetry as a fallen medium in the view of many contemporary moralists; or a tune reflecting the archaism of medieval culture for readers of later periods. At the moment of their inception as in the course of their transmission, Old French texts signify all the more as their soundscapes bring additional resonance to the *logos* of narration by either reinforcing or undercutting (via the parasitic action of *paralogos* and *diabolos*) the intended message of a story. This is a highly sophisticated literary tradition,[1] as evidenced by the polysemy of the Old French

[1] The sophistication of early French literature is confirmed—albeit indirectly—by the scientific definition of homophony in terms of an "illusory continuity." Experiments show that

noise in evoking a cross-sensory mode of cognition, or by the realistic effect of homophony in registering the unstable character of human transactions.

I set out to assess the role that Old French texts impart to audition in conditioning experience of the world and interaction with others. As I hope to have shown, phonic phenomena in this literary tradition sonorously concretize the highs and lows of human nature in the latter's capacity to transcend or destroy itself. Implicitly, these textual soundscapes alert their listening public about the danger of overemphasizing either the upper or the lower part of our twofold self at the risk of putting us off balance. The interest of this sonoscopic depiction of self and society is also linked to the fact that it enables us to hear, in a virtually unadulterated form, the resounding character of communication. At the core of the moralists' concern is precisely the vibrancy of this orally-communicated tradition in its capacity to feed man's worst impulses, evidence of which is the glorification of violence in epic songs and chivalric romances. And the question arises: is noise understood as perturbation the distinctive mark of an orally-based culture? Does this imply that a culture ceases to be "noisy" as it becomes literate?

Although such issues lie beyond the scope of this book, the concomitance they seem to establish between literacy and visualism does at this point warrant some degree of consideration. Three recent scholarly works acknowledge, by their very titles, the role of visual imagery in articulating a conception of self and creation specific to literate culture. Analyzing the production and consumption of the "book" in fourteenth-century France, Claire Richter Sherman (*Imaging Aristotle*) demonstrates how noble and lay readers relied on illustrated manuscripts (and, hence, on verbal and visual representation) to meditate and debate on issues relating to history, politics, and cognition. In a study significantly entitled *The Color of Melancholy* (trans. Lydia G. Cochrane [Baltimore: Johns Hopkins University Press, 1997]) Jacqueline Cerquiglini-Toulet explores the subject of books as the receptacles in which fourteenth-century poets sought metaphorically to preserve their texts and ensure the commemoration of their names. The monumental investigation of the techniques and figures employed by poets in late medieval and early Renaissance France leads François Cornilliat (*"Or ne mens": Couleurs de l'Eloge et du Blâme chez les "Grands Rhétoriqueurs"* [Paris: Champion, 1994]) to describe the authors' use of the "colors of rhetoric" as a repeated attempt to illustrate and reveal the iridescent light of truth and beauty. That visionscape and colorscape are the cornerstones of artistry and cognition in literate culture is corroborated by the production of illuminated manuscripts that each constitute "a

---

an interference (or "masker") is perceived as such if its noise is too loud. A successful masker is thus a sound that "fills in the background in such a way that there is no longer any spectral shape defined against the white canvas of silence": Albert S. Bregman, *Auditory Scene Analysis. The Perceptual Organization of Sound* (Cambridge, MA: MIT Press, 1990), 27, 392. In its literary application, a masker is a parasitic interference that is too subtle to be detected.

treasure to hold and behold as well as to read" (Krieger, *Ekphrasis*, 116).[2] Following the example, introduced earlier in Latin textuality, of word-separated texts in encouraging "the transition from oral to visual modes of book production," illuminated manuscripts designed for the consumption of lay readers in the later Middle Ages facilitated visually the swift conversion of signs into words.[3] Attention to space here discloses a desire to escape from temporality and overcome the ephemeral and transitory nature of the spoken word. As in the case of John's Revelation, the fluctuations of time are held in check to the extent that space prevails, fixing the world in an order conducive to reflection and introspection.

At the same time, the realm of "silent"[4] and private reading as practiced by the laity from the mid-thirteenth century on is not without its dangers, one of which is the possible (ab)use of images for personal delectation. As both Saenger and Camille point out, the emergence of an increasingly individual sphere of reading goes hand in hand with the beginnings of pornography: whence the rise of a mode of censorship whose goal was to prevent readers from turning into voyeurs. From demonic grotesques to tortures of naked female martyrs down to scenes of human coupling, fifteenth-century censors proceeded to edit and expurgate, by excising or emasculating, any image that could run counter to decency and fascinate the reader (in connection with the alternative meaning of "fascinum" as phallus). Our culture "of shame and modesty" arrived in this way, and with it, "visual conformism, a policing of the gaze, that is fundamental to modernity."[5] It is obvious, therefore, that the development of literacy and the ensuing centrality

[2] Krieger adds: "The very word 'illumination,' with all of its connotations of Platonic light, encouraged the letter, as well as the word and the text into which it opened, to take on a transcendent character that could allow it to make its transcendent claims": *Ekphrasis*, 116.

[3] Paul Saenger, *Space Between Words: The Origins of Silent Reading* (Stanford: Stanford University Press, 1997), 252. On *scriptio continua* see also M. B. Parkes, *Pause and Effect* (Aldershot: Scolar Press, 1992), 9–29.

[4] Reading in the Middle Ages was not unconditionally silent to the extent that this activity entailed pronouncing aloud the written signs of a text. Moreover, the practice of "silent" reading does not mark the definitive triumph of sight over voice. As Hans Ulrich Gumbrecht observes, even for the poets of the late Middle Ages—and Gumbrecht cites Eustache Deschamps—"Plus seur est de parler que d'escripre" ("speaking is more reliable than writing"): "La voix comme forme: topique de l'auto-mise en scène dans la poésie lyrique aux XIVe et XVe siècles," in *L'Hostellerie de Pensée*, ed. Zink and Bohler, 215–32.

[5] Camille, "Obscenity Under Erasure," 152, 154. Camille links the birth of private reading and individualism to that of authoritarian scopic regimes which henceforth prescribe that which can or cannot be seen, thereby inaugurating the unholy alliance of vision, violence, and obscenity. Gail McMurray Gibson studies the connection between the seen and the obscene in the performance of medieval childbirth: "Scene and Obscene: Seeing and Performing Late Medieval Childbirth," *Journal of Medieval and Early Modern Studies* 29 (1999): 7–24. For Chidester (*Word and Light*, 132), the triumph of visualism dates from the sixteenth century, when "eyes and ears defined independent fields of discourse, knowledge, and power divorced from their [. . .] convergence and interpretation in any symbolic synesthesia."

of visualism did not entail the emergence of a henceforth "noiseless" society in the sense of harmonious democracy.[6]

Noise understood as perturbation is in reality a-historical; and perturbation itself is always ambivalent. Sounds may thus endanger the equilibrium of a human body, just as they may restore it. In antiquity, for example, experts in medicine from Pythagoras to Galen were firm believers in the curative value of sounds.[7] In more recent times, medical research has developed a method called sympathicotherapy, which relies on sonorous vibrations to stimulate cells, release the patient's tensions, and regenerate his or her organism.[8] Also noteworthy is the claim made by a number of contemporary scientific theories (some of which are briefly reviewed in the Introduction) that noise is a basic component of order.[9] Conversely, sounds may have devastating effects, ranging from such illnesses as

[6] Confirmation that violence is not exclusive to orally-based cultures has been drawn from the fact, expounded by Raynaud (*La Violence au Moyen Âge*, 55–56, 112), that there are few images of violence in thirteenth-century manuscripts, whereas they abound in manuscripts dating from the fourteenth and fifteenth centuries, as a reflection of the "cruelty" characterizing the period.

[7] Although medical theoreticians (e.g., Caelius Aurelian, fifth century B.C., and Soranus, first century A.D.) were not all in favor of musicotherapy, many believed in its healing value, consistent with a conception of music in terms of proportion. According to Herophilus (a famous Alexandrian doctor in the early third century B.C., whose work is lost and known only through citations by later authors), listening to music may regulate the rhythm of the pulse (eurhythmicity) and cure such pathologies as cacorhythmicity (when the pulse beats contrary to the norm) or pararhythmicity (when the rhythm of the pulse is not consistent with the patient's age): Jackie Pigeaud, *Folie et cures de la folie chez les médecins de l'antiquité gréco-romaine: la manie* (Paris: Les Belles Lettres, 1987), 152–62. During the medieval period, vocal or instrumental music was viewed as the best means to cure such mental disorders as frenzy, mania, and especially melancholy: Jean-Marie Fritz, *Le discours du fou au Moyen Age, XIIe-XIIIe siècles* (Paris: Presses Universitaires de France, 1992), 143.

[8] The method of sympathicotherapy was introduced in the 1880s by Doctor Bonnier. Recognizing the power of sounds in either paralyzing or curing his patients, Bonnier sought out the assistance of an individual gifted with excellent hearing in order to help him control his technique. To find this individual, Bonnier consulted Camille Saint-Saëns, who was then director of the Conservatory of Music in Paris.

[9] See the review—and criticism—of chaos theories (such as those developed by Jacques Monod, Edgar Morin, Henri Atlan, and Ilya Prigogine) by René Thom, "Halte au hasard, silence au bruit," *Le Débat* 3 (1980): 119–32. Thom contests the view according to which order derives from random fluctuations: although those play a role in determining the evolution that emerges from a variety of possibilities, they do not also create it.

tinnitus,[10] and such social plagues as noise pollution,[11] to such information glut as the "data smog" to which we are increasingly exposed.[12]

Audition and, in fact, the entire sensorium inspired, as we have seen, a similarly ambivalent treatment during the medieval period. On the one hand, the co-mingling of perceptual categories in religious synesthesia was viewed as a worthy mode of experiencing the divine in its all-encompassing reality. The ethical value assigned to *syn*esthesia indicates that here the senses operate transcendentally and contribute to the spiritualization of the human experience.[13] In the religious perspective, the emphasis is on the principle of synthesis in holding together (*syn*) and connecting all the elements of God's creation. Heaven consequently represents the promise of an ecstasy wherein the five senses combined will provide the soul with spiritual nutrient, be it the bread of angels (A. E. Nichols, "The Bread of Heaven," in *The Iconography of Heaven*, ed. Davidson, 40–68), the fragrance of Paradise (Clifford Davidson, "Heaven's Fragrance," 100–27), its brightness (Philip Butterworth, "The Light of Heaven," 128–45), or its music (Richard Rastall, "The Musical Repertory," 162–96).

By contrast, syn*esthesia* in its secular usage was viewed as a transgressive activity inasmuch as the emphasis is on the aesthetic pleasure that one derives from sensory interpenetration.[14] At the hands of secular entertainers, the co-mingling of perceptual categories capitalizes on *aesthesia* as, etymologically, the realm of both sensation and sensationalism. An example in the later Middle Ages is the

---

[10] Much more severe than what is known as the "cocktail party syndrome," tinnitus is an uncontrollable hissing or ringing in the ears. Relief comes in the form of hearing-aid devices: being fed with white noise, the brain is trained to treat the sounds of tinnitus as mere background noise, to be ignored as city dwellers ignore traffic sounds. Acknowledging that sounds are not all therapeutic, Pythagoras distinguishes between the trumpet, which irritates and agitates, and the soothing effect of the song: Jackie Pigeaud, *La maladie de l'âme* (Paris: Les Belles Lettres, 1981), 324.

[11] The earth creates such an amount of microwave noise (as generated by airport radars, garage-door openers, and cellular phones) that we may soon not be able to hear above our own din.

[12] It comes as no surprise that inventors like Ray Dolby (who rid the recording world of dirty sound) are perceived as modern heroes, nor that research centers are being created in order to analyze the problem of noise pollution. Nantes (France) shelters a center for the study of "Sonorous Surroundings and the Quality of Downtown Life"; and Paris an "Urban and Architecture Acoustics Group," sponsored by the University (Paris VI) and the National Center of Scientific Research (CNRS).

[13] John of Damascus can thus write of "embracing the icon with the eyes as well as the lips," and Plotinus speak of the mind "grasping" the figures represented in a distant mosaic: Nelson, "To Say and to See," 153.

[14] Thus Robert Mannyng warns against the good music produced by minstrels as being "harmful to the soul [because it] gives way to an appreciation of its beauties at a purely sensual level [and becomes] the path to carnal vice" (Rastall, "The Sounds of Hell," 114–15).

artist's freedom in composing, say, a figure "half-man, half-horse, as he pleases, according to his *fantasia*" (Camille, "Before the Gaze," 213). This definition of the artist also reflects, in my view, the concept of invention as practiced by court entertainers during the earlier Middle Ages. Authors of the mythical and imaginative literary tradition display their creativity in proportion to their talent in joining and connecting that which is supposed to remain separate and distinct. In a preceding chapter, I have described as *entremés* those secular artifacts which combine sensory modes in ways that undermine the hierarchical world view developed in the discourse of orthodoxy. From the latter's standpoint, the coupling of a horse and a man is an aberration, and its result, a monster that should either remain unseen and be relegated to the periphery (antipodes) of the rational world, or should be exposed (*monstrare*, to show) as a negative model exemplar.

And thus we are back, it seems, to visualism as an allegedly optimal means to achieve perspective and perspicacity. In reality, however, the monster's public exposure operates according to the scapegoating process on which social order is typically grounded. The primary function of exposure is thus to confirm the distinction between monster and viewers, that is, between difference and similarity. The resulting spectacle does not in that sense call upon the agency of a dispassionate and detached eye, for, although the onlookers are under the impression that they stand at a safe distance from the creature thus exposed, they are irremediably involved in the scene as active participants. As etymology reminds us, abstraction does not mean "taking leave" so much as it means "tearing" into pieces (Michel Serres, *Les cinq sens* [Paris: Grasset, 1985], 23), suggesting that true cognition is not an abstract exercise but should rely on tact, that is, on one's capacity to touch upon an idea and leave it intact.[15] In Serres' definition ("Noise," *Le Débat* 15 [1981]: 94–101, here 95), we recall, the true scholar is a cross-disciplinary navigator who brings together the past and the present, who remembers, and who *listens*. But if knowledge entails paying attention to the sounds of the world, then the problem is that our language is now noise-free, "exempt of tempests, sound, and fury," and sterile and icy "as a result of having chased away many a beautiful noisome phenomenon." Serres here plays on the title of a painting, "La Belle Noiseuse," which is supposed to become the masterpiece of Frenhofer, the protagonist of Balzac's *Le chef d'oeuvre inconnu* (1832). Like Pygmalion, Frenhofer seeks not only to depict a beautiful woman but also to give life to Beauty. His enterprise leads to absolute failure because the painting is a chaotic

[15] To the etymological connection between "touch" (tactile) and "tact" correspond the connections between hearing ("entendre") and understanding ("comprendre"), seeing ("voir") and knowing ("savoir"), smelling and feeling ("sentir"), and taste ("saveur") and knowledge ("savoir") in confirming the sensory basis of cognition. Playing on the word "sapere" in indicating both the act of tasting and the state of being wise, Nicholas of Cusa thus affirmed in 1450 that "nothing tastes sweeter to the intellect than wisdom": *Idiota de sapentia et de mente*, trans. M. L. Führer (Toronto: University of Toronto, Centre for Reformation and Renaissance Studies, 1989), 25.

accumulation of hues and colors that do not combine into shape but constitute a formless confusion. For Serres, the truth of Frenhofer's masterpiece resides in a disorder which, far from being negative, generates meaning and order according to chaos theory. In this perspective, noise is both harmony and fury; and the only true language is the one which remembers the dual character of culture as an open sea that may either unite or divide.

For lack of adequate competence, I leave to Serres the role of navigator between humanistic culture and scientific culture. More modestly, I suggest that Frenhofer's primary challenge lies in his attempt to translate noise into vision. If the "Belle Noiseuse" embodies the sonorous and vibrant reality of fluctuation, then its transcription into hues and colors cannot but freeze that which is supposed to move, modulate, and mutate creatively. In truth, any form of translation (including Frenhofer's pictorial language and my own incursion into the textuality of noise) ends in silencing, by fixing and shaping, or by dissecting and analyzing, the "noisome" fluidity of existence in the nautical sense of the word.

It takes a genius to sing of laughter in tears and seriously mock gravity. Such is the voice of François Villon in the fifteenth century, whose vitality and vibrancy are still perceptible even by our deficient ears, unaccustomed as those have become to listen to a text. Thus Villon begins his *Lais* (Legacy; 1456) by lamenting his fate at the hands of a cruel lady, because her deceptively sweet looks have made him prisoner with a glance ("Le regart de celle m'a prins," ed. Longnon and Foulet, l. 33). Borrowing the rhetoric of traditional love poetry, Villon evokes how he has become a martyred lover for having gazed at the beauty of his beloved. This agony prompts him to draw up his legacy and distribute one by one his meager possessions. To his friend and benefactor, Master Guillaume Villon, he will leave his renown (his "noise": "mon bruyt," l. 69), which in context seems to refer to the fame he achieved as courtly poet in the high style. *Bruyt*, then, appears to summarize the chronicle of Villon's life, in reference to the gaze of loving contemplation, to the lover's martyrdom in the face of an unresponsive beloved, to his ensuing creativity, down to the immortality of his name and, hence, his benefactor's name.

This seemingly noble discourse is at once undercut by Villon's selection of a word, *bruyt*, which evokes the murmur of rumor rather than the stridence of glory (*noise*). How could such a tiny sound guarantee the renown of either poet or benefactor? A response to this issue arises from the relatively minimal information we have on François, born Montcorbier, information which comes mainly from police records and draws a picture of scandalous behavior.[16] By 1456 his

[16] By the time he undertook to compose his *Lais* (1456), Villon had already been accused of having killed a priest (1455) and, a year later, of having stolen money from the College of Navarre. Later (1461), he will be forced to spend a summer in the prison of the bishop of Orléans, will be arrested in Paris for theft (1462), and will eventually be sentenced to death by

reputation was already well established, indicating that the "bruyt" alludes either to the slanders to which he owes his renown, or to the furtive existence that will ensure his survival. Not only does the word imply something other than the melodious or sonorous sounds of fame; it also is a wind of odorous significance, in reference to the stench produced by this type of bodily emission.[17] What Villon bequeaths is his body in its most pragmatic manifestation, and what his poem celebrates is life in its most realistic character. The "prison of love" ("tres amoureuse prison," l. 15) has, in reality, nothing to do with love but evokes, instead, the very real possibility that he will end in jail, a fate that will not effect the breaking of his heart ("mon cueur debriser," l. 16) so much as that of his body. Anticipating this event, Villon endeavors generously to distribute that which he does not possess, such as his renown to Guillaume, his heart in a casket to his beloved, and his sword, wealth, diamond, gloves, silk cape, and plump capon to the various dignitaries whose authority he endures. As to the poor souls of his sort, Villon bequeaths the Art of Memory ("l'Art de Memoire," l. 112), which is the poet's humorous way of allying with his companions in misfortune against any form of affectation, whether behavioral or stylistic in nature.

That memory equates here with pomposity and grandiloquence becomes clear when, later in the poem (ll. 286–304), Villon playfully confesses having lost any remembrance of those processes and devices which empower the true artist to write in the high style of poetry. The reason for his amnesia is the appearance of Lady Memory, who comes and steals from him every one of the categories that are the foundations of logic and thought, which she proceeds to hide in a chest of drawers.[18] Seemingly lamenting the loss of Opinion and other scholastic faculties of reason, Deduction along with Discrimination, Comparison, and Exposition, Villon surreptitiously celebrates the defeat of grandiloquence as delineated by the specific places which treatises on artificial memory assign to each internal sense. Forgetfulness of memorized knowledge (Oblivion) has for its benefit

hanging (1463). He was then thirty-two and henceforth vanished from history. For a recent list of scholarly works on Villon, see Jane H. M. Taylor, *The Poetry of François Villon: Text and Context* (Cambridge: Cambridge University Press, 2001), 207–25.

[17] Jean-Marie Fritz proposes a similar interpretation of Villon's "bruyt" as a noise of obscene significance: "L'horizon sonore de la poésie de François Villon," in *L'Hostellerie de Pensée*, ed. Zink and Bohler, 173–85, here 175.

[18] Villon now proceeds to detail the mental powers that are involved in transforming sense impressions into thought. This process entails the combined agency of common sense (*sensus communis*), imagination (*ymaginatio*, understood as the faculty to retain and process impressions), cognitive imagination (*cogitativa*) as the faculty to combine and connect, judgment (*estimativa*) as the faculty to perceive non-sensible intentions, and intellect (*vis memorativa*) as the highest of our internal senses: see Camille, "Before the Gaze," 200–1.

that it discloses the connection between each sensory perception ("montrer de sens l'aliance," l. 304),[19] as Sensation now awakens, stirring up Imagination, which in turn rouses all of Villon's organs and holds his upper part ("la souvraine partie," l. 299) in check. The rejection of bombast results in an experience of self as a unified being, alive and alert, open to the realm of sensible reality and hence all the more aware of the weight brought about by pretension. In Villon's experience, sentience is a matter of "sense and sensibility" or, more precisely, of senses and sensitivity. His simulated despair at having "forgotten" the art of memory bespeaks a contrary affirmation, wherein Villon claims his right to create his own "bruyt" so as to silence the noise of power and authority.[20]

Is Villon's claim supposed to be heard via oral transmission or through private reading? What kind of public did Villon mean to address? The vast scholarly corpus devoted to this singular poet proposes a variety of responses to those issues,[21] many of which point to the less than "popular" character of Villon's work (Taylor, *The Poetry of François Villon*, 3–5). Undoubtedly, only experts in literary, social, and religious conventions could fully appreciate his humorous take on those conventions and savor his sardonic assessments of contemporary dignitaries. It also appears that Villon intended to exclude from his public anyone who was uninitiated in the street-life of Parisian students, their taste for practical jokes and revelries, and their reliance on a peculiar jargon. Thus it may be that Villon the "vile" and "villain" had in mind to amuse his fellows in pleasure and misery by

[19] André Lanly (in Villon, *Oeuvres*, ed. idem [Paris: Champion, 1991], 76–77) proposes a reading of l. 304 ("montrer de Sens la liance") which provides an opposite interpretation of the role of Oblivion. In his view, forgetfulness of memorized knowledge has an alienating rather than connecting effect to the extent that it "binds" ("liance") one's rational faculty: for, according to Lanly, "Sens" designates here not the senses but the spirit (*anima intellectiva*).

[20] Villon's work (including the *Lais* and the *Testament*, written during the winter of 1461–1462) "stands out among all the medieval texts known to us as a particularly scorn[ful] albeit witty discourse which cries out for justice and finds it in the pleasure of the 'last word.' [What Villon claims is] the right to speak uninterrupted": Rouben C. Cholakian, "The (Un)naming Process in Villon's *Grand Testament*," *French Review* 66 (1992): 216–28, here 225. The pleasure of Villon's voice also has to do with its cross-sensory quality, inducing the poet to compose a ballad wherein he calls upon his five senses to speak in his favor, for the "tongue" alone is an insufficient advocate. The ballad, in which Villon asks for a three days' delay, is addressed to the court which pronounced his banishment from Paris in 1463 (ed. and trans. Galway Kinnell [Boston: Houghton Mifflin, 1977], 212–15, 242).

[21] See Robert D. Peckham, "The Current State of Villon Studies: Part XI," *Fifteenth-Century Studies* 23 (1997): 258–78.

providing them with *entremés* to be recited in taverns and accompany their drinking dark wine ("vin morillon," *Testament*, l. 2022).

Indeed, Villon's poems combine literacy and orality in ways that call attention to the aural power of his work.[22] Reminiscing over his imprisonment at the hands of the bishop of Orléans (in the summer of 1461), Villon begins his *Testament* with a sarcastic evocation of the dignitary as the cause of his many pains (ll. 5–30). The poet develops his satire through phonic ambiguity, an example of which is his use of a word ("seignant," l. 7: to sign or to bleed) which describes a typical gesture (episcopal blessing through the signing of the cross) at the same time that it invokes Thibaut's parasitic authority (bleeding the poor of the streets). A similar ambiguity occurs at the following line ("Soubz la main Thibault d'Aucigny") by means of an untraditional placement of the caesura, which ends in decapitating his persecutor ("Thi/bault"), whose beheaded body now focuses on the bishop's lowly function ("bault," or "baud," as debauched and lascivious). It is again through an unorthodox use of the caesura that Villon calls upon God's justice to inflict on Thibault the very fate that the bishop imposed on others ("Luy soit donc semblable a ce compte," l. 28). In severing the central word of the line ("sem/blable"), Villon expresses aurally his hope that God may be "without" forgiveness ("sem" heard as "sans") toward a man whose words never cohere with his actions, to such an extent that episcopal preaching is nothing other than rubbish, in reference to the claptrap ("blabla" as obtained through the conflation of "blable" and "a") which now resonates in the second part of the line. As indirectly voiced by Thibault ("l'Eglise nous dit," l. 28: "the Church tells us"), God's Word is transformed into self-interested discourse, but Villon manipulates in his turn the bishop's verbal manipulation by turning episcopal dignity and

[22] As Fritz notes ("L'horizon sonore," 173–85), what characterizes Villon's work is the preponderance of noisy phenomena, beginning with the "bruyt" that constitutes the first of the gifts he bequeaths in his *Lais*, down to the ring of the bell of the Sorbonne that concludes the poem. A similarly sonorous "horizon" is found in Villon's *Testament*, which opens with the fictitious romance of the *Pet au Deable* (the Devil's fart), which he gives to his father, and ends with an evocation of the bell of Notre-Dame. For Claude Thiry, by contrast, Villon's poetry is grounded on the visual: "François Villon, poète du visuel," in *L'Hostellerie de Pensée*, ed. Zink and Bohler, 439–57. On the basis of the lexicon established by André Burger (*Lexique complet de la langue de Villon* [Geneva: Droz, 1974]), Thiry thus underscores the prevalence of a visual imagery wherein showing ("faire voir") equates with understanding ("faire savoir"). The divergence between Fritz's aural perspective and Thiry's visual approach testifies to the complexity of the manuscript tradition in which Villon's work is preserved. The multiplicity of variants that characterizes this tradition indicates that "analyzing Villon's poetry remains an open process" (Thiry, "Poète du visuel," 441). The *Testament* has been called "as polyphonic as the music of his day": Robert D. Peckham, "Incorporational Mechanics for Patterns of Self-Imaging Discourse in Villon's *Testament*," cited from http://globegate.utm.edu/french/globegate_mirror/aubiovil.html.

sermon upside down.[23] In contrast to the bombast and pompousness characterizing the representatives of high society, in Villon's experience lightness of being equates with a capacity to distance oneself from the noise of rhetorical and social affectation. It is noteworthy that, in the passage from Jean de Meun quoted at the opening of this Conclusion, the warrior holding his sword "san fere noise" is Mendacity itself in its most stealthy and lethal skill.[24] At the opposite of authoritarian or eristic eloquence is Villon's realistic "bruyt" as well as the "douce et plessant" noise—mentioned in Guillaume de Lorris' version of the *Roman de la Rose*[25]—of those brooks which sing of life in terms of a harmonious fluency.

On the basis of Villon's work, we may hypothesize that phonic phenomena distinguish those texts which, regardless of their origin, date, and metric form, qualify as "popular" by virtue of the collective circumstances that preside over their transmission or reception. Whether of a high or low caliber, in my definition popular culture has for its chief characteristic that it expresses the wisdom of the *vox populi* in its most universal intuition. Mythical and imaginative literature refers in that sense to the power of *fantasia*—as cultivated, among others, by the authors of the early French tradition—in speaking the language of both body and mind. The acumen of many of the Old French texts analyzed in this book consists, therefore, in acknowledging the cross-sensory character of cognition in enabling us to make sense of the world. In the final analysis this book was not, after all, an acoustemological journey so much as an incursion into the synesthesic value of *symbolos* understood as the capacity to interact and connect. What does the study of noise (in its synesthesic function) tell us about literature, and what does literature tell us about noise? Both warn us against the sterile and icy effect of theoretical discourse in classifying and, hence, ossifying life's ambiguities. Both remind us of the need to repossess our mother tongues in their polyvalent significance. And both encourage us to recognize our fundamentally noisy nature such that noise can turn into a life-sustaining, sense-producing energy.

---

[23] Like the mock sermons analyzed by Merceron ("Obscenity and Hagiography," 338), Villon undermines from within "the linguistic fabric of religious discourse" by highlighting "any possible bawdy syllables in church Latin or in the French vernacular."

[24] The name of this allegory is Ben Celer ("Skillful Concealment," trans. Dahlberg).

[25] Jean de Meun's reinscription of Guillaume's Rose indicts the courtly tradition as a language of abusive and ultimately sterile eloquence; see Jean's description of "fole loquence" as a mode of speaking that *bret*, *crie*, *noise*, and *tence* (howls, shouts, quarrels, and attacks, ll. 12181–12182). By contrast, Guillaume beautifies reality, including the love experience, such that life is noiseless, and *noise* in the main melodious.

WORKS CITED

Primary Materials

Alan of Lille. *De planctu Naturae*. Trans. James J. Sheridan. *The Plaint of Nature*. Toronto: Pontifical Institute of Mediaeval Studies, 1980.

Alcuin. *Epistolae. Epistola* 166. *Patrologia Latina* 100: 437–38.

Ambrose of Milan. *De Paradiso*. Trans. John J. Savage. In *Saint Ambrose: Hexameron, Paradise, and Cain and Abel*, 287–356. New York: Fathers of the Church, 1961.

Apocalypse. Ed. Paul Meyer. "Version Anglo-Normande en vers de l'Apocalypse." *Romania* 25 (1896): 174–257.

———. Ed. H. A. Todd. "The Old French Versified Apocalypse of the Kerr Manuscript." *PMLA* 18 (1903): 535–77.

———. Ed. Yorio Otaka and Hideka Fukui. *Apocalypse Anglo-Normande (Cambridge Trinity College Ms. R. 16. 2)*. Osaka: Centre de Recherches Anglo-Normandes, 1977.

Aristotle. *The Complete Works of Aristotle. The Revised Oxford Translation*. Ed. Jonathan Barnes. 2 vols. Princeton: Princeton University Press, 1985.

Augustine. *City of God* (16. 31), trans. Demetrius B. Zema and Gerald G. Walsh. vol. 6. Washington, D. C.: Catholic University of America Press, 1962.

———. *Confessions*. Ed. and trans. Pierre de Labriolle. Paris: Les Belles Lettres, 1969.

———. *Contra Judeos, Paganos*. *Patrologia Latina* 42:1117–1130.

———. *De doctrina christiana*. Trans. D. W. Robertson. *On Christian Doctrine*. Indianapolis: The Library of Liberal Arts, 1981.

———. *De Genesi ad litteram*. *Patrologia Latina* 34: 219–486.

———. *De libero arbitrio* (3.25.74). *Patrologia Latina* 32: 1307.

———. *Expositions of the Psalms* (Ps. 54: 11). In *The Works of Saint Augustine*, trans. and notes Maria Boulding, 3 pt. 17: 64–65. Hyde Park, NY: New City Press, 2001.

———. *Tractatus in Johannem* (6: 10). *Patrologia Latina* 35: 1429–1430.

Balzac, Honoré de. *Le Chef-d'oeuvre inconnu*. Ed. Pierre-Georges Castex et al. *Balzac, La Comédie Humaine*, vol. 10. Etudes Philosophiques. Bibliothèque de La Pléiade. Paris: Gallimard, 1979. Trans. Anthony Rudolf. *Balzac. Gillette or The Unknown Masterpiece*. London: The Menard Text, 1988.

Bataille de Caresme et de Charnage. Ed. Grégoire Lozinski. Paris: Champion, 1933.

Bernard de Ventadorn. *Cansos*. Ed. and trans. Frederick Goldin. In *Lyrics of the Troubadours and Trouvères*, 126–59. Garden City, NY: Doubleday, 1973.

Béroul. *Roman de Tristan*. Ed. and trans. Jean-Charles Payen. In *Les Tristan en vers*, 3–141. Paris: Garnier, 1974.

Bible. *King James Version*. Comp. and ed. Spiros Zodhiates. Grand Rapids, MI: Baker Book House, 1984.

———. *Bible de Jérusalem*. Paris: Cerf, 1955.

———. *Bible Moralisée*. Ed. and comm. Gerald B. Guest. *Bible Moralisée. Codex Vindobonensis 2554 Vienna, Österreichische Nationalbibliothek*. London: Harvey Miller, 1995.

———. Genesis. *La Bible française du XIIIe siècle. Edition critique de la Genèse*. Ed. Michel Quereuil. Geneva: Droz, 1988.

———. Macé de la Charité. *Bible*. Ed. P. E. R. Verhuyck. *La Bible de Macé de la Charité*. Vol. 2: *Lévitique, Nombres, Deutéronome, Josué, Juges*. Leiden: University Press of Leiden, 1977.
———. *Novum Testamentum Graece et Latine*. Ed. Erwin Nestle. Stuttgart: Württembergische Bibelanstalt, 1964.
Bonaventure. *Itinerarium Mentis in Deum*. Ed. and trans. Philotheus Boehner. New York: The Franciscan Institute, 1956.
Browning, Robert. *The Pied Piper of Hamlin: A Child's Story*. Illus. Hope Dunlap. Chicago and New York: Rand McNally Co., 1910
Chanson de Roland. Ed. Gérard Moignet. Paris: Bordas, 1969.
Chrétien de Troyes. *Erec et Enide* (Paris, BN fr. 794). Ed. Mario Roques. Paris: Champion, 1973. Paris, BN fr. 1376. Ed. by Jean-Marie Fritz. In *Chrétien de Troyes. Romans*, 55–283. Paris: Librairie Générale Française, 1994.
———. *Le Chevalier de la Charrette* (Paris, BN fr. 794). Ed. Mario Roques. Paris: Champion, 1983.
———. *Perceval* (Paris, BN fr. 12576). Ed. William Roach. Geneva: Droz, 1959. Berne 354. Ed. Charles Méla. In *Chrétien de Troyes. Romans*, 937–1211.
———. *Yvain ou le Chevalier au Lion* (Paris, BN fr. 794). Ed. Mario Roques). Paris: Champion, 1982. Paris, BN fr. 1433. Ed. David F. Hult. In *Chrétien de Troyes. Romans*, 705–936.
———. *Romans*. Trans. D. D. R. Owen. London: Dent, 1987.
Dante. *Inferno*. Ed. and trans. Charles S. Singleton. *Dante Alighieri. The Divine Comedy*. Princeton: Princeton University Press, 1980.
Gautier de Coinci. *Miracles of the Virgin Mary*. Ed. V. Frederik Koenig. *Les Miracles de Nostre Dame par Gautier de Coinci*. 4 vols. Geneva: Droz, 1966–1970. See also *Passion de Sainte Christine*.
Girart de Vienne, Chanson de Geste. Ed. Frederic G. Yeandle. New York: Columbia University Press, 1930.
Guillaume de Lorris. *Roman de la Rose*. See Jean de Meun.
Henri d'Arci. *Visio sancti Pauli*. Ed. L.-E. Kastner. *Revue des Langues Romanes* 48 (1905): 385–95. See also *Vision of Saint Paul*.
Hesiod. *Theogony*, and *Works and Days*. In *Hesiod. The Homeric Hymns and Homerica*. Ed. T. E. Page et al. Trans. Hugh E. Evelyn-White. Loeb Classical Library. London: Heinemann, and New York: Macmillan, 1914.
Hildegard of Bingen. *Epistolarium. Patrologia Latina* 197: 145–382.
Hyginus. *Poetic Astronomia*, 2.14. Trans. Theony Condos. In *Star Myths of the Greeks and Romans: A Sourcebook*, 142. Grand Rapids, MI: Phanes Press, 1997.
Jacques de Vitry. "Ad potentes et milites." In Jacques Le Goff, *L'imaginaire médiéval*, 258–59. Paris: Gallimard, 1985.
Jakemes. *Roman du Castelain de Couci et de la dame de Fayel*. Ed. Maurice Delbouille. Paris: Picard, 1936.
Jean de Meun. *Roman de la Rose*. Ed. Felix Lecoy. 3 vols. Paris: Champion, 1982–1985. Trans. Charles Dahlberg. *The Romance of the Rose*. Hanover and London: University Press of New England, 1983.
Jean Renart. *L'Escoufle* (Paris, Arsenal 6565). Ed. Franklin Sweetser. *Jean Renart. L'Escoufle, roman d'aventure*. Geneva: Droz, 1974.
Jeu d'Adam. Ed. Paul Aebischer. Geneva: Droz, 1964.
John Chrysostom. *Homilies on Genesis*. Trans. Robert C. Hill. Fathers of the Church 82. Washington, D. C.: Catholic University of America Press, 1990.
Livy. *Ab urbe condita*. Ed. and trans. B. O. Foster. Loeb Classical Library. Cambridge, MA: Harvard University Press, 1961.

Lucretius. *De rerum natura.* Ed. T. E. Page and E. Capps. Trans. W. H. D. Rouse. *Of the Nature of Things.* Loeb Classical Library. London: William Heinemann, and New York: Putnam, 1932.

Macé de la Charité. *Bible.* See Bible.

Marie de France. *Lais.* Ed. Karl Warnke. Trans. Laurence Harf-Lancner. Paris: Librairie Générale Française, 1990. Trans. Robert Hanning and Joan Ferrante. *The Lais of Marie de France.* Durham, NC: The Labyrinth Press, 1982.

Ménagier de Paris. Le Ménagier de Paris, Traité de Morale et d'Economie Domestique composé vers 1393 par un bourgeois parisien. Ed. and trans. Georgina E. Brereton and Janet M. Ferrier. Paris: Librairie Générale Française, 1994.

Miracles de Notre-Dame de Rocamadour au XIIe siècle. Trans. Edmond Albe, intro. Jean Rocachet, pref. Régine Pernoud. Toulouse: Le Pérégrinateur, 1996.

Nicholas of Cusa. *The Layman on Wisdom and the Mind.* Trans. with introduction and notes by M. L. Führer. Toronto: University of Toronto, Centre for Reformation and Renaissance Studies, 1989.

Orphic Hymns. Trans. A. N. Athanassakis. Baltimore: Johns Hopkins University Press, 1976.

Ovid. *Metamorphoses.* Trans. Joseph Chamonard. *Ovide. Les Métamorphoses.* Paris: Flammarion, 1966.

Passion de Sainte Agnès. Ed. Alexander Joseph Denomy. In *The Old French Lives of Saint Agnes and Other Vernacular Versions of the Middle Ages*, 65–98. Cambridge, MA: Harvard University Press, 1938.

Passion de Sainte Barbara. Ed. Alexander Joseph Denomy. "An Old French Life of Saint Barbara." *Mediaeval Studies* 1 (1939): 148–78.

Passion de Sainte Catherine d'Alexandrie. Ed. Henry Alfred Todd. "*La Vie de sainte Catherine d'Alexandrie*, as Contained in the Paris Manuscript 'La Clayette'." *PMLA* 15 (1900): 17–73.

Passion de Sainte Christine. Ed. Olivier Collet. *Gautier de Coinci: La Vie de Sainte Christine.* Geneva: Droz, 1999. Ed. Andreas C. Ott. *Gautier de Coincys Christinenleben nach den beiden Handschriften zu Carpentras und Paris.* Erlangen: Verlag von Junge, 1922.

Passion de Sainte Foy. Ed. Alfred T. Baker. "Vie anglo-normande de sainte Foy par Simon de Wasingham." *Romania* 66 (1940–1941): 49–84.

Passion de Sainte Marguerite. Ed. Aristide Joly. *La Vie de sainte Marguerite, poème inédit par Wace.* Caen and Rouen: Mémoires de la Société des Antiquaires de Normandie, 1879: 215–22.

Peredur. Trans. Jeffrey Gantz. "Peredur Son of Evrawg." In *The Mabinogion*, 217–57. New York: Dorset Press, 1985.

Perlesvaus. Ed. William A. Nitze and T. Atkinson Jenkins. 2 vols. Chicago: University of Chicago Press, 1932–1937; repr. New York: Phaeton Press, 1972.

Philippe de Beaumanoir. *The "Coutumes de Beauvaisis" of Philippe de Beaumanoir.* Trans. F. R. P. Akehurst. Philadelphia: University of Pennsylvania Press, 1992.

Plato. *The Collected Dialogues.* Ed. Edith Hamilton and Huntington Cairns. Princeton: Princeton University Press, 1989.

Queste del Saint Graal. Ed. Albert Pauphilet. Paris: Champion, 1984. Trans. P. M. Matarasso. *The Quest of the Holy Grail.* Harmondsworth: Penguin Books, 1986.

Pseudo-Renaut de Beaujeu. *Lai d'Ignaure.* Ed. Rita Lejeune. *Le Lai d'Ignaure ou le Lai du Prisonnier.* Bruxelles: Palais des Académies, 1938. Trans. Paul Brians. In *Bawdy Tales from the Courts of Medieval France*, 37–49. New York: Harper and Row, 1972.

Robert Biket. *Lai du Cor.* Ed. C. T. Erickson. *The Anglo-Norman Text of "Le Lai du Cor".* Oxford: Anglo-Norman Text Society, 1973.

Robert de Boron. *Le Roman de l'Estoire dou Graal.* Ed. William A. Nitze. Paris: Champion, 1983.

———. [prose rendition]. *Le Roman du Graal, manuscrit de Modène, par Robert de Boron.* Ed. Bernard Cerquiglini. Paris: Union Générale d'Edition, 1981.

Roman de Renart (Ms. C: Paris, BN fr. 1579, and Ms. M: Turin, Bibl. roy., varia 151). Ed. Naoyuki Fukumoto, Noboru Harano, and Satoru Suzuki. *Le Roman de Renart.* Tokyo: France Tosho, 1983.

Roman de Robert le Diable. Ed. E. Löseth. *Robert le Diable, roman d'aventures.* Paris: Didot, 1903.

Roman de Silence. Ed. and trans. Sarah Roche-Mahdi. *Silence. A Thirteenth-Century French Romance.* East Lansing, MI: Colleagues Press, 1992.

Songs of Holy Mary of Alfonso X, the Wise. Trans. Kathleen Kulp-Hill. MRTS 173. Tempe, AZ: MRTS, 2000.

Tertullian. *De cultu feminarum.* Ed. and trans. Marie Turgan. Paris: Cerf, 1971.

Thomas. *Roman de Tristan.* Ed. and trans. Jean-Charles Payen. In *Les Tristan en vers*, 145–244. Paris: Garnier, 1974.

Vie de Saint Alexis. Ed. Maurizio Perugi. *La Vie de Saint Alexis.* Geneva: Droz, 2000. Ed. Christopher Storey. *La Vie de Saint Alexis.* Oxford: Blackwell, 1968. Ed. Gaston Paris. *La Vie de Saint Alexis.* Paris: Champion, 1872.

Vie de Saint Gilles. Ed. Gaston Paris and Alphonse Bos. *La Vie de saint Gilles par Guillaume de Berneville. Poème du XIIe siècle publié d'après le manuscrit unique de Florence.* Paris: Firmin Didot, 1881.

Vie de Saint Jehan Paulus. Ed. Charles A. Williams and Louis Allen. *The German Legends of the Hairy Anchorite, with Two Old French Texts of "La Vie de Saint Jehan Paulus".* Urbana: University of Illinois Press, 1935.

Vie de Sainte Marie L'Egyptienne. Ed. Edmond Faral and Julia Bastin. *La Vie de Marie l'Egyptienne.* In *Oeuvres Complètes de Rutebeuf*, 2: 9–59. Paris: Picard, 1969.

Vie de Sainte Osyth. Ed. Alfred T. Baker. "An Anglo-French Life of St. Osith." *Modern Language Review* 6 (1911): 476–502.

Vie de Sainte Thaïs. Ed. F. Nau. "Histoire de Thaïs." *Annales du Musée Guimet* 30 (1903): 51–114.

Villon, François. Ed. and trans. Galway Kinnell. *The Poems of François Villon.* Boston: Houghton Mifflin Company, 1977.

———. Ed. and trans. André Lanly. *Villon: Oeuvres.* Paris: Champion, 1991.

———. Ed. and trans. Barbara N. Sargent-Baur. *François Villon. Complete Poems.* Toronto, Buffalo, and London: University of Toronto Press, 1994.

———. *Lais.* Ed. Auguste Longnon. Rev. Lucien Foulet. *François Villon. Oeuvres.* Paris: Champion, 1932.

———. *Testament.* Ed. Barbara Nelson Sargent. New York: Appleton-Century-Crofts, 1967.

Visio Tnudgali. Ed. V. H. Friedel and Kuno Meyer. *La Vision de Tondale (Tnudgal). Textes français, anglo-normand et irlandais.* Paris: Champion, 1907.

Vision of Saint Paul. Ed. L. E. Kastner. "Les versions françaises inédites de la descente de saint Paul en enfer." *Revue des Langues Romanes* 49 (1906): 49–62, 321–51, 427–50. See also Henri d'Arci.

Voyage of Saint Brendan. Ed. Ian Short and Brian Merrilees. *The Anglo-Norman Voyage of Saint Brendan.* Manchester: Manchester University Press, 1979.

Wace. *Roman de Rou.* Ed. J. Holden. 3 vols. Paris: Picard, 1970–1973.

Secondary Materials

Accarie, Maurice. "La mise en scène du *Jeu d'Adam.*" *Senefiance* 7 (1979): 3–16.
Ackerman, Diane. *A Natural History of the Senses.* New York: Vintage Books, 1990.
Anzieu, Didier. *Le Moi-peau.* Paris: Dunod, 1995.
Arendt, Hannah. *The Life of the Mind.* New York and London: Harcourt Brace Jovanovich, 1977.
Armstrong, Grace M. "Questions of Inheritance: *Le chevalier au lion* and *La Queste del Saint Graal.*" *Yale French Studies* 95 (1999): 171–92.
Aronstein, Susan. "Rewriting Perceval's Sister: Eucharistic Vision and Typological Destiny in the *Queste del San Graal.*" *Women's Studies* 21 (1992): 211–30.
Arthuriana 7 (1997) and 12 (2002): special issues on *Le Roman de Silence.*
Attali, Jacques. *Bruits: essai sur l'économie politique de la musique.* Paris: Presses Universitaires de France, 1977. Trans. Brian Massumi. *Noise: The Political Economy of Music.* Minneapolis: University of Minnesota Press, 1985.
Auerbach, Erich. *Mimésis. La Représentation de la réalité dans la littérature occidentale.* Trans. Cornélius Heim. Paris: Gallimard, 1968.
Aurell, Martin, Olivier Dumoulin, and Françoise Thelamon, eds. *La Sociabilité à table: Commensalité et convivialité à travers les âges.* Rouen: Publications de l'Université de Rouen, 1992.
Bailie, Gil. "Crossing the Jordan 'Opposite Jericho'. Ethnocentrism as a Response to the Sacrificial Crisis." Lecture presented in a colloquium on Violence and Religion at Stanford University, Spring 1992.
Baldwin, Charles Sears. *Ancient Rhetoric and Poetic.* New York: Macmillan, 1924.
Bailly, Anatole. *Dictionnaire Grec-Français.* Paris: Hachette, 1950.
Baumgartner, Emmanuèle. *L'Arbre et le pain: Essai sur la "Queste del saint graal."* Paris: Sedes, 1981.
Baun, Jane. "The Moral Apocalypse in Byzantium." In *Apocalyptic Time,* ed. Albert L. Baumgarten, 241–67. Leiden: Brill, 2000.
Beckerling, Philippa. "Perceval's Sister: Aspects of the Virgin in *The Quest of the Holy Grail* and Malory's *Sankgreal.*" In *Constructing Gender: Feminism and Literary Studies,* ed. Hilary Fraser and R. S. White, 39–54. Nedlands, Western Australia: University of Western Australia Press, 1994.
Benoist, J. O. "Le Gibier dans l'alimentation seigneuriale." In *Manger et boire au Moyen Âge: Actes du Colloque de Nice (15–17 octobre 1982),* ed. Denis Menjot, 75–87. Paris: Belles Lettres, 1984.
Berlin, Brent, and Paul Kay. *Basic Color Terms: Their Universality and Evolution.* Berkeley and Los Angeles: University of California Press, 1969.
Biernoff, Suzannah. *Sight and Embodiment in the Middle Ages.* Houndmills: Palgrave Macmillan, 2002.
Birren, Faber. *The Story of Color from Ancient Mysticism to Modern Science.* Westport, CT: The Crimson Press, 1941.
Bloch, R. Howard. "Modest Maidens and Modified Nouns: Obscenity in the Fabliaux." In *Obscenity. Social Control and Artistic Creation in the European Middle Ages,* ed. Jan M. Ziolkowski, 293–307. Leiden: Brill, 1998.
———. "The Lay and the Law." *Stanford French Review* 14 (1990): 181–210.
Bloom, Harold. *The Western Canon: The Books and School of the Ages.* New York: Harcourt, 1994.

Blumenberg, Hans. "Light as a Metaphor for Truth. At the Preliminary Stage of Philosophical Concept Formation." In *Modernity and the Hegemony of Vision*, ed. David Michael Levin, 30–62. Berkeley, Los Angeles, and London: University of California Press, 1993.

Bohler, Danielle. "La Discrète." In *L'Hostellerie de Pensée. Etudes sur l'art littéraire au Moyen Âge offerts à Daniel Poirion par ses anciens élèves*, ed. Michel Zink and eadem, 75–84. Paris: Presses de l'Université de Paris-Sorbonne, 1995.

Bolman, Elizabeth S. "*De Coloribus*: The Meaning of Color in Beatus Manuscripts." *Gesta* 38 (1999): 22–34.

Bonting, Sjoerd L. *Chaos Theology. A Revised Creation Theology.* Ottawa: Saint Paul University, 2002.

Bost, Hubert. *Babel. Du texte au symbole.* Geneva: Labor et Fides, 1985.

Braudy, Leo. *The Frenzy of Renown: Fame and its History.* New York: Oxford University Press, 1986.

Bregman, A. S. *Auditory Scene Analysis: The Perceptual Organization of Sound.* Cambridge, MA: MIT Press, 1990.

Brown, Howard Mayer, and Richard Freeman. "Jannequin, Clément." In *New Grove Dictionary of Music and Musicians*, 12:795–99. 29 vols. London: Macmillan, 2001.

Brown, Peter. "Images as a Substitute for Writing." In *East and West: Modes of Communication*, ed. Evangelos Chrysos and Ian Wood, 15–34. Leiden: Brill, 1999.

———. *The Cult of the Saints: Its Rise and Function in Latin Christianity.* Chicago: University of Chicago Press, 1981.

Bruckner, Mathilda Tomaryn. "Rewriting Chrétien's *Conte du graal* – Mothers and Sons: Questions, Contradictions, and Connections." In *The Medieval Opus: Imitation, Rewriting, and Transmission in the French Tradition,* ed. Douglas Kelly, 213–44. Amsterdam and Atlanta: Rodopi, 1996.

———. *Shaping Romance. Interpretation, Truth, and Closure in Twelfth-Century French Fictions.* Philadelphia: University of Pennsylvania Press, 1993.

Brumble, David. *Classical Myths and Legends in the Middle Ages and Renaissance.* Westport, CT: Greenwood Press, 1998.

Brun, Jean. *L'homme et le langage.* Paris: Presses Universitaires de France, 1985.

Brundage, James A. "Obscene and Lascivious: Behavioral Obscenity in Canon Law." In *Obscenity. Social Control and Artistic Creation in the European Middle Ages*, ed. Ziolkowski, 246–59.

Bruyne, Edgar de. *Etudes d'esthétique médiévale.* 3 vols. Bruges: De Tempel, 1946.

Bullington, Rachel. *The Alexis in the Saint Albans Psalter. A Look into the Heart of the Matter.* New York and London: Garland Publishing, 1991.

Bumke, Joachim. *Courtly Culture. Literature and Society in the High Middle Ages.* Trans. Thomas Dunlap. Berkeley, Los Angeles, and Oxford: University of California Press, 1991.

Burger, André. *Lexique complet de la langue de Villon.* Geneva: Droz, 1974.

Burns, E. Jane. "Devilish Ways: Sexing the Subject in the *Queste del Saint Graal.*" *Arthuriana* 8 (1998): 11–32.

———. *Bodytalk: When Women Speak in Old French Literature.* Philadelphia: University of Pennsylvania Press, 1993.

———. *Arthurian Fictions: Rereading the Vulgate Cycle.* Columbus: Ohio State University Press, 1985.

Burton-Christie, Douglas. *The Word in the Desert. Scripture and the Quest for Holiness in Early Christian Monasticism.* New York and Oxford: Oxford University Press, 1993.

Busby, Keith. "*Fabliaux* and the New Codicology." In *The World and Its Rival: Essays on Literary Imagination in Honor of Per Nykrog*, ed. Kathryn Karczewska and Tom Conley, 137–60. Amsterdam and Atlanta: Rodopi, 1999.

Butterworth, Philip. "The Light of Heaven: Flame as Special Effect." In *The Iconography of Heaven*, ed. Clifford Davidson, 128–45. Kalamazoo, MI: Medieval Institute Publications, 1994.

Bynum, Caroline Walker. *Holy Feast and Holy Fast: The Religious Significance of Food for Medieval Women*. Berkeley and Los Angeles: University of California Press, 1991.

Caillois, Roger. *Babel. Orgueil, confusion et ruine de la littérature*. Paris: Gallimard, 1948.

Calame-Griaule, Geneviève. *Ethnologie et langage. La parole chez les Dogon*. Paris: Institut d'Ethnologie, 1987.

Camille, Michael. "Before the Gaze: The Internal Senses and Late Medieval Practices of Seeing." In *Visuality Before and Beyond the Renaissance*, ed. Robert S. Nelson, 197–223. Cambridge: Cambridge University Press, 2000.

———. "Obscenity under Erasure: Censorship in Medieval Illuminated Manuscripts." In *Obscenity. Social Control and Artistic Creation in the European Middle Ages*, ed. Ziolkowski, 139–54.

———. "Philological Iconoclasm: Edition and Image in the *Vie de Saint Alexis*." In *Medievalism and the Modernist Temper*, ed. R. Howard Bloch and Stephen G. Nichols, 371–401. Baltimore: Johns Hopkins University Press, 1996.

Casagrande, Carla, and Silvana Vecchio. *Les Péchés de la langue: Discipline et éthique de la parole dans la culture médiévale*. Trans. Philippe Baillet. Paris: Cerf, 1991.

Caviness, Madeline H. "Obscenity and Alterity: Images That Shock and Offend Us/Them, Now/Then?" In *Obscenity. Social Control and Artistic Creation in the European Middle Ages*, ed. Ziolkowski, 155–75.

Cazelles, Brigitte. *The Unholy Grail: A Social Reading of Chrétien de Troyes's 'Conte du Graal'*. Stanford: Stanford University Press, 1996.

———. "Bodies on Stage and the Production of Meaning." *Yale French Studies* 86 (1994): 56–74.

———. "Mots à vendre, corps à prendre, et les troubadours d'Aquitaine." *Stanford French Review* 7 (1983): 27–36.

———. *Le corps de sainteté. D'après "Jehan Bouche d'Or," "Jehan Paulus" et quelques vies des XIIe et XIIIe siècles*. Geneva: Droz, 1982.

———. *La faiblesse chez Gautier de Coinci*. Saratoga, CA: Anma Libri, 1978.

Cerquiglini-Toulet, Jacqueline. *The Color of Melancholy. The Uses of Books in the Fourteenth Century*. Trans. Lydia G. Cochrane. Baltimore: Johns Hopkins University Press, 1997.

Chidester, David. *Word and Light. Seeing, Hearing, and Religious Discourse*. Urbana and Chicago: University of Illinois Press, 1992.

Cholakian, Rouben C. "The (Un)naming Process in Villon's *Grand Testament*." *French Review* 66 (1992): 216–28.

Classen, Constance. *World of Sense. Exploring the Senses in History and Across Cultures*. London and New York: Routledge, 1993.

———. "Creation by Sound / Creation by Light: A Sensory Analysis of Two South American Cosmologies." In *The Varieties of Sensory Experience. A Sourcebook in the Anthropology of the Senses*, ed. David Howes, 239–55. Toronto, Buffalo, and London: University of Toronto Press, 1991.

Clemente, Linda M. *Literary "Objets d'Art": "Ekphrasis" in Medieval French Romance, 1150–1210*. New York: Peter Lang, 1992.

Cohen, Jeffrey Jerome. *Of Giants: Sex, Monsters, and the Middle Ages*. Minneapolis and London: University of Minnesota Press, 1999.

Combarieu, Micheline de. "Manger (et boire) dans le *Roman de Renart*." In *Manger et boire au Moyen Âge: Actes du Colloque de Nice (15–17 octobre 1982)*, ed. Menjot, 415–28.

Cormillat, François. *"Or ne mens". Couleurs de l'Eloge et du Blâme chez les "Grands Rhétoriqueurs"*. Paris: Champion, 1994.

Crescenzo, Richard. *Peintures d'instruction. La postérité littéraire des "Images" de Philostrate en France de Blaise de Vigenère à l'époque classique*. Geneva: Droz, 1999.

Crist, Larry S. "Gastronomie et pornographie dans les fabliaux." In *Continuations. Essays in Medieval French Literature and Language in Honor of John L. Grigsby*, ed. Norris J. Lacy and Gloria Torrini-Roblin, 251–60. Birmingham, AL: Summa Publications, 1989.

Cytowic, Richard E. *The Man Who Tasted Shapes*. New York: Putnam, 1993.

Dahan, Gilbert. "Le Jugement dernier vu par les commentateurs des *Sentences*." In *De l'art comme mystagonie: iconographie du Jugement dernier et des fins dernières à l'époque gothique*. Actes du Colloque de la Fondation Hardt tenu à Genève du 13 au 16 février 1994 sous la direction d'Yves Christe, 19–35. Poitiers: Centre d'Etudes Supérieures de Civilisation Médiévale, 1999.

Davidson, Clifford. "Heaven's Fragrance." In *The Iconography of Heaven*, ed. idem, 110–27. Kalamazoo, MI: Medieval Institute Publications, 1994.

———. "The Fate of the Damned in English Art and Drama." In *The Iconography of Hell*, ed. idem and Thomas H. Seiler, 41–66. Kalamazoo, MI: Medieval Institute Publications, 1992.

Denasi, Marcel. "Thinking is Seeing: Visual Metaphors and the Nature of Abstract Thought." *Semiotica* 80 (1990): 221–37.

Delisle, Léopold, and Paul Meyer. *L'Apocalypse en français au XIIIe siècle*. Paris: Didot, 1899.

De Looze, L. "A Story of Interpretations: The *Queste del saint graal* as Metaliterature." *Romanic Review* 76 (1985): 129–47.

Derrida, Jacques. *Margins of Philosophy*. Trans. Alan Bass. Chicago: University of Chicago Press, 1982.

Dillard, Annie. "Teaching a Stone to Talk" (1982). Repr. in *This Sacred Earth. Religion, Nature, Environment*, ed. Roger S. Gottlieb, 32–36. New York and London: Routledge, 1996.

Dimock, Wai Chee. "A Theory of Resonance." *PMLA* 112 (1997): 1060–71.

Doob, Penelope Reed. *The Idea of the Labyrinth from Classical Antiquity through the Middle Ages*. Ithaca and London: Cornell University Press, 1990.

Doueihi, Milad. *A Perverse History of the Human Heart*. Cambridge, MA: Harvard University Press, 1997.

———. "The Lure of the Heart." *Stanford French Review* 14 (1990): 51–68.

Duby, Georges. *Les trois ordres ou l'imaginaire du féodalisme*. Paris: Gallimard, 1978.

———. "Les 'jeunes' dans la société aristocratique dans la France du Nord-Ouest au XIIe siècle." *Annales, Economies, Sociétés, Civilisations* 19 (1964): 835–46.

Duffy, Patricia Lynne. *Blue Cats and Chartreuse Kittens. How Synesthetes Color Their Worlds*. New York: Henry Holt, 2001.

Elias, Norbert. *La dynamique de l'Occident*. Trans. Pierre Kamnitzer. Paris: Calmann-Lévy, 1975.

Emmerson, Richard Kenneth, and Ronald B. Herzman. *The Apocalyptic Imagination in Medieval Literature*. Philadelphia: University of Pennsylvania Press, 1992.

Faral, Edmond. *Les Arts Poétiques du XIIe et du XIIIe siècle*. Paris: Champion, 1962.

Fein, David A. "*Le Latin Sivrai*: Problematic Aspects of Narrative Authority in Twelfth-Century French Literature." *French Review* 66 (1993): 572–83.
Feld, Steven. "Waterfalls of Song: An Acoustemology of Place Resounding in Bosavi, Papua New Guinea." In *Senses of Place*, ed. idem and K. H. Basso, 91–135. Santa Fe: School of American Research Press, 1996.
Ferrante, Joan. "'*Scribe quae vides et audis*': Hildegard, Her Language and Her Secretaries." In *The Tongue of the Fathers: Gender and Ideology in Twelfth-Century Latin*, ed. David Townsend and Andrew Taylor, 102–35. Philadelphia: University of Pennsylvania Press, 1998.
Fishler, Claude. *L'Homnivore: le goût, la cuisine et le corps*. Paris: Odile Jacob, 1990.
Fladerer, Ludwig. *Johannes Philoponos, De Opificio Mundi: Spätantikes Sprachdenken und christliche Exegese*. Stuttgart and Leipzig: Teubner, 1999.
Folkerth, Wes. *The Sound of Shakespeare*. London and New York: Routledge, 2002.
Foucault, Michel. "L'oeil du pouvoir." In *Michel Foucault: Dits et Ecrits, 1954–1988*, ed. Daniel Defert, François Ewald, and Jacques Lagrange, vol. 2: *1976–1988*, 190–207. Paris: Gallimard, 2001.
Frank, Georgia. *The Memory of the Eyes. Pilgrims to Living Saints in Christian Late Antiquity*. Berkeley, Los Angeles, and London: University of California Press, 2000.
———. "The Pilgrim's Gaze in the Age Before Icons." In *Visuality Before and Beyond the Renaissance*, ed. Nelson, 98–115.
Franz, Marie-Louise von. *Patterns of Creativity Mirrored in Creation Myths*. Dallas: Spring Publications, 1972.
Freeman, Michelle. *The Poetics of Translatio Studii and Conjointure: Chrétien de Troyes's "Cligès"*. Lexington, KY: French Forum Publishers, 1979.
Freeman-Regalado, Nancy. "La Chevalerie Celestiel: Spiritual Tranformations of Secular Romance in *La Queste del Saint Graal*." In *Romance. Generic Transformation from Chrétien de Troyes to Cervantes*, ed. Kevin Brownlee and Marina Scordilis Brownlee, 91–113. Hanover, NH, and London: University Press of New England, 1985.
———. "*Des Contraires Choses*. La fonction poétique de la citation et des *exempla* dans le *Roman de la Rose* de Jean de Meun." *Littérature* 41 (1981): 62–81.
Fritz, Jean-Marie. "L'horizon sonore de la poésie de François Villon." In *L'Hostellerie de Pensée*, ed. Zink and Bohler, 173–85.
———. *Le discours du fou au Moyen Âge, XIIe–XIIIe siècles*. Paris: Presses Universitaires de France, 1992.
Gellrich, Jesse M. *The Idea of the Book in the Middle Ages: Language Theory, Mythology, and Fiction*. Ithaca and London: Cornell University Press, 1985.
Gibson, Gail McMurray. "Scene and Obscene: Seeing and Performing Late Medieval Childbirth." *Journal of Medieval and Early Modern Studies* 29 (1999): 7–24.
Gleiser, Marcelo. *The Dancing Universe. From Creation Myths to the Big Bang*. New York: Dutton/Penguin Putnam, 1997.
Gonzalez-Crussi, Frank. *The Five Senses*. San Diego, New York, and London: Harcourt Brace Jovanovich, 1989.
Gouttebroze, Jean-Guy. *Le Précieux Sang de Fécamp. Origine et développement d'un mythe chrétien*. Paris: Champion, 2000.
Grabes, Herbert. *The Mutable Glass: Mirror-Imagery in Titles and Texts of the Middle Ages and the Renaissance*. Cambridge: Cambridge University Press, 1982.
Gravdal, Kathryn. *Vilain and Courtois: Transgressive Parody in French Literature of the Twelfth and Thirteenth Centuries*. Lincoln and London: University of Nebraska Press, 1989.

Graves, Robert. *The Greek Myths.* Volume 1. Harmondsworth: Penguin Books, 1960.
Grazia, Margreta de. "Homonyms Before and After Lexical Standardization." *Deutsche Shakespeare-Gesellschaft West Jahrbuch* (1990): 143–56.
Gregory, Timothy E. *Vox Populi: Popular Opinion and Violence in the Religious Controversies of the Fifth Century A. D.* Columbus: Ohio State University Press, 1979.
Gressman, Hugo. *The Tower of Babel.* New York: Jewish Institute of Religion Press, 1928.
Grieco, Allen J. "Le Thème du coeur mangé: l'ordre, le sauvage et la sauvagerie." In *La Sociabilité à table: Commensalité et convivialité à travers les âges*, ed. Aurell, Dumoulin, and Thelamon, 20–28.
Gross, Kenneth. *Shakespeare's Noise.* Chicago and London: University of Chicago Press, 2001.
Guerreau-Jalabert, Anita. "Les Nourritures comme figures symboliques dans les romans arthuriens." In *La Sociabilité à table: Commensalité et convivialité à travers les âges*, ed. Aurell, Dumoulin, and Thelamon, 35–40.
Gumbrecht, Hans Ulrich. "La voix comme forme: topique de l'auto-mise en scène dans la poésie lyrique aux XIVe et XVe siècles." In *L'Hostellerie de Pensée*, ed. Zink and Bohler, 215–32.
Gutton, Jean-Pierre. *Bruits et sons dans notre histoire: essai sur la reconstitution du paysage sonore.* Paris: Presses Universitaires de France, 2000.
Hagstrum, Jean H. *The Sister Arts: The Tradition of Literary Pictorialism and English Poetry from Dryden to Gray.* Chicago: University of Chicago Press, 1958.
Hahn, Cynthia Jean. *Portrayed on the Heart: Narrative Effect in Pictorial Lives of Saints from the Tenth through the Thirteenth Century.* Berkeley: University of California Press, 2001.
———. "*Visio Dei*: Changes in Medieval Visuality." In *Visuality Before and Beyond the Renaissance*, ed. Nelson, 169–96.
Haidu, Peter. *The Subject of Violence: The "Song of Roland" and the Birth of the State.* Bloomington: Indiana University Press, 1993.
Hall, Edward T. *The Hidden Dimension.* Garden City, NY: Anchor Books, 1982.
Harris, William V. *Ancient Literacy.* Cambridge, MA: Harvard University Press, 1989.
Hart, Mickey, and Fredric Lieberman. *Planet Drum.* New York: Harper Collins, 1991.
Harvey, Susan Ashbrook. *Holy Women of the Syrian Orient.* Berkeley: University of California Press, 1987.
Holsinger, Bruce. "The Color of Salvation. Desire, Death, and the Second Crusade in Bernard of Clairvaux's Sermons on the *Song of Songs*." In *The Tongue of the Fathers. Gender and Ideology in Twelfth-Century Latin*, ed. Townsend and Taylor, 156–86.
Horowitz, Jeannine. "La diabolisation de la sexualité dans la littérature du Graal au XIIIe siècle, le cas de la *Queste del Graal*." In *Arthurian Romance and Gender*, ed. Friedrich Wolfzettel, 238–50. Amsterdam and Atlanta: Rodopi, 1995.
Howes, David, ed. *The Varieties of Sensory Experience. A Sourcebook in the Anthropology of the Senses.* Toronto, Buffalo, and London: University of Toronto Press, 1991.
Hsia, Yun. "Whiteness Constancy as a Function of Difference in Illumination." *Archives of Psychology* 40 (1943): 5–63.
Hunt, Tony. *Villon's Last Will: Language and Authority in the Testament.* Oxford: Clarendon Press, 1996.
Huot, Sylvia. "Troubadour Lyric and Old French Narrative." In *The Troubadours: An Introduction*, ed. Simon Gaunt and Sarah Kay, 263–78. Cambridge: Cambridge University Press, 1999.

Ions, Veronica. *Indian Mythology*. New York: Peter Bedrick Books, 1984.
Jacoff, Rachel. "The Hermeneutics of Hunger." In *Speaking Images. Essays in Honor of V. A. Kolve*, ed. R. F. Yeager and C. C. Morse, 95–110. Asheville, NC: University of North Carolina Press, 2001.
Jaeger, Stephen C. *The Origins of Courtliness. Civilizing Trends and the Formation of Courtly Ideals, 939–1210*. Philadelphia: University of Pennsylvania Press, 1985.
Jager, Eric. *The Book of the Heart*. Chicago and London: The University of Chicago Press, 2000.
———. *The Tempter's Voice. Language and the Fall in Medieval Literature*. Ithaca and London: Cornell University Press, 1993.
James, Liz. *Light and Colour in Byzantine Art*. Oxford: Clarendon Press, 1996.
James-Raoul, Danièle. *La parole empêchée dans la littérature arthurienne*. Paris: Champion, 1997.
Jay, Martin. *Downcast Eyes: The Denigration of Vision in Twentieth-Century French Thought*. Berkeley, Los Angeles, and London: University of California Press, 1993.
———. "Scopic Regimes of Modernity." In *Vision and Visuality*, ed. Hal Foster, 3–28. Seattle: Bay, 1988.
Jeanneret, Michel. *Des mets et des mots: banquets et propos de table à la Renaissance*. Paris: Corti, 1987.
Jeanroy, Alfred. "Le théâtre religieux en langue française jusqu'à la fin du XIVe siècle." *Histoire Littéraire de la France* 39 (1962): 169–258.
Jeay, Madeleine. "Consuming Passions: Variations on the Eaten Heart Theme." In *Violence against Women in Medieval Texts*, ed. Anna Roberts, 75–96. Gainesville: University Press of Florida, 1998.
Jenks, Chris. "The Centrality of the Eye in Western Culture: An Introduction." In *Visual Culture*, ed. idem, 1–25. London: Routledge, 1995.
Johnson, Paul. *A History of the Jews*. New York: Harper and Row, 1987.
Jones, Robin F. "A Medieval Prescription for Performance: *Le Jeu d'Adam*." In *Performing Texts*, ed. Michael Issacharoff and idem, 101–15. Philadelphia: University of Pennsylvania Press, 1988.
Joshua, Essaka. *Pygmalion and Galatea: The History of a Narrative in English Literature*. Aldershot, Hants, Engl. and Burlington, VT: Ashgate, 2001.
Kaeuper, Richard W., ed. *Violence in Medieval Society*. Woodbridge, UK, and Rochester, NY: Boydell Press, 2000.
———. *Chivalry and Violence in Medieval Europe*. Oxford: Oxford University Press, 1999.
Karras, Ruth Mazo. "*Leccherous Songys*: Medieval Sexuality in Word and Deed." In *Obscenity. Social Control and Artistic Creation in the European Middle Ages*, ed. Ziolkowski, 233–45.
Kay, Sarah. "The Sublime Body of the Martyr: Violence in Early Romance Saints' Lives." In *Violence in Medieval Society*, ed. Kaeuper, 3–20.
Keen, Maurice. *Chivalry*. New Haven and London: Yale University Press, 1984.
Kelly, Douglas. *The Art of Medieval French Romance*. Madison: University of Wisconsin Press, 1992.
———. *Sens and conjointure in the "Chevalier de la Charrette."* The Hague: Mouton, 1966.
Kingsley, David R. *The Sword and the Flute. Kali and Krsna, Dark Visions of the Terrible and the Sublime in Hindu Mythology*. Berkeley, Los Angeles, and London: University of California Press, 1975.
Kinoshita, Sharon. "Heldris de Cornuälle's *Roman de Silence* and the Feudal Politics of Lineage." *PMLA* 110 (1995): 397–409.

Kittay, Jeffrey, and Wlad Godzich. *The Emergence of Prose: An Essay in Prosaics*. Minneapolis: University of Minnesota Press, 1987.
Krieger, Murray. *Ekphrasis: The Illusion of the Natural Sign*. Baltimore: Johns Hopkins University Press, 1992.
Krueger, Roberta L., ed. *The Cambridge Companion to Medieval Romance*. Cambridge: Cambridge University Press, 2000.
———. "Questions of Gender in Old French Courtly Romance." In *The Cambridge Companion to Medieval Romance*, ed. eadem, 132–49.
———. *Women Readers and the Ideology of Gender in Old French Verse Romance*. Cambridge: Cambridge University Press, 1993.
Lacy, Norris J. "The Evolution and Legacy of French Prose Romance." In *The Cambridge Companion to Medieval Romance*, ed. Krueger, 167–82.
———. ed. *Medieval Arthurian Literature: A Guide to Recent Research*. New York: Garland Publishers, 1996.
Laurioux, Bruno. *Les Livres de cuisine médiévaux*. Turnhout: Brepols, 1997.
Law, Vivien. *Grammar and Grammarians in the Early Middle Ages*. London: Longman, 1997.
———. *The Insular Latin Grammarians*. Woodbridge: Boydell Press, 1982.
Leach, Maria. *The Beginning. Creation Myths Around the World*. New York: Funk and Wagnalls, 1956.
Le Goff, Jacques. *L'imaginaire médiéval*. Paris: Gallimard, 1985.
Leroi-Gourhan, André. *Le geste et la parole*. Paris: Albin Michel, 1964.
Leupin, Alexandre. *Barbarolexis. Medieval Writing and Sexuality*. Cambridge, MA: Harvard University Press, 1989.
Levin, David Michael. Introduction to idem, *Modernity and the Hegemony of Vision*, 1–29. Berkeley, Los Angeles, and London: University of California Press, 1993.
———. *The Listening Self. Personal Growth, Social Change and the Closure of Metaphysics*. London and New York: Routledge, 1989.
Lévi-Strauss, Claude. *The Raw and the Cooked*. Trans. John and Doreen Weightman. New York: Harper & Row, 1990.
———. *The Origin of Table Manners*. Trans. John and Doreen Weightman. New York: Harper & Row, 1978.
Lewes, Ulle Erika. *The Life in the Forest: The Influence of the Saint Giles Legend on the Courtly Tristan Story*. Chattanooga, TN: Tristania Monograph Series, 1978.
Lewis, Clive Staples. *The Magician's Nephew*. New York: Macmillan, 1955.
———. *Perelandra*. New York: Macmillan, 1944.
———. *The Screwtape Letters*. New York: Macmillan, 1942.
Lewis, Suzanne. *Reading Images. Narrative Discourse and Reception in the Thirteenth-Century Illuminated Apocalypse*. Cambridge: Cambridge University Press, 1995.
———. "The English Gothic Illuminated Apocalypse, *lectio divina*, and the Art of Memory." *Word and Image* 7 (1991): 1–32.
Lincoln, Bruce. *Myth, Cosmos, and Society. Indo-European Themes of Creation and Destruction*. Cambridge, MA: Harvard University Press, 1986.
Lombard-Jourdan, Anne. *Fleur de Lis et Oriflamme. Signes célestes du royaume de France*. Paris: Presses du Centre National de la Recherche Scientifique, 1991.
———. *"Montjoie et saint Denis!": Le centre de la Gaule aux origines de Paris et de Saint-Denis*. Paris: Presses du Centre National de la Recherche Scientifique, 1989.
Looper, Jennifer E. "Gender, Genealogy, and the 'Story of the Three Spindles' in the *Queste del Saint Graal*." *Arthuriana* 8 (1998): 49–66.

Lorcin, Marie-Thérèse. "Manger et boire dans les fabliaux: rites sociaux et hiérarchie des plaisirs." In *Manger et boire au Moyen Âge: Actes du Colloque de Nice (15–17 octobre 1982)*, ed. Menjot, 227–37.

Lowden, John. *The Making of the "Bibles Moralisées", 1: The Manuscripts; 2: The Book of Ruth.* University Park, PA: Pennsylvania State University Press, 2000.

McCracken, Peggy. *The Curse of Eve, the Wound of the Hero: Blood, Gender, and Medieval Literature.* Philadelphia: University of Pennsylvania Press, forthcoming.

———. "Mothers in the Grail Quest: Desire, Pleasure, and Conception." *Arthuriana* 8 (1998): 35–48.

———. "'The Boy Who Was a Girl': Reading Gender in the *Roman de Silence*." *Romanic Review* 85 (1994): 517–36.

McGinn, Bernard. *Visions of the End: Apocalyptic Traditions in the Middle Ages.* New York: Columbia University Press, 1979.

McKinnon, James. *Music in Early Christian Literature.* Cambridge: Cambridge University Press, 1987.

McLuhan, Marshall. *The Gutenberg Galaxy: The Making of Typographic Man.* Toronto: University of Toronto Press, 1962.

MacCoull, L. S. B. "Notes on Philoponus' Theory of Vision." *Byzantion* 67 (1997): 558–62.

Maclagan, David. *Creation Myths. Man's Introduction to the World.* London: Thames and Hudson, 1977.

Maddox, Donald. *Fictions of Identity in Medieval France.* Cambridge: Cambridge University Press, 2000.

———. "Pilgrimage Narrative and Meaning in Manuscripts L and A of the *Vie de Saint Alexis*." *Romance Philology* 27 (1973): 143–57.

Magnúsdóttir, Asdis R. *La Voix du cor: la relique de Roncevaux et l'origine d'un motif dans la littérature du Moyen Âge (XIIe–XIVe siècles).* Amsterdam and Atlanta: Rodopi, 1998.

Manlove, Colin. *Christian Fantasy from 1200 to the Present.* Houndmills: Macmillan, 1992.

Marin, Louis. *Food for Thought.* Trans. Mette Hjort. Baltimore and London: Johns Hopkins University Press, 1989.

Marks, Lawrence E. *The Unity of the Senses: Interrelation Among the Modalities.* New York: Academic Press, 1978.

Matoré, Georges. *Le vocabulaire et la société médiévale.* Paris: Presses Universitaires de France, 1985.

Mendel, Arthur P. *Vision and Violence.* Ann Arbor: University of Michigan Press, 1992.

Menjot, Denis, ed. *Manger et boire au Moyen Âge: Actes du Colloque de Nice (15–17 octobre 1982).* Paris: Les Belles Lettres, 1984.

Mennell, Stephen. *All Manners of Food. Eating and Taste in England and France from the Middle Ages to the Present.* Urbana and Chicago: University of Illinois Press, 1996.

Merceron, Jacques. *Le Message et sa fiction: La communication par messager dans la littérature française des XIIe et XIIIe siècles.* Berkeley, Los Angeles, and London: University of California Press, 1998.

———. "Obscenity and Hagiography in Three Anonymous *Sermons Joyeux* and in Jean Molinet's *Saint Billouart*." In *Obscenity. Social Control and Artistic Creation in the European Middle Ages*, ed. Ziolkowski, 332–44.

———. "Cooks and Messengers: Food and Language in Twelfth- through Thirteenth-Century French History and Literature." *Chronica* (Medieval Association of the Pacific) (Fall 1992): 39–40.

Meyer-Baer, Kathi. *The Music of the Spheres and the Dance of Death.* Princeton: Princeton University Press, 1970.

Mikhaïlova, Milena. *Le présent de Marie*. Paris: Diderot Editeur, 1996.
Minkowski, Helmut. *Aus dem Nebel der Vergangenheit steigt der Turm zu Babel: Bilder aus 1000 Jahren*. Berlin: Rembrandt-Verlag, 1960.
Mitchell, W. J. T. "Eye and Ear: Edmund Burke and the Politics of Sensibility." In *Iconology: Image, Text, Ideology*, ed. idem, 116–49. Chicago: University of Chicago Press, 1986.
Morawski, Joseph, ed. *Proverbes français antérieurs au XVe siècle*. Paris: Champion, 1925.
Mueller, J.-D. "Pygmalion, höfisch mittelälterliche Erweckungsphantasien." In *Pygmalion: Die Geschichte des Mythos in der abendländischen Kultur*, ed. Mathias Mayer and Gerhardt Neumann, 465–95. Freiburg: Rombach, 1997.
Nelson, Robert S. "To Say and to See: Ekphrasis and Vision in Byzantium." In *Visuality*, ed. idem, 143–68.
———. ed. *Visuality Before and Beyond the Renaissance*. Cambridge: Cambridge University Press, 2000.
Newman, Barbara. *From Virile Woman to WomanChrist. Studies in Medieval Religion and Literature*. Philadelphia: University of Pennsylvania Press, 1995.
Nichols, Ann Eljenhom. "The Bread of Heaven: Foretaste or Foresight?" In *The Iconography of Heaven*, ed. Davidson, 40–68.
Nichols, Stephen G. "Seeing Food: An Anthropology of Ekphrasis and Still Life in Classical and Medieval Examples." *Modern Language Notes* 106 (1991): 818–51.
———. "The Light of the Word: Narrative, Image, and Truth." *New Literary History* 11 (1989): 535–44.
———. *Romanesque Signs. Early Medieval Narrative and Iconography*. New Haven and London: Yale University Press, 1983.
Nickle, R. W. D. *Light and Colour: Emblematic of Revealed Truth*. London: Hodder and Stoughton, 1889.
Nirenberg, David. *Communities of Violence: Persecution of Minorities in the Middle Ages*. Princeton: Princeton University Press, 1996.
O'Keefe, Katherine O'Brien. *Visible Song: Transitional Literacy in Old English Verse*. Cambridge: Cambridge University Press, 1990.
Ong, Walter J. *Orality and Literacy. The Technologizing of the Word*. London and New York: Routledge, 1995.
———. *Interfaces of the World: Studies in the Evolution of Consciousness and Culture*. Ithaca: Cornell University Press, 1977.
Owen, Douglas David. *The Vision of Hell: Infernal Journeys in Medieval French Literature*. Edinburgh: Scottish Academic Press, 1970.
Pächt, Otto, C. R. Dodwell, and Francis Wormald. *The St. Albans Psalter (Albani Psalter)*. London: The Warburg Institute, 1960.
Page, Christopher. *The Owl and the Nightingale. Musical Life and Ideas in France, 1100–1300*. Berkeley and Los Angeles: University of California Press, 1989.
Palmer, Barbara D. "The Inhabitants of Hell: Devils." In *The Iconography of Hell*, ed. Davidson and Seiler, 20–40.
Parker, Patricia. *Shakespeare from the Margins: Language, Culture, Context*. Chicago and London: University of Chicago Press, 1996.
Parkes, M. B. *Pause and Effect*. Aldershot: Scolar Press, 1992.
Pastoureau, Michel. *Figures et couleurs: études sur la symbolique et la sensibilité médiévales*. Paris: Le Léopard d'Or, 1986.
———. *Traité d'héraldique*. Paris: Picard, 1979.
Paulson, William R. *The Noise of Culture. Literary Texts in a World of Information*. Ithaca and London: Cornell University Press, 1988.

Payen, Jean-Charles. "Une Poétique du génocide joyeux: Devoir de violence et plaisir de tuer dans la *Chanson de Roland*." *Olifant* 6 (1979): 226–36.

Peckham, Robert D. "The Current State of Villon Studies: Part XI." *Fifteenth-Century Studies* 23 (1997): 258–78.

Pickens, Rupert T. "History and Meaning in the *Lais* of Marie de France." In *Studies in the Seven Sages of Rome and Other Essays in Medieval Literature Dedicated to the Memory of Jean Misrahi,* ed. Hans R. Runte, Henri Niedzielski, and William L. Hendrickson, *201–11*. Honolulu: Educational Research Associates, 1978.

———. "La Poétique de Marie de France d'après les Prologues des Lais." *Lettres Romanes* 32 (1978): 378–84.

Pigeaud, Jackie. *Folie et cures de la folie chez les médecins de l'antiquité gréco-romaine: la manie.* Paris: Les Belles Lettres, 1987.

———. *La maladie de l'âme. Etude sur la relation de l'âme et du corps dans la tradition médico-philosophique antique.* Paris: Les Belles Lettres, 1981.

Planche, Alice. "La Table comme signe de la classe: le témoignage du *Roman du Comte d'Anjou* (1316)." In *Manger et boire au Moyen Âge: Actes du Colloque de Nice (15–17 octobre 1982),* ed. Menjot, 239–60.

Potkay, Monica Brzezinski, and Regula Meyer Evitt. *Minding the Body: Women and Literature in the Middle Ages, 800–1500.* New York: Twayne, 1997.

Rastall, Richard. "The Musical Repertory." In *The Iconography of Heaven, ed.* Davidson, 162–96.

———. "The Sounds of Hell." In *The Iconography of Hell*, ed. Davidson and Seiler, 102–31.

Raynaud, Christiane. *La Violence au Moyen Âge, XIIIe–XVe siècle, d'après les livres d'histoire en français.* Paris: Le Léopard d'Or, 1990.

Reichler, Claude. *La Diabolie. La séduction, la renardie, l'écriture.* Paris: Minuit, 1979.

Rhodes, J. T., and Clifford Davidson. "The Garden of Paradise." In *The Iconography of Heaven*, ed. Davidson, 69–109.

Rindisbacher, Hans J. *The Smell of Books. A Cultural-Historical Study of Olfactory Perception in Literature.* Ann Arbor: University of Michigan Press, 1992.

Rivlin, Robert, and Karen Gravelle. *Deciphering the Senses. The Expanding World of Human Perception.* New York: Simon and Schuster, 1984.

Rockwell, Paul Vincent. *Rewriting Resemblance in Medieval French Romance: "Ceci n'est pas un graal."* New York and London: Garland, 1995.

Rorty, Richard. *Philosophy and the Mirror of Nature.* Princeton: Princeton University Press, 1979.

Rouhi, Leyla. *Mediation and Love: A Study of the Medieval Go-Between in Key Romance and Near-Eastern Texts.* Leiden, Boston, and Köln: Brill, 1999.

Roy, Bruno. "Getting to the Bottom of St. Caquette's Cult." In *Obscenity. Social Control and Artistic Creation in the European Middle Ages*, ed. Ziolkowski, 308–18.

Russell, Jeffrey Burton. *Chaucer and the Trivium: The Mindsong of the Canterbury Tales.* Gainesville: University Press of Florida, 1998.

———. *A History of Heaven: The Singing Silence.* Princeton: Princeton University Press, 1997.

Russell, Robert D. "A Similitude of Paradise: The City as Image of the City." In *The Iconography of Heaven*, ed. Davidson, 146–61.

Sacks, Oliver. *Seeing Voices. A Journey into the World of the Deaf.* Berkeley, Los Angeles, and London: University of California Press, 1989.

Saenger, Paul. *Space Between Words: The Origins of Silent Reading.* Stanford: Stanford University Press, 1997.

Saly, Antoinette. "Les dénouements du *Didot-Perceval* et de la *Queste del Saint Graal*." *PRIS-MA* (= Pour une Recherche sur l'Imaginaire et le Symbolique au Moyen Age) 28 (1998): 193–203.

Sargent-Bauer, Barbara Nelson. "'Avis li fu': Vision and Cognition in the Conte du Graal." In *Continuations. Essays in Medieval French Literature and Language in Honor of John L. Grigsby*, ed. Lacy and Torrini-Roblin, 133–61.
Scarry, Elaine. *The Body in Pain. The Making and Unmaking of the World.* New York and Oxford: Oxford University Press, 1985.
Schafer, R. Murray. *The Soundscape: Our Sonic Environment and the Tuning of the World.* Rochester, VT: Inner Traditions International, 1993.
Schmitt, Jean-Claude. *La raison des gestes dans l'Occident médiéval.* Paris: Gallimard, 1990.
Scully, Terence. "The *Sen* of Chrétien de Troyes's *Joie de la cort.*" In *The Expansion and Transformation of Courtly Literature*, ed. Nathaniel B. Smith and Joseph T. Snow, 71–94. Athens, GA: University of Georgia Press, 1980.
Seiler, Thomas H. "Filth and Stench as Aspects of the Iconography of Hell." In *The Iconography of Hell*, ed. Davidson and idem, 132–40.
Serres, Michel. *Les cinq sens.* Paris: Grasset, 1985.
———. *Genèse.* Paris: Grasset, 1982. Trans. Geneviève James and James Nielson. *Genesis.* Ann Arbor: University of Michigan Press, 1995.
———. "Noise." *Le Débat* 15 (1981): 94–101.
———. *Le parasite.* Paris: Grasset, 1980.
———. *Hermès IV: La distribution.* Paris: Minuit, 1977.
Sheingorn, Pamela. "'Who can open the doors of his face?': The Iconography of Hell Mouth." In *The Iconography of Hell*, ed. Davidson and Seiler, 1–19.
Shepkaru, Shmuel. "To Die for God: Martyr's Heaven in Hebrew and Latin Crusade Narratives." *Speculum* 77 (2002): 311–41.
Sherman, Claire Richter. *Imaging Aristotle. Verbal and Visual Representation in Fourteenth-Century France.* Berkeley, Los Angeles, and London: University of California Press, 1995.
Shipley, Joseph T. *Dictionary of Word Origins.* Totowa, NJ: Littlefield, Adams and Co., 1967.
Smith, Bruce R. *The Acoustic World of Early Modern England: Attending to the O-Factor.* Chicago: University of Chicago Press, 1999.
Solterer, Helen. "Dismembering, Remembering the Châtelain de Couci." *Romance Philology* 46 (1992): 103–24.
Spearing, A. C. *The Medieval Poet as Voyeur. Looking and Listening in Medieval Love-Narratives.* Cambridge: Cambridge University Press, 1993.
Stanesco, Michel. "Cligés, le chevalier coloré." In *L'Hostellerie de Pensée*, ed. Zink and Bohler, 391–402.
Steiner, George. *After Babel. Aspects of Language and Translation.* New York and London: Oxford University Press, 1975.
Stewart, Garrett. *Reading Voices: Literature and the Phonotext.* Berkeley and Los Angeles: University of California Press, 1990.
Stewart, Ian. *Does God Play Dice? The New Mathematics of Chaos.* London: Penguin Books, 1989.
Stock, Brian. *The Implications of Literacy: Written Language and Models of Interpretation in the Eleventh and Twelfth Centuries.* Princeton: Princeton University Press, 1983.
Stone, Gregory B. *The Death of the Troubadour. The Late Medieval Resistance to the Renaissance.* Philadelphia: University of Pennsylvania Press, 1994.
Stones, Alison. "Seeing the Grail. Prolegomena to a Study of Grail Imagery in Arthurian Manuscripts." In *The Grail. A Casebook*, ed. Dhira B. Mahoney, 301–66. New York and London: Garland Publishing, 2000.

Strauss, Erwin. *The Primary World of the Senses: A Vindication of Sensory Experience.* Trans. Jacob Needleman. London: Collier Macmillan, 1993.
Sullivan, Blair. "The Unwritable Sound of Music: The Origins and Implications of Isidore's Memorial Metaphor." *Viator* 30 (1999): 1–13.
Sutherland, Elizabeth. *Five Euphemias: Women in Medieval Scotland, 1200–1420.* New York: St. Martin's Press, 1999.
Taylor, Andrew. "Was There a Song of Roland?" *Speculum* 76 (2001): 28–65.
Taylor, Jane H. M. *The Poetry of François Villon: Text and Context.* Cambridge: Cambridge University Press, 2001.
Thiébaux, Marcelle. *The Stag of Love: The Chase in Medieval Literature.* Ithaca: Cornell University Press, 1974.
Thiry, Claude. "François Villon, poète du visuel." In *L'Hostellerie de Pensée*, ed. Zink and Bohler, 439–57.
Thom, René. "Halte au hasard, silence au bruit." *Le Débat* 3 (1980): 119–32.
Thomasset, Claude. "Des jeunes filles accidentellement muettes." In *L'Hostellerie de Pensée*, ed. Zink and Bohler, 459–66.
Todorov, Tzvetan. *Poétique de la prose.* Paris: Seuil, 1971.
Townsend, David, and Andrew Taylor, eds. *The Tongue of the Fathers: Gender and Ideology in Twelfh-Century Latin.* Philadelphia: University of Pennsylvania Press, 1998.
Truax, Barry. *Acoustic Communication.* Norwood, NJ: Ablex, 1984.
Tyerman, Christopher. "Proteus Unbound: Crusading Historiography." In idem, *The Invention of the Crusades*, 99–126. Toronto and Buffalo: University of Toronto Press, 1998.
Tyler, Stephen. "The Vision Quest in the West, or What the Mind's Eye Sees." *Journal of Anthropological Research* 40 (1984): 23–40.
Van Coolput, Colette-Anne. "La poupée d'Evalac ou la conversion tardive du Roi Mordrain." In *Continuations. Essays in Medieval French Literature and Language in Honor of John L. Grigsby*, ed. Lacy and Torrini-Roblin, 163–72.
Van Deusen, N. "Music, Rhythm," and "Musica, De." In *Augustine Through the Ages*, ed. A. D. Fitzgerald et al., 572–74, 574–76. Grand Rapids: Eerdmans, 1999.
Vance, Eugene. *Mervelous Signals. Poetics and Sign Theory in the Middle Ages.* Lincoln and London: University of Nebraska Press, 1986.
Vincensini, Jean-Jacques. *Pensée mythique et narrations médiévales.* Paris: Champion, 1996.
Vinge, Louise. *The Five Senses: Studies in a Literary Tradition.* Lund: Publications of the Royal Society of Letters, 1975.
Visser, Margaret. *Much Depends on Dinner. The Extraordinary History and Mythology, Allure and Obsessions, Perils and Taboos of an Ordinary Meal.* New York: Collier Books, 1988.
Vitz, Evelyn Birge. *Orality and Performance in Early French Romance.* Cambridge: Boydell and Brewer, 1999.
Wagner, Anthony Richard. *Heralds and Heraldry in the Middle Ages. An Inquiry into the Growth of the Armorial Function of Heralds.* London: Humphrey Milford for Oxford University Press, 1939.
Webb, Ruth. "*Ekphrasis* Ancient and Modern: The Invention of a Genre." *Word and Image* 15 (1999): 7–18.
White, Catherine L. "Women and Their Fathers in Three French Medieval Literary Works (*Le Roman de Silence*, *Erec et Enide*, and *Le Livre de la Cité des Dames*)." *Medieval Feminist Newsletter* 24 (1997): 42–45.
Wodak, Ruth. *Disorders of Discourse.* White Plains, NY: Addison Wesley Longman, 1996.

Zink, Michel, ed. (with Danielle Bohler). *L'Hostellerie de Pensée. Etudes sur l'art littéraire au Moyen Âge offerts à Daniel Poirion par ses anciens élèves.* Paris: Presses Universitaires de France, 1995.
———. *La Prédication en langue romane avant 1300.* Paris: Champion, 1976.
Ziolkowski, Jan, ed. *Obscenity. Social Control and Artistic Creation in the European Middle Ages.* Leiden: Brill, 1998.
Zumthor, Paul. *Essai de poétique médiévale.* Paris: Seuil, 1968.
———. *La lettre et la voix. De la "littérature" médiévale.* Paris: Seuil, 1987.

INDEX OF PRIMARY AUTHORS AND WORKS